ROBERT EDWIN PEARY

AN ARCTIC IDYLL : GREENLAND

Frontispiece

ROBERT EDWIN PEARY

A Record of his Explorations
1886-1909

BY

J. GORDON HAYES

"I was looked upon with contempt, like a man who should project a journey to the moon, but yet with a respectful interest, like one setting forth for the inclement Pole."—ROBERT LOUIS STEVENSON, *Travels with a Donkey*.

"I mentioned our design to Voltaire. He looked at me, as if I had talked of going to the North Pole, and said, ' You do not insist on my accompanying you ? '—' No, sir.'—' Then I am very willing you should go.' "—J. BOSWELL, *Journal of a Tour to the Hebrides*.

LONDON
GRANT RICHARDS & HUMPHREY TOULMIN
AT THE CAYME PRESS LIMITED, 21 SOHO SQUARE, W.

Printed in Great Britain by
NEILL & CO., LTD., EDINBURGH.

PREFACE

THE introductory remarks are too long for a preface and will be found in Chapter I.

Lady Shackleton has again gracefully permitted me to reproduce some of Sir Ernest's photographs, Nos. 4, 5, 6, and 7 having been taken on the *Endurance*. I wish also to thank Dr Lauge Koch of Copenhagen for Nos. 1, 2, and 3, as well as for Chart No. 4; and the Royal Geographical Society, whose officials are unfailingly helpful, for the other charts. The use of the books mentioned in the short Bibliography is gladly acknowledged.

As photographs of *Arctic* pack ice are unobtainable, *Antarctic* views necessarily are given. The differences between the two are slight, except for the summer thawing in the north, and this does not apply to the present subject. A fair idea of the conditions found on the Arctic pack can be obtained from the Weddell Sea ice.

I beg to thank the Librarian of Congress for his courtesy in verifying a document of the United States Government at Washington, D.C.

I am greatly indebted to the late Chief Geographer of Canada, Mr James White, for his gift of the official "Ninth Report of the Geographic Board," with its splendid charts, and for other assistance; also to Admiral Sir James Fergusson, K.C.B., K.C.M.G., for being good enough to read Chapter X of the present work; to Captain Hall, of Omaha, for the kindly gift of his book, and to Mr William E. Shea, F. Am. Geog. Soc., of Washington, for his interest and help, which included copies of his articles in the Boston *Independent*, and for reading through the proofs of this book.

Lastly, it gives me much pleasure to acknowledge, for the second time, the kindness of Mr Grant Richards.

Storridge Vicarage,   J. G. H.
   Malvern, July 1929.

As the last proofs were going to the printers I received a letter from an American gentleman who has "no hesitation in saying that the bulk of Peary's book *The North Pole* . . . at least 80 per cent., and probably more" was written by him. He prefers, if possible, to remain anonymous. He was not on the expedition. The internal evidence of the letter is far from convincing.

I do not think there is any record of Peary admitting such a claim as this to *authorship*. He published the book in his own name. He wrote in the first person throughout. He knew that the world believed him to be its author, and he never corrected this perfectly proper and legitimate belief. Whether he actually wrote it or not, he and he alone could be held responsible for the accuracy of its contents.

The explanation appears to be that this gentleman was Peary's amanuensis, but it will take time to clear everything up. That Peary inscribed a deliberate lie on his title-page is simply incredible.

J. G. H.

21st September 1929.

CONTENTS

    * The chapters marked with an asterisk are somewhat technical
and may be omitted by the general reader.

CONTENTS

SCHEDULES

TABLES

ILLUSTRATIONS

CHARTS AND DIAGRAMS

A SHORT GLOSSARY OF GLACIOLOGICAL TERMS

Term.	Definition.	Authority.
Continental Ice	"The ultimate result of the profound glacierisation of a large land-mass. . . . All, or the majority, of the irregularities of the surface of the land are swamped by the accumulation of ice."	R. E. Priestley
Crevasse	A deep rift or fissure in the ice of glaciers and other land-ice formations.	
Disturbed Ice	Any ice that is torn and contorted into chaotic elevations and depressions. The commonest term for this is *Pressure* (which see).	
Drift	An abbreviation of : (1) drifting or drift snow, which is wind-driven snow, as in a blizzard. (2) The motion of sea ice, ships, etc., due to the wind or ocean currents.	
Drift Ice	"Loose, very open pack, where water preponderates over ice."	J. M. Wordie
Fast Ice	"Sea ice while remaining fast in the position of growth . . . met only along coasts where it is attached to the shore, or over shoals."	Priestley and Wordie
Floe	"Any area of sea ice, other than fast ice."	Wordie
Glacier	"A field or stream of ice, formed . . . from compacted snow."	*Standard Dictionary*
Glaciology	The science of ice forms and phenomena.	
Ice	The crystalline or fibrous solid formed by the freezing of water and by molecular changes in *névé* (which see) from a crystalline to a granular structure. (See *Snow*.)	
Ice Cap	"A continuous covering of ice, *névé*, or snow, such as occurs in polar lands."	Dr H. R. Mill
Ice Disturbance	(See *Disturbed Ice*.)	

Term.	Definition.	Authority.
Ice Field	1. Applied to sea ice, is " an area of pack ice of such extent that its limits cannot be seen from a ship's masthead." 2. Any large area of land ice, as snow-field, firn-field, or *névé*-field.	Wordie and Priestley
Ice Foot	" A sheath of ice adhering along the shores of Polar lands."	Sir Douglas Mawson
Ice Sheet	A convenient term for any large area of ice, especially land ice.	
Igloo	An Eskimo snow dwelling.	
Inland Ice	An obsolescent term for *Continental Ice* (which see) and other forms of land ice. The usual term for the continental ice of Greenland.	
Lead or Lane	" A navigable passage through pack ice." It is customary to speak of these channels as leads even when covered with young ice.	Wordie
Névé	" The compacted snow of a snowfield ; a stage in the transition between soft, loose snow and glacier ice."	Mawson
Pack Ice	" *Sea Ice* (which see) which has drifted from its original position."	Priestley and Wordie
Pack, The	" The term used to denote the main belt of derived sea ice which, in the Arctic, fills the Polar Sea. . . . The term is used more generally to mean any area of pack ice, however small."	Priestley and Wordie
Pressure Ice	—or more usually *Pressure*—is either land or sea ice, forced upward above its normal level, downward beneath that level, or both. Such ice is said to be *disturbed*. In sea ice, pressure is classified by Wordie into : (1) Bending of young ice. (2) Tenting of heavy floes. (3) Rafting, which is the commonest. (See *Pressure Ridges*.)	
Pressure Ridges	Commonly abbreviated to *Pressure*, and formerly, in sea ice, termed hummocks. They are elevations of disturbed and disrupted ice forced above the normal surface of floes.	

GLOSSARY

Term.	Definition.	Authority.
Sea Ice	All ice formed on the surface of the sea. It does not include icebergs, which are land-born, of *névé*.	Wordie
Snow	A solid formed by the condensation of water-vapour. Its structure is granular or crystalline, formed of minute plates and prisms. Every form of land ice is composed of snow, after it has been transformed into *névé*.	Based on C. S. Wright
Tide Crack	" Produced by the movement of the ice under the influence of the tide. A tide crack may be single, but it is commonly double, triple, or even fourfold.	Priestley

CHAPTER I

INTRODUCTION

" Be sure you get your facts right. Then go ahead."
PRESIDENT HOOVER.

1. DURING the preparation of some sledging statistics, a few years ago, I found that Admiral Peary held the world's record for speed. This would have been remarkable under any conditions, for he was fifty-three years of age at the time; but what made this record almost, if not quite, incredible was that the conditions under which it was made were known to have been unfavourable to high speeds. A careful examination of his return from the North Pole to Bartlett's last outward camp was made, for it was here that the marvellous speed was recorded, and the results were communicated, in the form of a lecture, to the Manchester Geographical Society. The scope of this inquiry was somewhat extended in preparing the lecture for publication in the Society's Journal; the Journal being sent, in accordance with the excellent custom of these learned societies, to many parts of the civilised world.

Some little interest was aroused in the United States and Canada by this lecture. Several well-known explorers and geographers most kindly corresponded with me on the subject. Mr V. Stefansson was good enough to write, from New York, several letters of great value and interest. He had been a friend of Peary, yet he said: "As far as the published evidence goes you have the best of the Peary argument."

The Chief Geographer to the Canadian Government sent me a mass of new data. Mr Edwin Swift

Balch, the eminent Philadelphian jurist and geographer; a captain in the Royal Navy who had spent his life doing hydrographical work, and others, opened up an interesting and pleasant correspondence.

Most of these communications were in support of my position, and none was antagonistic to it. Meanwhile, I had been fortunate in making the acquaintance of several members of Captain Scott's and Sir Ernest Shackleton's scientific staffs, who are among the greatest living authorities on most polar problems. They had devoted, I found, some attention to Peary's records and had arrived, quite independently, at similar conclusions to myself.

No one who has set his hand to the plough relishes the idea of turning back; hence the present book. Other writings on the subject were unheard of until my own conclusions were formed; and no other work, to my knowledge, is concerned exclusively with Peary the *explorer*. Commander Green has produced a good biography of Peary the *Man*,[1] well written and authoritative, though we cannot agree with all its statements; but it is purely a personal appreciation, with the emphasis very strongly laid on the hero's struggles to attain his life's ambition. The geographical work done by Peary is scarcely mentioned, and only in its adventurous aspect. The biography is frankly uncritical, and scatters praise with a lavish hand; its character is "popular."

Our purpose may well be introduced by Mr Apsley Cherry-Garrard, when he wrote of "the atmosphere of hero-worship" into which Captain Scott's men were plunged on their return from Antarctica, as follows: "That atmosphere was very agreeable; but it was a refracting medium through which the expedition could not be seen with scientific accuracy. . . . Whilst we knew what we had suffered and risked better than

[1] *Peary the Man who Refused to Fail*, Fitzhugh Green (Putnam, 1926).

anyone else, we also knew that science takes no account of such things." [1]

Admiral Peary's name may suffer from the effects of a similar exotic atmosphere unless a serious attempt is made to find out precisely what he has done. He was an explorer with a world-wide reputation. He spent all the best years of his life on Arctic expeditions, and was one of the greatest civilised sledge travellers who ever lived. Thousands of people have been fascinated and thrilled by his daring exploits and hair-breadth escapes. He was received with unquestioning glorification on his return from his last expedition; but "*science takes no account of such things.*"

The geographical and scientific work Admiral Peary accomplished must be distinguished and separated, clearly and definitely, from the mere plaudits of the market-place. It appears that this has not been done. Peary has never been focussed into the geographical field of vision. The actual results of permanent value that he acquired have not, hitherto, been considered and assessed in the calm and dispassionate, if somewhat critical, light of a geographer's study.

The main purpose of this book is to do this, by a comprehensive survey of Peary's life work, with special reference to his geographical discoveries and explorations.

2. President Hoover's motto, quoted at the head of this chapter, may be better than he knows. It is the basis of all true research, and as such it is to be our guiding principle throughout the task we are now beginning. If all the President's fellow-countrymen had followed it, this book would not be written.

Another American facetiously remarked that facts "are the framework of history, not the drapery." No one could build a durable edifice with soft fabrics; their purpose is decoration. Our purpose is truth. In pursuance of this ideal, we will begin, after a few

[1] *The Worst Journey in the World*, Apsley Cherry-Garrard, p. 61.

more words of necessary introduction, with a glance at the field of action.

Captain Amundsen wrote: "Admiral Peary was the first man ever to reach the North Pole. 'But,' you may ask, 'how do you know he reached it? You have only his word for it. . . . Peary, with his technical knowledge, could easily have faked his records.' Nevertheless, I know Admiral Peary reached the Pole. The reason I know it is that I know Peary. What you say about his ability to fake his observations is perfectly true. The answer to any doubt on that score is simply that Peary was not that kind of man. The character of the explorer, therefore, is always the best evidence of the truth of his claim of achievement." [1] Amundsen added: "The foregoing paragraphs have been written chiefly to illuminate the only comment I feel called upon to make on the Cook-Peary controversy: *Polar records must be read in the light of the antecedents of the explorers*" (his italics). This we will now proceed to do. We have nothing to do with the Cook-Peary controversy, but everything to do with "the antecedents" of Admiral Peary. We must delay only to make a rapid survey of his theatre of operations.

[1] *My Life as an Explorer*, R. Amundsen, p. 225 (Heinemann, 1927).

CHAPTER II

PEARY'S ARCTIC [1]

*" If the predominant note in the tropics is wealth and luxuriance of
life, in the polar regions it is magnitude of physical processes."*
R. N. RUDMOSE BROWN.
The Polar Regions.

1. SOME acquaintance is necessary with the lands and
waters over which Admiral Peary travelled if his
movements are to be followed intelligently. We are
faced, however, with the peculiar difficulty that there
is no single and well-marked boundary, at once convenient and generally accepted, between the Arctic
and the North Temperate Zone.

The Arctic Circle is not of much practical use. It
is, of course, an arbitrary and imaginary line drawn
round the globe, with a radius of 1408 geographical
miles from the North Geographical Pole; its latitude
being 66° 32′ north of the Equator.[2] The Circle is
purely a theoretical line, and actually divides nothing
material, hence it is now seldom referred to.

The Gulf Stream carries temperate conditions
north-eastward to within the Circle, and the East
Greenland Current (to give no other example) bears
the polar ice hundreds of miles southward into the
Temperate Zone. For these and other reasons *the
southern limit of the sea ice* has been suggested as a
suitable boundary over the water spaces, while *the
timber line* may be said to perform the same office on
land. This will suffice for our present purpose.

[1] See Chart No. 1. The term " Arctic Regions " is now obsolescent.

[2] It may be advisable to note here that there are 60 geographical
miles, or minutes of latitude, to a degree, and 360 degrees form a
circle.

The chief and central feature of the Arctic is its ocean, which occupies, round the North Pole, a corresponding, non-concentric position to that occupied by Antarctica round the South Pole, its area being similar, also, though a little greater, or about 5½ million square miles. The Arctic Ocean is approximately 2700 miles [1] in length from Canada to Europe and 1600 miles wide between Greenland and Siberia, these distances being measured in straight lines across the Geographical Pole.

The greater part of the circumference of this ocean is formed by the northern coastlines of Europe and Asia, of Canada with its Arctic islands, and of Greenland. Within the rim are numerous other islands as well as archipelagoes. The periphery of the Arctic Basin is remarkable in having only one opening of considerable width, the Greenland Sea, which connects the surface waters of the Arctic and Atlantic Oceans; and only two other narrow and navigable channels leading southward. One of these is Bering Strait, and the other consists of a chain of waterways, the best known of which is the southernmost, Smith Sound. As we shall hear much of these channels, we must note that Smith Sound lies between Greenland and Ellesmere Island. It leads northward into Kane Basin, and this basin successively into Kennedy Channel, Hall Basin, and Robeson Channel, the last of which debouches into the Arctic Ocean.

This ocean is unique among the oceans of the world in occupying such a land-locked basin. It is of abysmal depth, or as much as 2000 fathoms in its deepest parts. Much more oceanographical research is needed in this ocean. Too many expeditions have rushed aimlessly about over its frozen surface, while the world remained in ignorance of the rudimentary facts concerning the

---

[1] All miles in this book are English statute miles, of 1760 yards, except where geographical miles are mentioned. The latter will be also referred to as " minutes."

KENNEDY CHANNEL

facing p. 6

mass of water and ice that lay beneath. The surface is formed of floating ice, known as pack ice and ice floes,[1] of which we shall hear a great deal. The normal thickness of the ice, apart from pressure ridges, may be anything up to about twenty feet. The floes, especially during the summer, become intersected by numerous channels and pools of open water, and the whole pack is continually drifting about.

2. There are two North Poles, the one magnetic and the other geographical. The North Magnetic Pole is more than a thousand miles from the North Geographical Pole, and is not an imaginary point, but a large and variable area, over the different parts of which, at different times, the vertical magnetic needle points downward at an angle of 90° to the horizontal. The horizontal needle of the compass points towards the Magnetic Polar Area with continual variation; it gets more and more sluggish and useless the nearer this area is approached, because of the increased downward pull.

Our main concern will be with the North Geographical Pole, and it will be referred to as the North Pole, or simply as the Pole. This Pole is better understood than the Magnetic Pole, and is, of course, the imaginary point, in the Northern Hemisphere, where the meridians, or lines of longitude, meet. It is also the northern end of the imaginary axis on which the earth revolves. It is not situated very near the middle of the Arctic Ocean, but lies amid the ice floes at a distance of nearly 500 miles from the north of Greenland and Grant Land.

The Arctic is divided, by some geographers, into two parts: the Eastern Arctic, or that lying to the north of the Old World, and the Western or Canadian Arctic, which includes also Greenland. Admiral Peary never visited the Eastern, nor the greater part of the Western, Arctic; his journeys being restricted

[1] See the Glossary of Glaciological Terms.

to a comparatively small segment of the latter, or a portion of the Greenland Quadrant. He did not visit Southern, or the greater part of Eastern, Greenland. This country is by far the largest purely Arctic land-mass. A few miles to the west of it lies Ellesmere Island, to the west and south-west of which is the Sverdrup Archipelago.[1] We shall become better acquainted with these lands as we proceed.

3. Australia being, oceanographically, a continent, Greenland is the largest island in the world, with an area of half a million square miles. It is probably unique in being claimed by one nation, Denmark, while another and kindred nation, Norway, disputes its sovereignty. A *modus vivendi* has been found in an agreement that extends until 1944. Greenland is chiefly remarkable, physically, from being, like Antarc-tica, though on a smaller scale, in its ice age. The land, except for a strip along the greater part of the coast, is entirely submerged by snow, hardened, be-neath a few feet of the surface, into ice. The correct glaciological term for this colossal ice-sheet is con-tinental ice, but it is usually, in Greenland, referred to as the inland ice. It covers about 86 *per cent.* of the land, and "reaches the sea in many places, forming the coast for considerable stretches." [2] The maximum thickness of this ice-cap, as it is also called, is said to be 4000 feet. Its surface rises gradually, from the coast or a short distance inland, to a height of about 8000 feet in the interior. Nearly the whole of this country, therefore, is a huge snow plateau, second only, in area and height, to the Antarctic Plateau, and one of the most sterile waste places on the earth.

Ellesmere Island is part of the Dominion of Canada. It is about 500 miles long from north to south and, like Cæsar's Gaul, is divided into three parts: Grant Land,

---

[1] The latest authentic maps of this district are those of the Canadian Government. See *Ninth Report of the Geographic Board.*
[2] *Geographical Journal,* December 1928, p. 513.

in the north; Grinnell Land, in the centre; and King Oscar Land, in the south. The width of this island varies from 50 to 300 miles; its coast being very much indented by long fjords. It is similar to Greenland in this, also in being ice-capped; but it is dissimilar in the possession of one fertile area, 150 miles long and 40 miles wide.[1] This oasis is the Lake Hazen valley of Grinnell Land. We shall often hear of the northern, or oceanic, coasts of both Greenland and Grant Land; they form adjacent portions of the rim of the Arctic Basin. From these coasts Peary made all his attempts to reach the Pole.

The length of a single day in the Arctic, as in the Antarctic, is twelve months. The sun, in the highest latitudes, remains above the horizon for several months. The duration of the seasons varies with the latitude. Continual daylight is followed by months of twilight and darkness, when the moon shines continually for ten or twelve days, in fine weather, and brightens the long period of gloom. The cold, on the surface of the Arctic Ocean, is not as severe as in Siberia, but the polar winds intensify the effect of frost on all organisms.

4. *The character of the pack ice* on the polar ocean being the decisive factor in any attempt to reach the North Pole by sledge, we must take a general view of it now, and leave for a later chapter a closer consideration of its special conditions on Peary's routes.

The first characteristic of this ice is its *continual motion*. This fact must be grasped thoroughly, clearly, and decisively. Its evidence is seen in the annual flow of the ice to the south, especially in the East Greenland Current; in the drifting of the *Jeannette*, the *Fram*, and other ships; in the Siberian driftwood found on the shores of Greenland; in the observations and experience of all travellers on its surface, and in other evidence that need not be given here.

It has been established that the motive power of

[1] *Three Years of Arctic Service*, Greely, vol. i, p. 415.

the pack ice is, mainly if not exclusively, the wind, and as it blows from all points of the compass, the ice drifts in every direction. When, however, the winds from one quarter preponderate, the equivalent of a current is set up. In some localities there is no definite drift in any one direction. Dr Nansen found that, while the north-westerly drift of the *Fram* prevailed, the ship was driven shorter distances to all points of the compass.

One important effect of the wind, in moving the ice floes, is the formation of water channels. These extend in all directions. On any line of progress over the pack, most of the channels will appear more or less at right angles to the route, because few others are met with.

The main seasonal effect on these channels is that of summer, which opens them out into mighty waterways; and of winter, or of frost at any time, which glazes them over with ice. The evidence of Nansen and Cagni is very clear: that the amount of open water in the pack increases with advancing summer, till the ice is covered with a network of channels and pools of all sizes. This is the annual disintegration of the pack.

The second obstacle to the progress of a sledge party over the pack is that of the pressure ridges. These were termed hummocks in the past; but as they are caused by the pressure of the ice they are now known as "pressure," with or without the additional words "ice" or "ridges." A normal icefield is a comparatively level, central surface bounded on all sides by these ridges, which are long, irregular mounds of disrupted ice, forced up by the grinding of the floes against each other and extending along their sides.

The polar pack presents almost an infinite number of variations from the normal field of ice. These variations extend from miles of continuous pressure ridges, without any level surfaces, to miles of flat plains with, perhaps, only distant ridges in sight; but extensive level areas are rare. The average condition of the ice may be said to present a goodly mixture of "up and downs," with some level areas and at least a few channels. The changes, however, are continuous and often remarkable, Cagni finding level expanses in May, on his return journey, slightly to the west of latitudes that were covered with pressure on his outward journey in March.

Dr Rudmose Brown has well said: "It is the pack ice that closes the polar sea to navigation and guards the inner secrets of the Arctic Basin." [1] All attempts to reach the North Pole by sledge must be made over this somewhat chaotic kind of surface, which, in addition to its special character just mentioned, has areas of soft snow, and of snow hardened by the wind, as in all polar lands.

Travellers over the pack have no difficulty in obtaining water from old sea ice. It cannot be too well known that "sea ice is not, strictly speaking, frozen sea water, because the freezing is a selective process in which most of the saline matter is discarded." [2] The result is that ice from the summits of high pressure ridges contains very little salt, and is commonly used for culinary purposes.

Although the Arctic is beyond the northern limit of large trees, many dwarf shrubs, with grasses and flowers, flourish on the land; they even luxuriate over large areas. This vegetation supports herds of reindeer and polar oxen. These wild oxen are better known as musk oxen; but the use of this term seems unsuitable, as there is no flavour of musk about them. [3] Mr Stefansson suggests the name "Ovibos." Polar bears and foxes roam for hundreds of miles over the pack, as well as on land. Wolves are found in some Arctic countries, as also are hares and smaller mammals.

[1] *The Polar Regions*, Dr Rudmose Brown, p. 59.
[2] *Ibid.*, p. 62.
[3] See *New Land*, O. Sverdrup, vol. i, p. 35.

Whales, seals, and walrus abound in the waters, and the Arctic coasts frequently are haunted by innumerable birds.

We may now be informed sufficiently to follow Admiral Peary's career as an explorer. It falls into three main periods: (1) Greenland, 1886–95; (2) the *Windward* Expedition, or journeys from a base in the Smith Sound district, 1898–1902; (3) the *Roosevelt* Expeditions, or journeys from Cape Sheridan, 1906–09.

CHAPTER III

THE GREENLAND EXPEDITIONS

" Let us probe the silent places, let us see what luck betide us ;
Let us journey to a lonely land I know.
There's a whisper on the night-wind, there's a star agleam to guide us,
And the wild is calling, calling . . . let us go."

ROBERT W. SERVICE.
Songs of a Sourdough.

1. THE RECONNAISSANCE OF 1886. 2. PEARY'S COMPLAINT
AGAINST NANSEN. 3. THE EXPEDITION OF 1892. 4. THE
EXPEDITION OF 1893–1895.

1. ROBERT EDWIN PEARY was born at Cresson Springs,
Pennsylvania, in 1856. His great-grandfather, Stephen
Pierre, had migrated from the south of France. The
family were successful barrel manufacturers. Robert
entrusted his mother with the secret of his subsequent
career in a letter he wrote, about the year 1880: "I
shall not be satisfied that I have done my best until
my name is known from one end of the world to the
other." [1] His consuming desire, throughout his life,
was fame; and his use of the term "one end of the
world" is curious, as it seems to have foreshadowed
the North Pole.

In 1881 he joined the civil engineering corps of
the United States Navy and worked on the Nicaraguan
Canal. Four years later, he tells us, he lighted upon
a paper on Greenland, and the Arctic *virus* entered
his soul, as it has entered the souls of hundreds of
young men with red blood in their veins. Where
Peary differed from most men of his age was that
here he saw his path to glory.

[1] *Peary the Man who Refused to Fail*, p. 33.

13

The first and the second steps that he took to carry out his desires have been taken by others. He devoured all the literature on the subject, and then read a paper on Greenland, in April 1886, before the National Academy of Science. After that, Peary's specific character began to appear; a month later he set off on his first expedition. This was a reconnaissance of the inland ice. He was accompanied on this adventure by the Danish Lieutenant Maigaard.

The ice-cap, at a height of about 2000 feet above sea-level,[1] was reached by means of a fjord in Disco Bay. An easterly course was set towards the interior. On attaining a height of 3000 feet a gale came on. No tents being carried, the two men lay in the shelter of the sledges and were soon buried in the snowdrift.

Peary made a study of Arctic clothing. His practice was to dress in furs, and usually to dispense with both tent and sleeping-bag. This Spartan system was more successful than may be imagined, and we shall hear of it again.

On this occasion Peary and Maigaard left their sledges on the inland ice, and returned to their camp on the fjord to await better weather. On 5th July they set off once more. After digging the sledges out of the snow, Peary broke through into his first crevasse through not wearing snowshoes. On the 6th he and his companion camped at a height of about 4100 feet, the distance inland not being given. The outward journey was pursued for ten days more, until a height of about 7525 feet was reached. This is probably an uncorrected aneroid reading. Here the two men were completely snowed under for forty-eight hours, and had to turn back after penetrating, Peary said, nearly a hundred miles from the edge of the inland ice. The return was made in safety.

2. *Peary's Complaint against Nansen.*—It was surely unnecessary for Peary to compare the exploits of other

[1] All Peary's heights appear to be merely aneroid readings.

explorers unfavourably with his own, and it was certainly unwise to do so. Yet he affirmed that Nansen, in 1888, carried out suggestions that he himself had made in 1886; and he complained of "the forestalling of my work [*i.e.* his work of 1892, shortly to be dealt with] which," he added, "was a serious blow to me."[1] The unfavourable comparison we shall return to later.

Circumstances were not favourable to Peary's scheme; but history records certain facts he does not mention. These we must now consider.

A great name should be introduced with due decorum. Dr Nansen has contributed so much to the advancement of human knowledge that, in his own special territory, the Arctic, he stands almost without compeer. He was the father of modern polar exploration.

In 1882 he gazed upon the unexplored east coast of Greenland, and thought of attempting to reach it. The idea of penetrating into the interior flashed through his mind, but did not take definite shape until the following year. In the autumn of 1883 he formed his plan "of an expedition crossing Greenland on 'ski' from coast to coast,"[2] though he was unable actually to prepare for this venture until 1887. Peary had never heard of Greenland until three years after Nansen, as he looked upon its virgin snows, had conceived the idea of its exploration. Nansen's plan of crossing the inland ice anticipated Peary's programme of 1886 also by three years. Peary's insinuations, therefore, were quite unfair; for while it was possible for him to have copied from Nansen, Nansen could not have copied from him. This, however, is not the end of the matter.

None but accurate scientists should provoke such men as Nansen; for he has shown that the altitude

[1] *Northward over the Great Ice*, p. 37.
[2] *The First Crossing of Greenland*, vol. i, pp. 3-4.

Peary claimed to have reached on the inland ice was much too high. He has shown, further, that Peary could not have known, with any certainty, where he turned back on the ice-cap. Nansen wrote: "Peary's longitude was only based, as it seems, on some observations of altitude taken with the theodolite about noon on 19th July. The expression 'circum-meridian sights,' which both he and Maigaard use, is not quite clear in itself. These so-called 'simple altitudes' are, besides, notoriously uncertain for longitude reckonings. The chronometer, too, had come to a standstill, and an ordinary watch, which Peary declares to have been very trustworthy, was used in its place; but, as far as I can see from his account, no observations were taken subsequently by the coast to determine this timepiece's accuracy.

"The distance of a hundred miles from the margin of the ice cannot, therefore, be considered as established beyond all doubt." [1]

Most polar explorers have been navigators, and thus able to fix their positions on open plains with professional accuracy. Others have been scientists who, from their special training, have had no difficulty in acquiring at least as much skill as the navigators in the art of taking observations for latitude and longitude. The latter, not infrequently, have taken professed navigators with them on their journeys. Peary, by profession, was neither scientist nor navigator. He was a civil engineering assistant and never had to navigate a vessel in his life, in the course of his duty. It was a pity he did not. The records brought back from newly discovered lands are almost useless unless they are accurate.

Peary was one of the most daring pioneers who ever drove a sledge; and only two or three modern explorers have spent more years in the Arctic than he did. He was fascinated by the unknown into which

[1] *The First Crossing of Greenland*, vol. i, pp. 505–506.

he plunged with commendable boldness. He had practical abilities to carry out the impulses of his powerful will. Above all, he worshipped at the shrine of Fame. His methods of navigation, however, were slipshod, as we shall see more particularly in a later chapter. He did not possess, either by nature or training, a scientific mind, and it would appear that he never learnt the need of accuracy in determining his position or altitude. Thus, to this day, it is unknown how far or how high he got on the inland ice during his first reconnaissance, and consequently no use can be made of the information he brought back.

3. *The Expedition of* 1892.—Peary returned to his dockyard work and was unable to obtain leave of absence from the Navy, after his first venture, until 1891. In June of that year he set out on his first North-Greenland expedition with five assistants. Of these, Dr F. A. Cook, the honorary surgeon and anthropologist, afterwards became the most widely known; though Eivind Astrup, the young Norwegian, was Peary's sole companion on the daring journey made in 1892.

The plan of the expedition was to establish a Base in Whale Sound, Western Greenland, and from there to cross the inland ice to the unknown north-east coast. Full credit must be given to Peary for this enterprise. We will not linger with him over the detailed work he did in the neighbourhood of his station, but follow him at once across the ice-cap.

He was most emphatic, during his earlier expeditions, as to the advantages of small sledging units. His reasoning appears to have been correct, though it will be omitted here as the subject will receive special attention later.[1] We shall see, to our surprise, that Peary completely altered his views, and adopted large units, on his last expedition.

He gives an imposing list of surveying and other

[1] Chapter XI.

instruments, chronometers, barometers, etc., taken on the trip of 1892. This was a graceful tribute to science; there is no indication that the instruments were overworked. Peary claimed to be the first Arctic explorer who used an odometer, fixed to the back of a sledge, for registering the distance travelled. No tent was taken, and the sleeping bags were thrown away "at the end of three weeks." [1] The rations per man per day included 16 oz. of pemmican, and amounted to 2½ lb.

Peary never adopted the excellent custom of the greatest explorers who publish their daily diary or journal. This custom is commendable, because it establishes the *bona fides* of the traveller, who obviously has nothing to hide, and who usually presents his original journal to some scientific society, where it is carefully preserved and consulted by students.

Peary, instead of doing this, published stories of his travels, and his original journals are secret documents; but we shall deal with this more fully in its place. At present we are concerned only with the fact that the account he produced of his first great journey omitted all mention of many days, as will be seen on Schedule No. 1.[2] It must not be assumed from this that there was anything to conceal; for the record of this journey appears to be candid. The point is that Peary's method of telling a tale, instead of letting his diary speak for itself, is an appeal to the public rather than to students, hence it cannot fail to be regarded by the latter with some little suspicion.

On 30th April, 1892, Dr Cook, Gibson, Astrup, and some Eskimos were sent with two sledges and twelve dogs to haul supplies up to the inland ice. Peary followed them on 3rd May. A week was occupied in transporting the loads to a height of about 2500 feet, near the edge of the ice-cap. The difficulties to be

[1] *Northward over the Great Ice*, vol. i, p. 283.
[2] See pp. 22–23.

surmounted are shown by the time taken to advance the first twenty-six miles. This distance was not accomplished, owing to blizzards, steep slopes, and soft snow, until 15th May. The gradient then became easier and the daily marches began to lengthen out.

When the party was fairly upon the inland ice, the course was set north-east, true,[1] with the purpose of missing several inlets that extended inland from the north-west coast of the country. That they were not missed may have been due to their not having been surveyed completely, or to faulty navigation, or to both. Peary had much difficulty, delay, and danger, during the journey, from the crevasses that lay round the head of each inlet.

On 17th May he reached the ice-divide between Whale Sound and the Humboldt Glacier, at 5000 feet, and began to descend. On 25th May the supporting party of Dr Cook and Gibson was sent back with two dogs and twelve days' rations. Peary and Astrup proceeded with thirteen dogs, the loads being light, or about 77 lb. per dog. The men helped to pull when necessary.

Their north-eastern course led them into the heart of the unknown. It was very courageous, therefore, to press forward as they did, though courage is common to all pioneer exploration. There was no need for Peary to claim, apart from its questionable taste, that this journey was superior to Nansen's first crossing of Greenland, for Nansen actually ran much greater risks. Peary never in his whole life attempted anything, for the sake of discovery, as dangerous as Nansen's crossing of the East Greenland Current. The return over the thin ice of the large channel, in 1906, was as great a risk, perhaps, but to take this risk was the only chance of life. On all Peary's crossings of the ice-cap he knew his course was approximately parallel to the coast for the greater part of the

[1] *I.e.* on the Geographical and not the Magnetic Pole.

distance, so that he could reach the sea, if in difficulties, very quickly. Nansen's only hope lay at the
end of his journey; he "burnt his boats."

The head of Petermann Fjord was seen on 31st
May, and Peary swerved ten miles eastward to avoid
it. This did not enable him to escape the crevassed
region, where he was involved for two or three days.
The summit of the next ice-divide was at a height of
5700 feet. St George's Fjord came into view on 8th
June, and a week was spent in its locality; for two days
a blizzard raged, in which it was impossible to travel.
This was followed by a three days' struggle among
crevasses. Only ten miles were made in eight days.
Sherard Osborne Fjord appeared on 18th June with
the inevitable crevasses; but escape to the east here
was more successful, in spite of breaking through the
lids of several of these chasms.

New land was seen to the N.W., N., and N.E.
on 22nd and 23rd June. The height of the inland
ice was then said to be about 6000 feet. The next
two days, presumably 24th and 25th June, are not
mentioned; there may have been nothing to record.
On the 26th the entrance to a fjord was seen to the
N.N.W. The course was changed to E., and next
day to S.E., as Peary was headed off by his new land.
Three days are here missed out of the record, except
to say that the S.E. course was maintained, following
the edge of the land.

On 1st July an opening appeared in the shore
mountains and Peary descended towards it, over
steep gradients. The land was reached by crossing a
moraine. Here bird and animal life, rejoicing in the genial
warmth of the sun, was found. The hunting of polar
oxen occupied most of Peary's time in his new country.

He wrote: "If, as I had for some days suspected,
this channel [1] actually stretched from Lincoln Sea to

[1] Peary did not make it clear what channel he referred to. He
showed a " Peary Channel," that we shall hear of again, on his map.

the Arctic Ocean on the N.E. coast of Greenland, was I to fail now to fathom its secret and take home the news that the northern extension of the mainland had at last been found? It was certain that we had no reserve of provisions that would warrant us in making any considerable sojourn in the region." [1]

In writing of the *certainty* of scant food Peary answered his own question. He did fail to fathom the geographical secrets of the land he had discovered, particularly with reference to the channel, for fresh meat was an absolute necessity at that time, though hunting was not the purpose of the expedition. This purpose, unfortunately, had to take second place to hunting for beef. Peary did his best to explore the land, and he tramped many weary miles to obtain a good viewpoint. This he found, at last, on an eminence 3800 feet high, that he named Navy Cliff. Here he built a cairn and left his record, fixing the point by observation at "81° 37′ 5″ N. latitude and 34° 5′ W. longitude." [2]

He made the kind of mistake common to pioneers, but to an uncommon extent, in misunderstanding the character of many of the land-forms and waterways he had discovered. He thought he had reached the ocean coast, and that he saw "islands beyond the mainland." [3] He named one chapter of his book "Northernmost Greenland," [4] which it was not; though such errors are not uncommon, as we have said, with pioneers. He plotted a large bay on his map, which he named Independence Bay; also a great channel, probably the channel already referred to, that insulated an extensive mass of the northernmost part of Greenland. These features will be seen on Chart No. 2. [5]

[1] *Northward over the Great Ice*, vol. i, pp. 329–330.
[2] *Ibid.*, vol. i, p. 348.   [3] *Ibid.*, vol. i, p. 335.
[4] *Ibid.*, vol. i, chap. xii, p. 329.
[5] In pocket.

SCHEDULE No. I

McCormick Bay to Independence Fjord

1892.		Miles.
May 3	Peary left Redcliffe ; supporting party left on 30th April	? 15
4 } 5 }	Carrying loads up to Cache Camp at edge of inland ice, 2525 ft.	2½
	(6th and 7th not mentioned ; probably same as 4th and 5th)	?
8	Blizzard ; unable to leave Cache Camp	0
9	Blizzard ; struggled a few, probably six miles through it	? 6
10	Relaying up steep gradients, through soft snow (11th to 14th apparently the same ; distance probably 15 miles)	3
		? 15
15	Reached summit at last	?
16	" Real journey on ice-cap " began ; 16 dogs ; course N.E. true	5
17	Crossed 5000-foot divide and descended into Humboldt Glacial Basin	7
18	In Humboldt Glacial Basin	12
19	Saw land between Rensselaer Harbour and Humboldt Glacier	20
20	Still descending	20
21	Deflected 5 miles east ; short march ; built igloo ; blizzard	?
22	Blizzard for 48 hours ; height about 3500 feet	0
23	Storm had hardened surface	20
24	Last march of supporting party ; 130 miles from sea	20
25	Peary and Astrup proceed with 13 dogs ; loads 1000 lb. ; short march	?
26	Sledge broken and repaired ; height about 3500 feet to here	10
27	Soft and deep snow ; ascending out of Humboldt Glacier Basin	15
28	Snow worse ; blizzard ; built igloo ; one dog killed	3
29	Cross ice-divide	15
30	Snow harder ; land seen to N.W. ; descend into Petermann Basin	20
31	Deflected 10 miles east ; head of Petermann Fjord seen	5
June 1	Camp Petermann, 4200 ft. ; obs. and bearings ; warm, clear, calm	0

1892.		Miles.
June 2	Petermann Mts. in sight; crevasses; course E. 10 miles	?
3	Course N.E.; mts. still seen; surface "comparatively level"	?
4	Gradual ascent; snow softer and deeper	?
5	Crossed Petermann and Sherard Osborne divide, 5700 feet	?
6	Snow harder; following wind	19½
7		21
8	Camped in view of St George's Fd. after rapid descent	21
9	Blizzard, buried in drift snow	0
10	,, ,, ,,	0
11	Trapped among crevasses; climbing steep	
12	slopes on S.E. course; 15 miles of northing lost	?—15
13	Course N.E.; crevasses; fog; 18 hours' delay	0
14	Sledge broken	4
15	Rise of temperature causes stickiness; camped 2 days	6
16	In camp, overhauling sledges; 75 lb. discarded	0
17	Relaying	6¼
18	Sherard Osborne Fjord seen; deflected N.E. then E.	16½
19	Crevasses; blizzard	8
20		18½
21	Tired, helping dogs to pull	18
22	New land seen to N.W., N., and N.E.; sun warm	20½
23	New land; New Fjord to N.W., 6000 feet	20
24	(Not mentioned)	?
25	,, ,,	?
26	Course E.; descending; half march; drift	10
27	Course S.E.	10
28	(Not mentioned, except that course was still S.E.	?
29	(Not mentioned, except that course was still S.E.)	?
30	(Not mentioned, except that course was still S.E.)	?
July 1	Course N.E.; descend from 5000 ft.; land reached; 8 dogs left	?
	Total distance given	502½

We shall give particular attention to Peary's discoveries in this district when recording the visits of other explorers to it.

The return journey was begun with "eight well-fed dogs," and the two men were satisfied with beef, having killed several polar oxen. They started on 7th to 8th July, travelling by "night" to avoid the glare of the sun. The "corrected elevation" on the 11th was said to be about 7300 feet. They were held up for the next two days by a blizzard. Most of the daily marches were of about twenty miles. On 3rd August thirty-five miles were covered, with five dogs, on a falling gradient. Next day the great journey ended.

The distance travelled on this trip is said to have been 1200 miles. This is probable, as a straight line along the route measures 500 miles. The speed on the outward journey averaged less than 10 m.p.d. Peary was premature in claiming, as the principal result of this expedition, "the delineation of the northern extension and the insularity of Greenland." [1] He virtually accomplished this a few years later; but he felt the need of "boosting" his first enterprise as much as possible, to raise funds for completing the work. He had merely glimpsed his new land, and at once set about the inception of a more pretentious expedition, to explore, and possibly to make an accurate survey of, his discoveries.

4. *The Expedition of* 1893–95.—The Second North Greenland Expedition proved, through no fault of its leader, a failure. Peary struggled most bravely, though ineffectually, against one misfortune after another. He was deprived of nearly all his men, his dogs, and his stores.

On 6th March, 1894, his party of eight men, with eighty dogs, started for the same objective as in 1892. His purpose, on reaching Independence Bay, was to split the party into three small units: three men to go

[1] *Northward over the Great Ice*, vol. i, p. 438.

north; three others to proceed to the south and east, as far as Cape Bismarck; and two men to remain with the dogs, surveying and hunting. All this was well planned.

Before the first week of the journey was ended, men and dogs began to fail. A succession of blizzards, at a height of 5000 feet, reduced the party by 23rd March to four men, the others having returned. Another storm, during the first week in April, and an epidemic among the dogs, made it necessary to abandon the trip. They turned back on 10th April after travelling 128 miles. The stores were *cached* and marked with a 14-foot bamboo driven 2½ feet into the snow. An empty biscuit tin was attached to the top of the bamboo and the depot was visible from a distance of 2½ miles. Its position was fixed by observations. Other depots were left nearer the station. Only twenty-five dogs survived, and all Peary's assistants, except Lee and Henson, his negro servant, returned to civilisation.

The depots were to be revisited in October as part of the preparation for a second attempt, in 1895, to cross the inland ice. Blizzard after blizzard delayed this journey, and when the position of the main depot, according to Peary's observations, was reached, nothing could be seen of it. The most careful search proved unavailing. The stores were either buried in snow, as Peary supposed, or he failed to find their exact location; possibly both these causes contributed to the disaster. "All my essential supplies," he wrote, "for the next spring's sledging journey, nearly a ton and a half in all, including every ounce of my alcohol and pemmican, were irrevocably and for ever buried. . . . I was almost stunned by my loss; I felt like a man shipwrecked upon an uninhabited shore." [1]

Very few, even of the boldest, explorers would have persisted, after this misfortune, in making the journey; but Peary was "the man who refused to fail," and he merely cried: "The fates and all Hell are against me,

[1] *Northward over the Great Ice*, vol. ii, pp. 295-296.

but I'll conquer yet! " [1]   Food and fuel, of inferior
kinds, could be improvised, though the chances now
were heavily loaded against successfully negotiating
the double journey. To embark upon it was a gamble
with death, and the prospect of being able to do any
useful work was infinitesimal. Only two months'
allowance, of any supplies, were available. If the
inland ice were crossed in half this time, the party
would be absolutely dependent upon finding game
before returning. Not the slightest margin existed
for contingencies; indeed, unless circumstances were
favourable, there would be little hope of returning.

On 1st April 1895 Peary, Lee, and Henson started
on this hazardous journey. "Equipment and rations
were both makeshifts. . . . We knew that we were
relying solely upon our own exertions and the Almighty.
. . . Whatever accidents or mishaps befell, there
would, there could be no rescuing party." [2]   The
winter station, when they left it, was deserted.

At a speed of over 20 m.p.d. the party reached the
position of the lost depot. A smaller depot, containing biscuits and milk, was recovered; only three
inches of the pole were projecting above the snow.
There were then three sledges and forty-two dogs.
A course was set to avoid the crevassed areas, and a
height of 7670 feet was said to have been averaged
for one week. When 500 miles had been accomplished only seventeen dogs remained, and these, as
Peary said, went to the dogs literally. There was
nothing else but dog-meat for the surviving dogs to
eat, and in a few days more only eleven dogs survived,
three of which were not strong.

Land was then sighted. On reaching it, no recent signs of polar oxen appeared. It was decided
to stake everything on finding them. "We were
taking our lives in our hands," Peary wrote. He

[1] *Peary the Man who Refused to Fail*, p. 145.
[2] *Northward over the Great Ice*, vol. ii, pp. 438–439.

secured about half a dozen of the beasts, but no geographical, cartographical, or any other work was done. The journey was wasted.

Peary's little party started for home on 1st June with about a fortnight's full rations, *plus* nine dogs and nine cartridges, for the 500-mile run. Particular attention is directed to this journey, for reasons that will appear more fully in a later chapter; not that we are given many details of the daily marches, but because it was a race with death.

Peary considered that the prospects of the three men getting back, at the expense of the dogs, were good, if the weather was reasonable. Schedule No. 2 [1] shows most of the particulars of this journey. Lee began to fail after the first few days; this was a dreadful handicap for the others. He was heavily dosed with quinine, peptonoids, hot tea, and brandy. These stimulants got him along with only one day's complete rest. On 7th June one of the two remaining sledges was abandoned, with the hope that the other and lighter sledge would make "the remaining 400 miles without breaking." [2] On the 11th the men were obliged to help the five remaining dogs to drag the sledge. They then had "nineteen days' half-rations of biscuit, tea, and milk," and were about half-way across the inland ice. They were unable to travel as much as 21 m.p.d., but usually they accomplished twenty miles. A few blizzards, that did not last many hours, shortened some of the marches, but improved the surface by hardening it. The sledge-runners were iced to increase the glide. The dog-meat was tough and tasteless. The last ice-divide was crossed on 22nd June, and the party began to descend from the plateau. They then felt safe, though only one dog remained, and next day only four biscuits, which were then eaten. The dog was given some sealskin boots and survived. Thus

[1] See next page.
[2] *Northward over the Great Ice*, vol. ii, p. 512.

they reached the station in a state of terrible exhaustion, but the race with death was won.

This was one of the "worst journeys in the world" made in the polar regions. There have been many journeys in which men suffered more, but few when such risks were taken. It was one of the worst, not only because of its peril and hardship, but because it accomplished nothing, beyond proving the strength of Peary's character. No results could possibly be obtained under the circumstances, and all the risk was run for nothing. Everything had to be concentrated upon an endeavour to save life. Twenty-five marches were made, on the return, in twenty-four days, which averaged 20·7 miles a day. There were no detours on this journey. A little compass-sledge was used to keep the course in thick weather; this saved three days, and possibly the whole party. The meteorites were then brought home to cover the defeat. Peary's short cut to fame, up to this time, had not proved a success.

Schedule No. 2

Independence Fjord to Whale Sound

1895.		Miles.
June 1	Left moraine and climbed slope ; wind and drift	?
2	Rations for 14 days ; 9 dogs ; 6000 feet ;[1] fine	20
3	Fine	25¼
4	"A fair march " ; probably nearly 20 miles ; fine	?
5	All troubled with feet and legs ; wind and drift	?
6	Lee failing, doped ; loose and deep snow ; fine	?
7	Lee still unwell ; 2 dogs fail ; frost-fog ; fine	17½
8	Lee worse ; large sledge abandoned ; bad surface ; fine	20
9	Lee incapable ; heavily doped ; obs. " Lodge nearly 400 miles "	4
10	Lee better ; weather thick	20
11	Third dog shot	?

[1] The highest altitude given is " nearly 8000 feet " (*Northward over the Great Ice*, vol. ii, p. 518).

1895.		Miles.
June 12	Fourth dog shot; about half-way; 9½ days' rations left	20½
13	Fifth dog shot; on a slight decline; sun warm	20½
14	(Not mentioned, except distance)	20½
15	Blizzard caused several hours' delay	20½
16	Last dog-food eaten; warmth increases friction	20½
17	Short march owing to blizzard	?
18	Blizzard hardened surface	21½
19	Heavy pulling; snowing, then stiff head wind	10½
20	(Not mentioned; probably about 20 miles)	?
21	Two dogs left; probably about 20 miles	?
22	One dog left; now feel safe; probably about 20 miles	?
23	Four biscuits left; soft snow, wind, and drift	17½
24	Reach the Lodge; one dog left	20

CHAPTER IV

THE *WINDWARD* EXPEDITION

" Unlike the dreaming prehistoric world, ours . . . has devoted its best energy and treasure to the sovereign purpose of detecting error and vindicating entrusted truth."

LORD ACTON.
Lectures on Modern History.

1. INCEPTION DIFFICULTIES. 2. EVENTS FROM AUTUMN 1898 TO SPRING 1900. 3. THE SLEDGING SEASON OF 1900. 4. INACCURATE CHARTING. 5. EVENTS FROM JUNE 1900 TO END OF EXPEDITION.

1. PEARY had announced his intention of trying for the North Pole on his last Greenland expedition.[1] When this was over he took up the project more seriously and decided to use the Smith Sound route. He began his report on the *Windward* Expedition of 1898–1902 as follows: "In January 1897 I promulgated my plan for an extended scheme of Arctic exploration, having for its main purpose the attainment of the North Pole." [2]

A Norwegian expedition happened to have planned, a little before Peary, another four years' campaign, and, unfortunately, with the design of also using the Smith Sound route. Four months prior to the above date, or in September 1896, Captain Otto Sverdrup had undertaken to command the Second *Fram* Expedition. He wrote: "Together with Dr Nansen and my owner I agreed on the following route, which

[1] *Northward over the Great Ice*, vol. ii, p. 550.
[2] *Nearest the Pole*, p. 295. According to a conversation reported by Commander Green, Peary announced his plan about June 1896 ; but in this conflict of evidence Peary's statement as given above must be regarded as " official."

was to be up Smith Sound and Kane Basin, through Kennedy and Robeson Channels, and as far along the north coast of Greenland as possible before wintering. From there we were to make sledge expeditions to the northernmost point of Greenland, and as far down the east coast as we could attain. *There was no question of trying to reach the Pole* " [1] (our italics).

Captain Sverdrup was a particularly capable leader for such an exploration. His record is well worth consulting by any who are unfamiliar with it.[2] Our knowledge of the region he had planned to investigate was delayed for many years, if we are not yet the losers, because he was prevented from carrying out his programme.

The *Fram* sailed on 24th June 1898 and reached Smith Sound on 16th August. When Peary heard of Sverdrup's expedition, he raced to get there first, and won by a few days. There was plenty of room, according to their published plans, for both these expeditions; they were complementary. Moreover, Peary was the interloper; though he had a perfect right to use this route to the Pole. He showed the greatest annoyance, however, and wrote: "The introduction of a disturbing factor in *the appropriation by another of my plan and field of work* necessitated the chartering of an auxiliary ship." [3] The statement italicised was, of course, untrue.

Sverdrup withdrew, as soon as he could, into Jones Sound. Peary, personally, assumed an antagonistic and even offensive attitude towards Sverdrup, who had done nothing wrong. We cannot altogether avoid these matters; for Peary, as we shall see, would not leave Sverdrup alone. He might, indeed, have been a formidable competitor; not for the Pole, but in the

[1] *New Land*, vol. i, p. 1.
[2] See Nansen's *First Crossing of Greenland* and *Farthest North*, as well as Sverdrup's *New Land*.
[3] *Nearest the Pole*, p. 296.

reaping of important results. Peary must have been afraid that his dream of fame, dispersed by the forces of nature in Greenland, would be endangered by the presence of Sverdrup. No consideration for the rights of other explorers caused Peary any concern.

It would seem as if nature punished Peary for this. He had a terrible time during the four years of this expedition. We will leave it at that, with the remembrance that the two expeditions were planned independently; that Peary's main object, the North Pole, was not on Sverdrup's programme; and that the purpose of the Norwegian expedition to explore the north coast of Greenland was the only item that clashed, and this only with one of Peary's subsidiary aims, and one that he had not publicly avowed. The want of a little reasonableness resulted in "the publication of quite erroneous maps for many years." [1]

2. *Events from Autumn* 1898 *to Spring* 1900.— Unfavourable ice-conditions prevented the *Windward* from advancing farther north than Cape D'Urville, which is about 700 miles from the North Pole. Peary expected to sledge this distance by working supplies forward to an advanced base on, or near, the coast of the Arctic Ocean. This would be nearly half-way to his goal, on paper. His immediate need, in the autumn of 1898, was fresh meat; and he combined with the hunting as much useful work as possible, by mapping the parts of Grinnell Land that were in the neighbourhood of the ship. He was feverishly anxious to forestall the Norwegian surveyors in all debatable land; but he should have made sure that his maps were better than theirs. When the two are compared, the inferiority of Peary's charting is evident. [2]

The polar campaign began by sledging northward in the light of the winter moons; the first reconnaissance being begun on 29th October. Fort Conger, General Greely's station, was the objective, and

[1] *The Lands of Silence*, p. 380.   [2] See also p. 192.

supplies were advanced some distance towards it during the November moon. Peary sledged from Cape Wilkes, while returning from the first trip, a distance of seventy miles in a straight line, in one long march of "23 hours and 20 minutes, or 21 hours 30 minutes actual travelling time." [1] Peary estimated this march at ninety miles, which would necessitate an average speed of over 4 m.p.h. This is possible, as there were *no loads* on the sledges and it was a beaten track. Dr MacMillan, Peary's assistant, subsequently sledged one hundred miles in twenty-four hours over Melville Bay, but Peary's performance may be the record for moonlight sledging.

On 20th December another start was made for Fort Conger. Peary reached there on 6th January, 1899, in a critical condition. The winter blizzards, in the darkness, during the last week of this journey, nearly caused the loss of the party. The men groped and stumbled through a chaos of rugged ice. The temperature was down to —63° F. Peary's feet were frostbitten and his toes had to be amputated. He was lashed on a sledge on 18th February and taken, by moonlight and twilight, back to the *Windward*. The minimum temperature during this journey was —65° F. The ship was reached on the 28th; a distance of 250 miles in eleven days, or 22·7 m.p.d.

The final amputation of Peary's toes was performed on 13th March. He started for Fort Conger with more supplies on 19th April, riding again on a sledge, for his right foot had not healed. The journey was made in ten days at 25 m.p.d. Peary then twice attempted to cross Robeson Channel to Greenland, but the ice was unfavourable. One of his wounds that had not healed began to look unhealthy; so on 23rd May Conger was left for the *Windward*. This well-beaten track was covered in six days [2] at an average of over 41½ m.p.d., which may be a record,

[1] *Nearest the Pole*, p. 304.   [2] *Ibid.*, p. 312.

to continue its exploration; and he hoped to link up the Independence Bay district he had discovered in 1893 with Lockwood's farthest.

Fort Conger was left on 15th April and Robeson Channel crossed. Rough ice, open water, and storms were daily hindrances to progress along the Greenland coast. The Black Horn Cliffs were passed on very thin ice. "Lockwood's cache and cairn" at Cape Bryant were found to have been scattered by bears; but the record at Lockwood Island was recovered "in a perfect state of preservation." From here, after naming Cape Washington, Lockwood had turned back. Peary, therefore, was the discoverer of the coast beyond this island.

He did not tarry long, for he yearned to pass Cape Washington and see country that was altogether his own by discovery; and this he accomplished, from Lockwood Island, in one march. He rejoiced to find that a more northerly cape existed, previously unseen by man. It is the northernmost point of Greenland, and received the name Cape Morris Jesup. Here "variation and latitude sights were taken," and then Peary set off towards the Pole across the ice of the Arctic Ocean.

He had not been on the pack before at any distance from land, and was now to find out what kind of sledging surface it would present. He found out very quickly. The first night he camped "a few miles from land," possibly on ice that was aground. He gave no more than sixteen lines of description to the rest of his northward journey. The second and third days were foggy, and the going was over "gigantic, wave-like drifts of hard snow." On the fourth day after leaving land the air was clear, but it was "frightful going—consisting of fragments of old floes, ridges of heavy ice thrown up to heights of twenty-five to fifty feet, crevasses and holes masked by snow; the whole intersected by narrow leads of open water." [1]

[1] *Nearest the Pole*, p. 327.

The prospect from a pinnacle, "some fifty feet high," showing no improvement, Peary turned back from here, after taking observations and bearings of the newly discovered coast. The land could not have been far away and was reached in one march. We are not told what distance he went on the pack, but his route, as marked on the chart, scales about fifteen or sixteen miles.

The foregoing was an experience of historic importance in Peary's life. His first meeting with the polar pack was a short skirmish with the most formidable opponent he had to meet in his attempts to reach the North Pole. His relation to the pack-ice was the greatest factor in all his subsequent journeys. Somewhat as Whymper assailed the Matterhorn and Mallory Mt. Everest, so Peary faced the polar pack. It was his great antagonist that he had to overcome. We shall see whether the man or the ice finally conquered.

His first encounter showed that the odds were heavily in favour of the ice. Peary had done all distances, with light sledges, up to about 80 m.p.d., and with full loads, over 20 m.p.d., over other ice. On the polar pack his average was not more than one-fifth of this latter figure. His first assault, therefore, on his grim adversary, was repulsed decisively if not ignominiously.

As Peary pursued his way eastward into the unknown, along the coast that he was the first man to see, he had solid food for thought. Two seasons now remained in which to attain the Pole; but how could any man reach it across such ice? Were all his hopes to be shattered?

This four-years' expedition had been planned on one main assumption, drawn from an experience of several years in Greenland and on the frozen waterways of its western coast. This assumption, which was perfectly reasonable, was that an average speed of about ten miles a day could be maintained all the

Independence Bay, calling it Independence Fjord"; [1] it was not a Sound.

Captain Mikkelsen went out to try and recover Erichsen's diary, and was in North-east Greenland from 1909 until 1912. He succeeded in finding a long message from the ill-fated explorer, containing these words: "We drove westward, with 23 dogs, until the 1st of June, reaching Peary's Cape Glacier, and discovered that the Peary Channel *does not exist* (his italics), Navy Cliff being connected by land with Heilprin Land." [2] Peary's incorrect map very nearly cost the lives of Mikkelsen and his companion, who intended returning through the mythical "Peary Channel."

Sir Clements Markham adds, in a footnote: "Peary's point at the place he calls 'Navy Cliff,' where he says he saw the sea and called it 'Independence Bay,' is over a hundred miles from the sea or any bay. He may have seen the end of the long, narrow fjord which Erichsen discovered, but his channel across Greenland does not exist." [3]

Mr Knud Rasmussen became anxious for the safety of Mikkelsen, and organised, in 1911, a most efficient expedition, with the double purpose of searching for the lost explorer and carrying out scientific work. "Prominent among the scientific objects of the expedition," wrote its leader, "was that of exploring and surveying the supposed Peary Channel." [4] One of the finest sledge journeys on record was made across the inland ice, on a course approximately parallel to, and a little south of, Peary's previous routes. The outward journey to Danmark Fjord was 628 miles in length, and the greatest height attained, 7231 feet, makes Peary's highest altitude of nearly 8000 feet [5] extremely improbable.

[1] *Lost in the Arctic*, p. 192.   [2] *Ibid.*, p. 192.
[3] *The Lands of Silence*, p. 373.
[4] *Report of the First Thule Expedition*, 1912, p. 286.
[5] *Northward over the Great Ice*, vol. ii, p. 518.

Rasmussen and his companion, Peter Freuchen, found that Peary's "Independence Bay" was a long fjord, and "in the place of the supposed Peary Channel there is an extensive ice-free upland, abounding in game." [1] They saw "an open stretch of snowless land just where the map (Peary's) showed the dotted line of a channel. Greenland was thus in unbroken connection with Peary Land." [2]

Rasmussen added: "Mylius Erichsen had already, in 1907, discovered that the Peary Channel did not exist; he could not then, however, as we know, support his statement by actual survey of the base of the fjord owing to the lateness of the season. And Einar Mikkelsen, who turned back and started for home on reaching the mouth of Danmark Fjord, was likewise unable to carry out the work. To him must, however, be ascribed the credit of connecting Mylius Erichsen's name with the discovery. . . . It remained for Freuchen and myself to furnish, by our surveys, final proof as to the correctness of Mylius Erichsen's discovery." [3]

Freuchen wrote: "All idea of a Peary Channel filled with glacier ice had to be relinquished"; [4] and a little later: "This must be the hollow which Peary and Astrup looked out over in 1892 without being able to see down into it. The country rises again, however, a little farther in." [5]

The last explorer to visit this district was Lauge Koch, in 1921. He most inexplicably puts the following heading to a section of his report: "We rediscover Peary Channel." [6] He gives no record of the rediscovery of the channel, for the very good reason that it is not there! His excellent map shows

---

[1] *Geographical Journal*, December 1913, p. 546.
[2] *Report of the First Thule Expedition*, 1912, pp. 321–322.
[3] *Ibid.*, 1912, p. 327.   [4] *Ibid.*, 1912, p. 362.   [5] *Ibid.*, 1912, p. 364.
[6] *Report on the Danish Bicentenary Jubilee Expedition*, 1920–23, p. 95.

a diminutive fjord, named Bronlund Fjord, leading westward into a valley, Wandel Valley, which contains a lake, and ends in the Astrup Glacier; the inland ice occupying all the western half of the land where Peary installed his great channel. Koch did not penetrate far up Wandel Valley, but his health was not good at the time of his visit.

Peary said that he "had now and then caught glimpses of the frozen channel" through "rifts in the mountains." [1] He may have seen the lake, but he did not go near the valley, which he magnified and extended into a huge arm of the sea, insulating a large mass, 200 miles long and 130 miles wide, of the most northerly part of Greenland.

His record was found on Navy Cliff. From here he said: "We saw stretching away to the horizon the great icefields of the Arctic Ocean." [2]

Excuses and explanations, when mistakes are found out, are easily made; but the major features of a chart are either correct or incorrect; and they may bear some general resemblance to nature without the chart being accurate. Peary's map of his discoveries in this district (*Northward over the Great Ice*, vol. i, p. 353) was so grossly incorrect as to be misleading and dangerous. This was acknowledged by the United States Government, in 1915, when Peary's charts were "officially cancelled and withdrawn," on the grounds, *inter alia*, that they "erroneously show waterways that do not exist and lands that are really deep sea, while lands that do exist are omitted altogether." [3]

This part of our subject must be concluded before becoming open to the charge of flogging a dead horse, though all the evidence on Peary's bad mapping of this

---

[1] *Northward over the Great Ice*, vol. i, pp. 345–346.

[2] *Ibid.*, vol. i, p. 343 ; see also pp. 347, 357.

[3] *The Congressional Record*, January 1916, p. 1092 and following pages.

WANDEL VALLEY

facing p. 42

district has not been given. Mr Rasmussen is one of our latest authorities on Northern Greenland, and he was a great admirer of Peary, yet the truth compelled him to write: "Peary had come to wrong conclusions with regard to places like Nordenskjöld Fjord and de Long Fjord, not to mention Independence Fjord." [1] Rasmussen pleads excuses for Peary as a pioneer. Our business is to record the facts. The most impartial examination of Peary's work cannot evade the truth that he engraved major geographical features upon his maps that bore no resemblance to nature, and even some that had no material existence. Pioneers often make slight mistakes and are readily forgiven; but Peary built up grandiloquent claims upon foundations so insecure that they have now been wiped out.

5. *Events from June* 1900 *to End of Expedition.*— Peary returned to Fort Conger on 10th June, 1900, having found that the Greenland route to the Pole was impracticable. One of the principal reasons he gave for this was "the comparatively rapid motion of the ice as it swung round the northern coast into the southerly setting East Greenland current." [2] Subsequently he found his more westerly route from Grant Land somewhat, though not considerably, better. It never occurred to him that on a still more westerly course he might have found an even greater improvement in the ice conditions. There is a certain amount of evidence for this, but it would be out of place here. Peary met with serious difficulties on every journey he made between land and the Pole.

The next ten months of his record are a blank, except for hunting. He intimates that the winter was spent at Fort Conger, and then expressly states that, on 5th April, 1901, he started, with only twelve dogs, on his "northern trip." [3] This was his delicate

---

[1] *Greenland by the Polar Sea*, p. 155 ; see also pp. 17, 154.
[2] See p. 236.
[3] *Nearest the Pole*, p. 334.

manner of stating that he set out for the Pole, without sufficient supplies to carry him one quarter of the distance to it. The attempt was most feeble. After going about fifty miles, apparently in four days, he turned back from Lincoln Bay without setting foot on the pack-ice. He said that he had no chance of reaching the Pole.

An air of mystery hangs over this sledging season. Weakness seemed to overcome Peary after his return to Fort Conger in June 1900. The following ten months were completely wasted, no exploratory work being attempted. Apart from the nerveless attempt of April 1901, nothing was undertaken seriously for nearly two years. We have no need at present to speculate on the cause of this, but it may be relevant to notice that usually Peary worked in "fits and starts." He wasted two entire seasons, those of 1899 and 1901, during the four years of this expedition; the former as the result of his unbalanced zeal when first he came north, and the latter without any reason being apparent. He had inherited, presumably, a highly emotional nature, that need have been no serious disadvantage; but he tried to represent himself as a man of granite. His alternating action and inaction suggest rubber as a more appropriate simile.

On 17th April, 1901, he started southward for the ship, which he reached on 6th May. The 300 miles on this journey averaged 15 m.p.d. with light sledges. The rest of the year was spent, apparently, in preparing for the final attempt on the Pole. The period of weakness lasted until the following spring.

Peary set out from Payer Harbour for the last time on 6th March, 1902. The journey to Fort Conger was accomplished in fourteen days, at 21 m.p.d., with full loads. On the 24th he started for the Pole from Fort Conger, and left the land at Cape Hecla on 6th April. His description of the pack-ice should be observed carefully, because the seasonal changes are small, and the general conditions vary little, in the same locality, from year to year. We shall see, also, that similar difficulties were encountered on each of the last three attempts. Peary himself has made us quite familiar with the conditions on his routes to the Pole.

The first obstruction met with, on leaving Cape Hecla, was soft snow in which "the dogs wallowed belly deep." [1] At about two miles from land, "areas of rough ice . . . compelled us to exaggerated zigzags and doubling on our track. It was easier to go a mile round." Some "heavily rubbled old ice" ended the first day's march.

The next day the party "came upon a zone of old floe fragments deeply blanketed with snow . . . the dogs floundering, almost useless . . . now lifting the sledges bodily . . . veering right and left, doubling in our track." Occasionally there were better patches, but men and dogs were thoroughly exhausted after about six miles on this day, which was "a fair sample of our day's work." [2]

The next day mentioned is 12th April, when a blizzard buried the dogs and set the floes in motion. On the 13th two channels deflected them off their course as much as 90°, "until an area of extremely rough ice prevented us from following (the second channel) farther." They were held up for over a day by this channel, which Peary called the "Grand Canal." On crossing it, on the 14th, he entered "a zone of high parallel ridges of rubble ice covered with deep snow," and it took "some time" to find "a practicable pass through this barrier." He next had to cross "extremely rugged and heavy old floes" covered with soft and deep snow. Sixteen hours' toil advanced the party "two or three miles."

[1] *Nearest the Pole*, p. 341.
[2] *Ibid.*, p. 342. Peary, *apparently*, always refers to geographical miles made good on the course, but he does not say so.

On the 15th they passed over "heavy old floes slowly moving eastward," and had to wait, frequently, "for the pieces to crush close enough together to let us pass." Peary was then "compelled to bear away due east by an impracticable area," and, lastly, he was "brought up by a lead some fifty feet wide. From this on, one day was much like another. . . . Fog and stormy weather also helped to delay us." [1]

Our main purpose in these citations is to ask how much should be added to the latitude distance for all the deviations. We are not told if the daily distances given were those actually travelled, though on his later journeys Peary always referred to the distance *made good* on his course, which was much less. He did not give the latitude of Cape Hecla, but the Canadian Government maps show it at about 82° 50′ N. As he turned back in latitude 84° 17′ N., he made 87 geographical miles of northing. A geographical mile is nearly 267 yards (or 15 per cent.) longer than an English statute mile; hence, 100½ statute miles were gained towards the Pole.

Schedule No. 3 [2] shows how little information we have been given with reference to this journey over the pack. It is clear, however, that the deviations from the meridian of Cape Hecla were serious. Twice in the sixteen days' advance Peary wrote of travelling at *right angles* to his course, and twice of even *doubling back*. One-third is a common addition for deviations from the straight line, but on this journey 40 *per cent.* must be nearer the truth. Assuming this amount, Peary travelled 140 miles at an average of about 8 m.p.d., for 6 m.p.d. of northing made good. [3]

He found that the pack to the north of Grant Land was not much better, as a sledging surface, than it was off the Greenland coast, but he found again that the

---

[1] *Nearest the Pole*, p. 343.   [2] Page 49.
[3] For further references to the amount of deviation from the course, see pp. 145–149.

prevailing drift of the ice was from west to east, and this made the more westerly route safer, as there was less danger of being swept into the East Greenland Current. The ice conditions, at the turning-point in latitude 84° 17′ N., were similar to those encountered during the journey, and *the sound of pressure came from the north.*

The Grant Land route to the Pole lay across very active ice. Peary's opinion was that the floes he heard in motion, to the north of latitude 84° 17′ N., "were crushing together under the influence of the wind or, what was perhaps more probable from the long continuation of the noise, the entire pack was in slow motion to the east." [1]

Particular attention is directed to Peary's description of the character of the pack on this first serious attempt to reach the Pole. There is not the slightest reason to doubt it. If we are granted little general information about the oceanic stage of the journey, we are given a fairly full account of the ice-conditions; indeed, Peary wrote little else. This was perfectly normal and natural, for the pack, as we have seen, was his most formidable antagonist.

When turning back, on 21st April, 1902, Peary wrote: "I hurried our departure in order to utilise as much of our tracks as possible before they were obliterated." The westerly wind that was blowing would fault the trail, so laboriously broken on the outward journey. "We lost it repeatedly," the account continues, "when we would be obliged to quarter the surface like bird dogs." [2]

The most fundamental factor was the movement of the pack, which caused pressure ridges and broke the backward trail. Peary found out these things, and he appeared to find also that the prevailing direction of the drift was from west to east. To counteract this, he set his course from Cape Hecla approximately

[1] *Nearest the Pole*, p. 344.   [2] *Ibid.*, pp. 344–345.

N.N.W. The longitude of his most northerly point on this journey was three or four degrees to the west of the cape. Had he travelled northward on the Hecla meridian he would have been obliged to return on a south-westerly course to reach his starting-point, otherwise he would have been carried towards the embouchure of Robeson Channel.

Only one storm worthy of mention occurred during the outward journey, and this appears to have lasted less than one day, yet the ice was very active as Peary advanced. One open channel had become, on the return, "a huge pressure ridge, which I estimated," wrote Peary, "to be from 75 to 100 feet high." [1] We shall hear of this monster again. Here, naturally, the trail was faulted. Peary found the picking up of his outward track a mental strain. He dare not camp for more than "a few hours," he wrote, "for I recognised that the entire pack was moving slowly, and that our trail was everywhere being faulted and interrupted by new pressure ridges and leads, in a way to make our return march nearly, if not quite, as slow and laborious as the outward one." [2]

This condition of the ice unfortunately was normal, for Peary proceeded: "The following marches were much the same," and at the "Grand Canal" the place was "almost unrecognisable." Some of the experienced Eskimos, two marches from here, "had been hopelessly bewildered, and wandered, apparently, for at least a day without finding the trail." A new road had to be made, but next day the old tracks were picked up.

Further quotations to the same effect could be given, but would be superfluous for the purpose of proving the character of the pack. Peary left no doubt in the minds of his readers that—

(1) The activity of the pack was his greatest difficulty, and made many additional miles of travel necessary.

[1] *Nearest the Pole*, p. 345. [2] *Ibid.*, p. 345.

SCHEDULE No. 3

1902.	Lat. N.		Miles.
April 6	82° 50′	Left Cape Hecla	5
7	..	Deep snowdrifts; axes used; fine	c. 5–7
8			?
9	..	(Not mentioned, except that the 7th was " a fair sample ")	?
10			?
11			?
12	..	Westerly gale ; no march	o
13	..	Deflected west ; then held up by " Grand Canal "	
14	..	..	2–3
15	..	" Daily advance . . . steadily decreasing "	?
16			?
17			?
18	..	(Not mentioned)	?
19			?
20			?
21	84° 17′ 27″ and 99° W.	Observation	?
22	..	Turned back	—

87 geo. miles of latitude in 16 days=5·4 m.p.d.
100·5 stat. miles=6·2 m.p.d.

(2) His next great hindrance was the roughness of its surface, which caused further delay and extra travel.

(3) The prevailing drift of the pack was from west to east.

(4) The difficulty of returning by the outward track was so very great as to become impossible after the lapse of many hours.

Fort Conger was reached on 3rd May, and left for the ship on the 6th. The contrast between the speed attained on this last stage of the journey, which was about 27 m.p.d., and that on the polar pack, of about *one-quarter* this daily distance, is sufficiently instructive, and should be remembered. Thus ended this important expedition.

It had not been very successful. Enormous depots had been laid on the route, but Peary had not been able to get very far beyond them. The absence of ability, in failing to push out any great distance beyond Fort Conger, is conspicuous. The severe character of the Arctic pack-ice was the final cause of failure.

CHAPTER V

THE FIRST *ROOSEVELT* EXPEDITION

" The obvious exaggerations of a mind giving a loose to its habitual impulses, and moulding all nature to its own purposes. . . . Hence his excessive egotism which filleth all objects with himself."

WILLIAM HAZLITT.
The Character of Rousseau.

1. THE CHARACTER OF THE RECORD. 2. CONSIDERATIONS PRELIMINARY TO THE POLAR JOURNEY. 3. THE POLAR JOURNEY TO STORM CAMP. 4. THE POLAR JOURNEY FROM STORM CAMP. 5. THE WESTERN JOURNEY.

1. PEARY returned in 1902 to his duty in the naval dockyards as "a faded romance, a broken bubble, an exploded theory. . . . Of course he had failed." [1] He was the last man, however, to be kept down for long, and the following year he was inspired by Captain Scott's deeds in Antarctica to begin planning another attempt on the Pole. In 1904 he was given 100,000 dollars for a new ship, and in July 1905 he sailed on what he expected to be his last expedition, for he was fifty years of age.

His book entitled *Nearest the Pole* [2] is the authority for this, as for the *Windward*, expedition; but his report of the latter is given somewhat in the form of an appendix to that of the first *Roosevelt* expedition. It is necessary before proceeding further to glance at this book and, in particular, to notice its most outstanding feature.

The published records of all the great explorers impress their readers by their transparent candour and sincerity. They never appear to be withholding

[1] *Peary the Man who Refused to Fail*, p. 234.   [2] Hutchinson, 1907.

information. They take their readers fully into their confidence and thus win their wholehearted interest and support. They trust us, upon occasion, with their inmost thoughts, and all their methods are described. They do their best to help others.

The contrast between all this and Peary's record of his penultimate expedition is complete. It is not pleasant to find that he is deliberately secretive; that he is withholding as much information as possible, and that he is giving his readers, grudgingly, like a miser, the very minimum that can be wrung from him. He appears, throughout this book, to be keeping back the cream of his account for some future and more worthy publication, but such has never appeared.

This want of candour, unfortunately, was deliberate. He travelled for the simple purpose of making his name resound from one end of the world to the other. This he believed he could accomplish by reaching the Pole, and he took every precaution not to help any possible competitor. He frankly admitted this, as Mr Stefansson has told us. "I once asked Peary why he had not published certain things that we were talking about, and his reply was, 'My dear boy, I am not printing anything until I have got the Pole.' It was only after he had reached the Pole . . . that he wrote his book, *Secrets of Polar Travel*." [1]

2. *Considerations Preliminary to the Polar Journey.* —The distance of the North Pole from the north coast of Grant Land is about 450 miles in a straight line. This is little more than half the length of Captain Scott's sledge journey to the South Pole; but the ice conditions on the two routes are almost totally different. Peary's route was harder than Scott's, thereby equalling, to some extent, its lesser

---

[1] *The Friendly Arctic*, p. 31. For several years it was impossible to obtain a copy of this book, and it has only been seen since the above was written. It merely enlarges, however, upon matters mentioned in the earlier works.

mileage. The distance actually travelled, moreover, on the ever-moving pack-ice is considerably in excess of that made good on a northerly course, so that the difference in the two efforts is still further reduced.

Peary's sledging experience in Greenland had enabled him to double his earlier speed over the inland ice, his first journey being made at an average of about ten, and his last at over twenty, miles a day. On beginning his trips along the coasts of Grinnell and Grant Lands, which formed the second stage of his sledging career, he found the conditions more troublesome than those he had successfully encountered on the ice-cap. He had to learn sledging lessons, in some particulars, over again. The type of sledge had to be totally different to negotiate the rougher track. He succeeded, for the second time, in overcoming his difficulties, and he did so to such purpose that his speed was again increased.

The third and last theatre of Peary's sledging operations proved the hardest of all. The higher speeds he had made normal along the ice-foot of the coasts were utterly unapproachable on the circumpolar pack. This was due, firstly, to the difficulty in picking the easiest course, when nearly every course seemed almost impracticable for sledging; secondly, to the obstacles necessitating continual detours and frequent excavations; thirdly, to the channels of open water, which imposed long and irritating delays and deviations; and lastly, to the movement of the ice carrying him, even when in camp, many miles off his course.

If any attempt to reach the Pole was to be made with any prospect of success, two improvements on Peary's previous arrangements were essential: a ship capable of transporting the expedition's base to the shore of the Arctic Ocean, and a pioneer party to break the arduous trail for the main advance. Both were provided in 1906 when Peary approached his most formidable antagonist, the polar pack, fully armed at last.

The *Roosevelt* was built for the express purpose of forcing her way through the ice-choked channels to the north-eastern coast of Grant Land; and this she did, though not without much difficulty and some damage. Cape Sheridan, the advanced base of the Nares Expedition, was reached on 5th September, 1905, and the autumn was spent in hunting.

During the winter the equipment for the polar journey was prepared. The dark months were passed satisfactorily, excepting for disease among the dogs. This might have been extremely serious had it not been checked in time and had not a very large factor of safety been provided for such a contingency: about 240 draught animals had been brought up from Smith Sound.

The campaign opened on 19th February, 1906; Point Moss, twenty miles west of Cape Hecla, being the point of departure from land. Five white men, twenty-one Eskimos, Henson (Peary's negro servant), and one hundred and twenty dogs set out for the Pole. The sledging system will be mentioned later. We need only notice, at present, that a pioneer party with three light sledges was sent over the pack on 28th February, while Peary brought up the rear of the long procession on 6th March.

He had written, after the return of the *Windward*, that from the "proposed winter quarters on the north shore of Grant Land . . . I should start due north [1] over the polar pack; . . . I should expect to accomplish the distance to the Pole and return in about a hundred days or a little more,[2] an average travel of about ten miles a day. This plan is the result of some twelve years of almost continuous experience in these latitudes." [3]

[1] He actually went west of north in 1906 ; see *The North Pole*, p. 4.

[2] This is repeated on p. 431 of the same volume ; see next note.

[3] Copy of letter to Secretary of U.S. Navy, dated 2nd September, 1903, in the *National Geographic Magazine*, vol. xiv, No. 10, October 1903, p. 379.

The distance from Grant Land to the Pole, in a straight line, was approximately 400 geographical miles. (Peary always referred to *geographical* miles.) He did not expect, from his previous experience, to be able to make good, on an average, more than about 8 m.p.d. of latitude. In this he showed sound judgment. The speed he hoped to maintain was about two or three miles a day more than he had accomplished on his last attempt over the polar pack; but in 1902 he had no pioneer party to break the difficult trail. The "average *travel* of about ten miles per day" (our italics) referred, of course, to the distance actually marched, including detours around obstacles and all deviations from the direct line. As 10 m.p.d. for "a hundred days or a little more" would make a total distance of at least 1000 miles, it is obvious that Peary expected his actual marching distance to be over 100 miles, each way, more than the direct air-line from land to the Pole. This was a very fair estimate, making an allowance of 25 *per cent.* for deviations. It was more optimistic than Nansen's experience would warrant, for his deviations amounted to an addition of about 40 per cent. to his straight-line distance. But, again, Nansen had no pioneers. We are now to see how far Peary's experience fulfilled his expectations.

We should notice, perhaps, before proceeding, that a distinct change comes over his record of this journey from page 130 of his *Nearest the Pole.* All his writings, up to this point, are normally lucid; but from the date of 13th April, 1906, in this account, the text becomes confused and unsatisfactory. It is necessary to mention this because of the difficulty in unravelling Peary's meaning.

3. *The Polar Journey from Point Moss to Storm Camp in Latitude* 85° 12′ *N.*[1]—Peary stepped on to the polar pack, on 6th March, 1906, with his whole column before him. The surface was "good at first,"

[1] Reference should be made to Schedule No. 4 at end of chapter.

but the "trail was tortuous" and "became extremely arduous." [1] It is important to follow closely his description of the ice conditions and to compare it with that of his previous trip from Cape Hecla. The news from the pioneer party was that "the ice was heavily rafted . . . and the trail faulted." The distance travelled is not given on one of the first sixteen days, but it is easily deduced from the latitudes, and averaged 3·4 geographical m.p.d. made good on a northerly course, for this period.

On 7th March there was good going at first; then "some skirmishing" became necessary to pick up the broken trail of the forerunners. At this time the ice became active, "leads and rafters began to form about us." The camp that night was subjected to a glacial bombardment, which shattered the igloos.

On the 8th the surface was good, "except where the movement of the ice had faulted the trail." The ice was still active, and again bombarded the camp and frightened the Eskimos.

The ice was "in motion everywhere" on the 9th, and the trail, in consequence, was disrupted. The advantage of having a pioneer party was largely discounted by the repeated faulting of the trail. Peary wrote: "We were steadily drifting eastward." He does not appear to mention what course he set on leaving land, but it is marked on the chart somewhat more to the west than his course of 1902; this was supposed to counteract the stronger drift to the east.

The ice was steadier on the 10th, "and the going comparatively good." These conditions continued, possibly, for a few days; but the 11th to 13th are scarcely mentioned, and the 14th is entirely omitted. The entry for the 15th is concerned only with supplies, and the 16th is not mentioned. Land was still

---

[1] *Nearest the Pole*, p. 102. The subsequent quotations follow from this.

"distinctly visible" on the 17th, "but not as far away as I could wish." This probably was why no distances were given; the progress had been extremely slow, fighting for every yard. After "a mile of fearfully rough ice" a perfect surface was reached. In spite of this, Peary complains next day, the 18th, that "it is aggravating not to be travelling faster," for his average, as we have seen, was only *one-third* of his estimated speed, and put the Pole quite out of the question, unless there was to be a rapid and permanent improvement in the ice.

The next two or three days (the 19th, 20th, and part of the 21st) are not mentioned, except for some general notes that may refer to them. This brings us to the "night of the 21st," when a fierce westerly wind began, which continued "all night and day of the 22nd and caused pronounced changes in the ice," splitting the floes and so forth. On this day we read another complaint of the slowness of the advance: "The work was not moving with the speed which I could have desired," though it moved smoothly.

The wind on this day held up all progress and upset the ice. On the 23rd a channel, "a hundred yards or more wide, gave us some trouble to negotiate, and at other places enormous pressure leads had been formed across the Captain's (Bartlett's) track. The northern ice in every instance had shifted to the eastward." [1]

The speed here suddenly increased to the highest rate Peary had yet attained on the pack. This was the first of four consecutive days on which it seems correct to assume that twelve geographical miles were made good on the course, basing the assumption on the following statement: "Ten years ago I would have called these marches fully fifteen miles each, now I hoped they were at least twelve." [2] Ten years before this he had not seen the pack-ice. If these marches were more than twelve miles each, the speed of the

[1] *Nearest the Pole*, p. 111.   [2] *Ibid.*, p. 112.

first sixteen days was less than 3·4 geo. m.p.d. This is
fixed by the latitudes, as we shall see.

On the 24th the temperature stepped down to
—60° F., or 92° of frost, which approaches the
record on all polar, north and south, journeys. On
the 25th the young ice of the previous day continued,
and then came some "old floes with hummocks on
them like ranges of hills." On the next day, "a
splendid march, over the finest going," was made;
this was the last of the four good marches of twelve
miles each. We must notice that Peary, at this time,
considered twelve miles "a good long march." [1] He
had never, before this, been able to accomplish more
than half this distance on the pack. He was then held
up for a week by a large channel, which will be considered in a later chapter.

On the 28th, "satisfactory observations with
sextant and transit gave latitude 84° 38′ and longitude
74° W., approximate variation 107½° W." [2] The
latitude of Point Moss is not given, but it appears to
be about 82° 55′ N. Reckoning it at this, the distance
to the large channel was 103 geographical miles made
good on the course, in twenty marches on twenty-one
days. The daily average of northing, therefore, as
far as this, was only 4·9 m.p.d. and 5·1 m.p. march,
whatever the distance actually travelled may have
been.

This speed, being only half Peary's estimate, made
the Pole impossible of attainment, because the journey
would take twice as long as the expedition was provisioned for. The pioneer party and Peary's increased experience had not combined to lengthen
appreciably the daily distance that could be wrung
from the relentless pack.

The channel was crossed on 2nd April and Henson sent ahead. Peary followed on the 3rd, crossing
several channels on young ice, and finding the snow

[1] *Nearest the Pole*, p. 114.   [2] *Ibid.*, p. 117.

softer and deeper on the old floes than it had been farther south. A blizzard then blew from the north until noon of the 4th, when the going was of a mixed character. The blizzard soon returned, and the trail, on the 5th, was "very difficult." The surface was bad, and the storm, now from the west, increased. The ice became active on the following day, and a full gale came on, holding up all progress for the next six days.

The wind backed a little to the south of west, but the camp was driven hard to the east. When, on 12th April, the gale ceased, Peary's observations gave his latitude as 85° 12' N. and "our longitude but slightly west of the ship at Sheridan." [1] This meant that the camp had been blown seventy miles to the east, if the route is marked correctly on the chart.[2] Assuming this to be so, the pack had drifted *more than eleven miles a day* before the gale. We shall hear of this again. It is now necessary to consider the latitudes and speeds.

The previous observations, at the large channel, on 28th March, had given latitude 84° 38' N. The average rate of progress, therefore, on the four days before the storm, was 8½ geographical miles of northing. The average speed from land, 137 miles away, to this point, was 5·7 m.p. *march*. The miles per *day*, including the days when no march was possible, were 3·6 for the thirty-eight days, or still very little more than one-third of Peary's estimate. Only one-third of the distance to the Pole had been covered in five weeks. More than *one-third* of the hundred days estimated for the whole journey had been spent in travelling *one-sixth* of the total distance. The estimate sent to the Secretary of the Navy had proved much too optimistic. The Pole clearly was unattainable.

[1] *Nearest the Pole*, p. 129.
[2] The longitude is incorrectly shown at the " Big Lead " ; see Chapter XIII, Sec. 2, p. 238.

4. *The Polar Journey from Storm Camp.*—Peary's narrative of this journey, as far as we have followed it, while leaving much to be desired, has been clear enough to give an outline of events. There has been much we should have liked to know, but we have been in no doubt as to what actually happened. A distinct change, as already intimated, comes over the story from this point.

When the blizzard ended, on 12th April, the expedition was in desperate straits. We are not told that the Pole was then, as it had been almost from the first, utterly beyond Peary's reach, but such was the undiluted truth. He had seven men with him, and scant supplies of food. He complained that "the party was larger than it need be,"[1] and that his supporting parties could no longer assist him. These disadvantages were not Peary's fault, they were due to the forces of nature, and particularly to the long blizzard. He was nearly at the end of his resources, and yet he was more than sixty miles behind Nansen's farthest north, of latitude 86° 14′ N., and eighty miles behind Cagni's record. These were the main facts of the situation.

Peary, however, scarcely touches on them. He writes, in bravado strain: "I had no occasion to think or worry, I knew already what I should do"; but that was merely to save his party from disaster, and if possible to make a new record. It is only *in extremis* that a commander abandons his gear; yet Peary at once abandoned, he said, "everything which we did not absolutely need"; and then, "bent every energy to setting a record pace."[2]

There is a decided similarity in his accounts between this point and where he sent Bartlett back, on his last expedition. On both occasions he had no white men with him, and on both only Henson and the Eskimos. On both he said there were few, if any,

[1] *Nearest the Pole*, p. 130.   [2] *Ibid.*, p. 130.

difficulties in the way of his further progress. On both occasions he claims to have done extraordinary, but unwitnessed, speeds, and on both his stories cease to be straightforward and become confused and dubious.[1]

Peary begins by saying that the blizzard had levelled all the irregularities of the surface: "North of Storm Camp we had no occasion for snowshoes or pickaxes." This is remarkable because, while the surface of the snow would be hardened, the blizzard could not flatten out the pressure ridges. On the contrary, it would set the ice in more rapid motion and make the conditions for travel worse than before. Every storm on the pack causes new pressure ridges, by grinding the floes together; yet these ridges were annihilated, according to Peary's account, to the north of Storm Camp. All difficulties vanished at this point, as if cut off with a knife. Peary, previously, had considered a speed of 12 m.p.d. to be, as it was, excellent progress. From now, under conditions that must have been worse rather than better, we are told that this party of eight men travelled *two and a half times* faster than this.

"The first march, of ten hours . . . placed us thirty miles to the good."[2] As if to buttress up this sweeping assertion, Peary added that his speed "was not less than three miles an hour." No child needs telling that thirty miles in ten hours is *precisely*, instead of "not less than," 3 m. per hour. It is remarkable that, immediately Peary leaves his white companions,

[1] Captain Hall points out, further, that on each occasion the dogs go faster when tired than when fresh; the goal is reached just before noon on sunny days; and that both Storm Camp and Bartlett's Camp are reached, on the return, in gales; while the only trouble, on both, is from snow-blindness. "All these things cannot," he writes, "in the nature of things, be coincidents. . . . Almost anybody could have invented something new for the second story" (*Has the North Pole been Discovered ?*, p. 303).

[2] *Nearest the Pole*, p. 131.

his speed suddenly should become nearly ten times as rapid as his previous average; that all the difficulties of the polar pack, which he himself had taught us were nearly insurmountable, should vanish like smoke, and that the state of the ice, to the north of Storm Camp, should have been, at that time, so utterly different from the state of the ice to the south of this latitude.

We are asked to believe that these eight men were able to travel nearly as far in one *hour* as they had recently travelled in one *day*, and that they could keep this up for ten hours. The four days at 12 m.p.d. had been an improvement on the previous average; but even compared with this speed the rate of progress, when all responsible witnesses are shaken off, jumps up to 2½ times as much as the previous best.

On the next day, 14th April, there was half a gale from the W.S.W. with much drift, but Peary set off through it at "a good pace." He wrote: "We travelled ten hours . . . and I felt that we had covered thirty miles more." [1] He had no proof of this distance. It would not be quite fair, perhaps, to lay much stress on his use of one word; but no accurate explorer would claim to have marched an unprecedented number of miles on the ground that he "felt" he had done so many. Peary never measured his distances on the pack. Sixty geographical miles is sixty-nine statute miles of northing in two days, *plus* deviations. We have seen that Peary's own estimate for these was an allowance of 25 per cent. extra mileage. This would bring the distance travelled in the two days up to 86¼ statute miles. Thus Peary claimed to have covered forty-three miles on each of these days. He was fifty years of age, with a party of eight men.

Detours, on the second day, are admitted, though naturally minimised. No less than eleven channels were crossed, but they "gave us," Peary wrote, "no

[1] *Nearest the Pole*, p. 131.

very serious trouble." [1] He admitted that he *only estimated* his distances on the polar pack. He was striving, at this time, furiously and almost savagely, to beat Cagni's record; this was his only hope of avoiding a complete fiasco. He would naturally, therefore, over-estimate his mileage. His latitudes, we shall find, put a very different complexion on the matter, and they contradict the evident suggestion of his story, that he was making, every day, a dash to his northernmost point at the highest speed.

On 15th April, the third day from Storm Camp, Peary said his speed "was not less than two and one-half miles per hour." [2] This is all we are told, and it conveys very little information. We are not told for how many hours this speed was maintained. An uncritical reader, having learnt that ten hours were marched on the previous two days, naturally would infer that twenty-five miles were travelled on this day. Peary may have intended to intimate this. If so, the difficulty of making even common sense out of the remainder of this remarkable story is increased, as we shall see.

The fourth day from Storm Camp, 16th April, is not mentioned; and the 17th is bequeathed no more than the one emphatic word "Hell!" This may have been designed as a terse and graphic description of the difficulties encountered, perhaps particularly with regard to high winds. On 18th April we read: "Travelled ten hours. We must be close to Abruzzi's highest now." [3] Again no distance for the day is given and no hourly rate.

The record that Peary was attacking was latitude 86° 34' N. made by Commander Cagni of H.R.H. the Duke of the Abruzzi's expedition in 1900. Peary evidently expected to be in about latitude 86° 30' N. on this day. If so, he would be seventy-eight miles from Storm Camp, and his average would have been

[1] *Nearest the Pole*, p. 131.   [2] *Ibid.*, p. 132.   [3] *Ibid.*, p. 133.

13 m.p.d. since leaving there. As, however, he claimed to have done thirty miles on the first and second days, only eighteen miles remained for the last four days, or an average of 4½ *miles a day*. This is very little for ten hours' marching, or, alternatively, for a speed of 2¼ m.p.h. Such is Peary's account of this portion of his journey, but we must return to his record.

The next day, 19th April, is not specifically mentioned; though a paragraph is inserted between the account of the 18th and that of the 20th telling us (as we are told in 1909, after Bartlett's dismissal) how much "the ice improved." Our main concern is to notice the statement that "our pace was heartbreaking. . . . As dogs gave out, unable to keep the pace, they were fed to others." [1] How could four or five miles a day, over improved surfaces, break down dogs which were capable of 30 m.p.d.?

The chronicle of the 20th reads: "Hurrying on . . . a forced march was made. Then we slept a few hours, and starting again soon after midnight, pushed on till a little before noon of the 21st." Thus "we had reached 87° 6′ N. latitude and had at last beaten the record." [2]

Nine marches had been made in the 8½ days from Storm Camp, in latitude 85° 12′ N., averaging 12½ m.p.m. and 13 m.p.d. As a degree was done on the first and second days, only fifty-four miles remained for the other 6½ days, which averaged, therefore, 8·3 m.p.d. Peary cannot have it both ways, and history must know which is true. Did he make a frantic rush? Or did he march at 8 m.p.d.? Which are we expected to believe? If the general purport of his account is to be credited, he must have reached a higher latitude than 87° 6′ N.; but as he was never known to *under*-estimate his own performances, we must accept this latitude as at least the highest, if it was not higher than, he reached in 1906. Hence, we can be sure that

[1] *Nearest the Pole*, p. 133.   [2] *Ibid.*, pp. 133–134.

his speed was not more than 8 m.p.d., and his story loses the impress of truth.

No normal man, inditing his own history, could write of 8 m.p.d. being a "heartbreaking pace" or a "forced march," especially after referring to a speed of 30 m.p.d. in much more modest terms. Moreover, if twenty-five miles were done on 15th April, as Peary seems to intimate, only twenty-nine miles remained for the last six days of this "reckless dash," or an average of 4·8 m.p.d.! These lower speeds of from 5 to 8 m.p.d. were at least possible; but *unless two days had been done at 30 m.p.d. Cagni would still have held the record.*

With regard to the outward journey as a whole, no daily distances are given on 41 out of the 47 days, or on 27 out of the 33 marches. The total latitude distance being 251 miles, the average speed from Point Moss to the turning-point was $5\frac{1}{3}$ m.p.d. This was little more than half of Peary's estimate, 10 m.p.d., and made the attainment of the Pole impracticable. At this speed, the journey would take nearly two hundred, instead of the estimated one hundred, days.

The average rate per *march* is not of much value, because it eliminates the greatest difficulties; it is little more than a species of intellectual conceit. Still, for what it may be worth, it was 7·6 m.p.m. for the outward journey.

The most valuable statistics of this attempt to reach the Pole, probably, are the following: If the two doubtful days of thirty miles each are eliminated, 191 miles were marched on the remaining forty-five days, when the average was 4·2 m.p.d. If the six days on which the distances are given be eliminated, the *average for* 41 *out of the* 47 *days* is seen to be *only* 3·4 *m.p.d.* Peary deliberately suppressed his speed on all but his best days, and these were no more than one-eighth of the total.

One conclusion emerges very clearly, that Peary was not, as he wished us to believe, the fastest traveller over the polar pack. Nansen, it is true, had averaged no more than four or five miles a day, but Cagni had maintained the splendid averages of 13½ m.p.d. for 241, and 6 m.p.d. for 600 miles. Cagni surpassed all Peary's *authentic* performances for long distances. Yet Cagni's best days were one of 28½, one of 22, two of 21, and six of 20 miles. These figures make Peary's 60 miles in two days quite incredible, for Cagni was a much better and faster sledger than Peary, and had a superior equipment. Nansen's best days were one of 25, one of 21, and three of 20 miles. There must be few men, if any, acquainted with this subject, who will believe that Peary did better than Cagni, especially when the startling fall in the speed for the remainder of the "dash" is remembered; while Peary tried to convey the impression that he was keeping up these high speeds as far as his turning-point. It is not suggested that 30 m.p.d. *of travel*, for one or two days, would be, under any circumstances, impossible. The suggestion is that, as we have nothing but Peary's assertion that this *latitude distance* was done, we like not the security.

The story of events beyond Storm Camp is too uncertain to rob Commander Cagni of his record. The Abruzzi expedition had four Europeans at the highest latitude, which seems to be well attested. We have nothing but Peary's word for his latitude of 87° 6′ N., and his record of the journey is unsatisfactory. That his unsupported word might be unreliable was seen by his mythical discoveries in Greenland, and we shall find that, unfortunately, these do not stand alone. It is uncertain how far he went beyond latitude 85° 12′ N.

One hoped that he may have intended his 30 m.p.d. to be route miles, which would have helped the averages of the succeeding days, but there seems no reason for assuming this. His usual, and apparently invariable, custom was to refer only to latitude distance, and on 13th April his phrase was: "Thirty miles to the good." Remembering his custom, this seems equivalent to "made good," or latitude distance.

That Peary's mind was confused while writing this part of his story is seen by a reference to p. 132 of his *Nearest the Pole*. We are told, near the top of the page, that he "camped beside an open lead." This he often did, in order to rest while the channel either closed or froze over. We are next given some incidents of that day's march, followed by a paragraph on other matters. Then he quotes from his journal, under date 18th April, saying, on the last line of the page, "No serious trouble was experienced in crossing the lead."

Unfortunately for his veracity he has missed out two days! These days were the 16th and 17th April, as will be seen by referring to Schedule No. 4.[1] "Yesterday, hell," has been attributed to the 17th, though Peary may have intended it to refer to the "violent wind and driving snow" twice mentioned in the first paragraph on this page. We shall not be expected to discuss such difficulties as these indefinitely, and must leave the matter here, with the warning that many worse difficulties than this will be found in Peary's last book.

Mr V. Stefansson, in a long and interesting letter to the present writer, said: "You say that Peary's 'narrative, fortunately, stands alone among the published journals of the heroic band of polar explorers' in various undesirable things which you proceed to enumerate. I suggest to you that you did not think so before you studied it so carefully, and you may not think it so different hereafter if you go on and study several others equally carefully.[2] . . . Why do you not study a few others? You may conclude eventually that there is not an equally high percentage of unexposed charlatans among any group of men

---

[1] Pages 79-81. [2] A complimentary passage is omitted.

whose names (to choose a random criterion) are in
the *Encyclopædia Britannica*."

Mr Stefansson's excellent suggestion has now been
carried out; but *without verifying* his supposition.[1]

5. *The Western Journey.*—Any suspicions that may
have been aroused by the story of the journey to the
north of Storm Camp, are supported by Peary's
narrative of his return to Cape Sheridan. This is a
traveller's tale of hairbreadth escapes, without reliable
data. There is only one event in it that will concern
us, and this is dealt with later.[2] No more need be
said now than that all dates are carefully, and even
ingeniously, suppressed. This must have been done
with some deliberate purpose, that we need not,
perhaps, attempt to fathom; though it may have been
thought necessary to remove every scrap of evidence
that could be used by scientists to check, and thereby
to prove or disprove, the authenticity of latitude
87° 6′ N.

Be that as it may, the most laborious circumlocu-
tions were adopted to avoid giving any dates, *e.g.*:
"The third march from Storm Camp," on p. 142;
"the second march south of the scar," on p. 143;
"the next march after we emerged from the southern
edge of the zone of shattered ice," on p. 147; "the
next march after sighting the land," on p. 148; "the
first march from the musk oxen," on p. 161. "Each
day," "every march," "several days," and "next
march" are among the more definite expressions used!
Even the date of the return to the *Roosevelt* is suppressed. Peary wrote: "I quote from my journal of
the next day,"[3] when he had not told us the date for
a month!

After such an exhibition as this we shall not be
expected to take the return journey seriously, and it

---

[1] See the " Critical Remarks " in *Antarctica : A Treatise on the
Southern Continent* (Richards Press, 1928).

[2] See p. 236.   [3] *Nearest the Pole*, p. 168.

is here omitted. Its omission must not be assumed to imply any desire to discredit the whole story, which may be true enough. The position is that the narrative, obviously, is too unreliable for any practical purpose. No one can build upon a quicksand.

The first date mentioned is long enough after reaching the ship to prevent anyone from working backward and making awkward discoveries. This date is 2nd June when Peary started west, along what he termed the "glacial fringe" of Grant Land. (The last date given was 21st April.) The purpose of the trip was "to fill in the unknown gap . . . between Aldrich's and Sverdrup's farthest." [1] We must notice that he admitted Sverdrup had preceded him on this coast. There would be no object in following Peary very closely on this journey.

The first point of interest arises when the new land is reached. Peary then writes on 17th June: "A day's march beyond Aldrich's farthest, and what I saw before me in all its splendid, sunlit savageness was *mine* [his italics], mine by right of discovery, to be credited to me and associated with my name, generations after I have ceased to be." [2]

One's first thought on reading this was that Peary was jesting, but he appears to have been perfectly serious. It may be remembered that he set out in life with the single purpose of making his name famous, as he wrote to his mother, "from one end of the world to the other."

On 18th June, when farther west, he wrote: "In to-day's march we passed the mouth of a black, precipitous-walled bay, some eight to ten miles wide at its mouth, with apparently several interior ramifications. *Mine!* " [3]

We now approach two matters of some slight interest in the history of geographical discovery. On

[1] *Nearest the Pole*, p. 174.   [2] *Ibid.*, p. 190.
[3] *Ibid.*, p. 192. Again his italics.

24th June Peary ascended to the summit of a promontory, that he called Cape Colgate, and considered the westernmost point of Grant Land. We have just seen how he admitted Sverdrup had discovered it, but this did not prevent the later explorer from renaming the headland, if it was the same one.

On Thursday, 8th May 1902, Captain Sverdrup's party reached here from the south, and named the N.N.W. point of Grant Land, Lands Lokh, or Land's End. Its latitude was given at 81° 40′ N. and its longitude is shown at about 92° W. on the Norwegian chart.[1] All that could be seen from here was Sverdrup's by right of discovery, and will remain to the credit of Norway while time shall last, though all these lands are claimed by the Dominion of Canada.

The geographical matters referred to above, and other matters, arise out of the following quotation. Peary was standing on the cape just mentioned and wrote: "From the summit . . . the view was more than interesting. East lay the wide, white zone of the icefoot; west, the unbroken surface of Nansen Strait, and beyond it the northern point of that western land which I saw from the heights of the Ellesmere Land ice-cap in July 1898, and named Jesup Land, though Sverdrup has later given it the name of Heiberger Land. South, over and beyond some intervening mountains and valleys, lay the southern reaches of Nansen Strait. North stretched the well-known ragged surface of the polar pack, and north-west it was with a thrill that my glasses revealed the faint, white summits of a distant land. . . ."[2]

Before considering these claims to the discovery of Axel Heiberg (Peary's "Heiberger") and Crocker Lands, the reader should refer to Map No. 2, from which he will see that Peary was nearly 90° in error

---

[1] *New Land*, vol. ii, p. 370.   [2] *Nearest the Pole*, p. 202.

as to his orientation. In other words, his cardinal points were wrong! The icefoot along which he had travelled trended, first, nearly true *north*, and then bore away in a north-easterly direction. To the *west* of where he stood, if he was at Land's End, lay the northern part of Crown Prince Gustav Sea, not Nansen Sound and Axel Heiberg Land; these were almost due *south*.

Peary was not referring to the magnetic orientation, which does not help us in this difficulty; for he was very near the magnetic meridian, which joins the Magnetic and Geographical Poles, and on which true south would be magnetic north. Peary's "west" was nearly magnetic north or true south, from Land's End. His orientation was a compromise between the true and the magnetic directions.

This is one of the most flagrant inaccuracies that even Peary committed, and shows how much reliance can be placed upon his statements. He was not the best man to seek for the North Pole, for he thought it lay somewhere along the 83rd parallel! "Crocker Land," that he said lay to the north-west, is shown north-west true on his chart; but this leaves nearly 170° between this "land" and Nansen Sound, which he thought was to the west, instead of the 45° that form half a quadrant. We shall return to this "land" again.

We have just read Peary's claim to have seen and named Axel Heiberg Land "from the heights of the Ellesmere Land ice-cap in July 1898." This date should be noticed. If we turn to p. 296 of *Nearest the Pole*, we read: "The *Windward* sailed from New York on the 4th of July 1898, and on the 7th I went on board the *Hope* at Sydney, C.B." On the next page we are told that "both ships steamed out of Etah," in Smith Sound, "on Saturday, 13th August." These dates are confirmed by Commander Green, who writes: "The *Windward* backed out from her dock on

Canal Street, New York, on 4th July 1898"; [1] also: "It was not until the 18th of August that the vessel staggered into a little patch of open water under Cape D'Urville. . . . Meanwhile Sverdrup had established himself in Rice Strait." [2] What is the most appropriate description of a man who will do a thing like this?

Peary knew he was on the high seas "in July 1898," but we can only assume that he wanted to claim priority to Sverdrup. Comment is needless. It is said, moreover, that Axel Heiberg Land is invisible from Peary's viewpoint on "the heights of the Ellesmere Land ice-cap."

Sverdrup crossed Ellesmere Land, to its western side, in April 1899. Isachsen, one of his staff, crossed in June of the same year and penetrated more than half-way down Bay Fjord, on the western coast. From here he saw across Eureka Sound to Axel Heiberg Land. The Norwegian Expedition moved, in the autumn of 1899, into Jones Sound, and completed the discovery of Axel Heiberg Land and all its neighbouring coasts, which were visited, charted, and named, from 1900 to 1902.

In July 1899 (and not 1898) Peary had ascended the glacier at the head of Sawyer Bay, "crossed the ice-cap to its western side" (?), "and from elevations of from 4000 to 4700 feet looked down upon the snow-free western side of Ellesmere Land, and out into an ice-free fjord, extending some fifty miles to the north-west." [3] This "ice-free fjord" must have been Cañon Fjord, and if Peary saw any land beyond it, this would be Grant Land.

On 1st July 1906 he waxed sentimental over leaving Axel Heiberg Land, writing: "I must confess to a feeling of sadness and regret at leaving. . . . The deer and hare feeding. . . . The call of the birds and

---

[1] *Peary the Man*, p. 172.   [2] *Ibid.*, p. 175.
[3] *Nearest the Pole*, p. 314.

the sound of running water . . . but I, *to whom it belongs* (our italics), should never see it again." [1]

Most people are prepared to stand a good deal from their heroes, as long as they seem worthy of devotion; but the quotation just given proved too much for at least one devout worshipper of Peary. It became necessary to revise one's whole estimate of the man. He knew that Sverdrup and his scientific staff had thoroughly explored the coasts of Axel Heiberg Land and the adjacent countries, four or five years before he touched its northern tip, and that they had carried out their work in a manner he was never able to achieve. He accepted Sverdrup's discovery of Nansen Sound and adopted the name bestowed upon it by its discoverer.

The second geographical matter that arises out of Peary's ruminations on the summit of Sverdrup's headland is the new country he claimed to have seen in the north-west, or possibly south-west. On or about 27th June Peary ascended another headland, that he thought was the northernmost point of Axel Heiberg Land, and said, from here "I could make out apparently a little more distinctly the snow-clad summits of the distant land in the north-west (?) above the ice horizon." [2]

Dr Donald B. MacMillan was one of Peary's assistants in 1909, and ardently admired his chief. In 1914 he (MacMillan) took an expedition to the north, for the purpose of exploring "Crocker Land"; Peary having gone as far as to christen his discovery. MacMillan's party went where the land should have been, according to the true orientation, but as it was not there, they went thirty miles farther, with the same result. "Crocker Land" has no existence. [3]

MacMillan wrote: "My hopes had ended in bitter disappointment." He thought Peary had been de-

[1] *Nearest the Pole*, p. 212.　　　　[2] *Ibid.*, p. 207.
[3] *Four Years in the White North*, p. 82, etc.

ceived by mirage; but another theory seems quite as reasonable, because based on Peary's own evidence. This is that, in accordance with the erroneous orientation, Isachsen Land was the country seen. On the assumption that Nansen Sound lay to the west of Land's End, this is quite possible, for Cape Isachsen is about 40° north of Svartevoeg, the northern point of Axel Heiberg Land. To expect "Crocker Land" in the true north-west is to do violence to Peary's whole sense of direction; but another matter now requires our attention.

Sverdrup, the discoverer, Peary, Dr Cook, and MacMillan, to mention them in chronological order, all visited the north of Axel Heiberg Land. Sverdrup went farther than this, and on 8th May 1902 reached, as we have seen, the north-western point of Grant Land. Here he wrote that he, "with some trouble collected enough stones to build a small cairn, which, at any rate, was not too small to be seen from the camping ground three minutes south of the spot." [1] On 10th May he called at Svartevoeg, which was included in his survey.

Four years later Peary said he hoped to find Sverdrup's cairn; he tried to do so "but without success, though we all searched the shore carefully." [2] He then crossed to what he believed was the most northerly point of Axel Heiberg Land, and wrote: "No previous cairn exists on or near this cape, nor does it appear from Sverdrup's narrative or his map that he reached this point." [3] Sverdrup had described his crossing of Nansen Sound, which he had discovered and named, from Land's End to Svartevoeg. This last point, he said, "we reached latish in the afternoon. . . . We pitched our tent up on the crack." [4] No mention is made of leaving a record here, but geological work was done, and the "high, steep cliff" of the point

[1] *New Land*, vol. ii, p. 370.   [2] *Nearest the Pole*, p. 202.
[3] *Ibid.*, p. 210.   [4] *New Land*, vol. ii, p. 371.

is described.   Next day the party went on to Kvitberg, or the White Mountain, on Nansen Sound.

Dr Cook was the third traveller to reach Svartevoeg, where he left a depot, two years after Peary's visit. Cook has given us the only photograph we have, and a good one, of the headland.   He wrote: "Svartevoeg is a great cliff, the northernmost point of Heiberg Land, which leaps precipitously into the Polar Sea. Its negroid face of black, scarred rocks frowns like the carven stone countenance of some hideously mutilated and enraged Titan savage."[1]   Cook added that, "a great deal of careful search and study was prosecuted about Svartevoeg, for here Peary claims to have a *cache*. . . . But no such *cache* was found, and I doubt very much if Peary ever reached this point."[2]   This, it will be seen, was the truth.

After another six years MacMillan comes.   As a supporter of Peary he is most anxious to find his old chief's record, and possibly no less anxious not to find the records of other explorers.   He and Commander Green, Peary's biographer, spent the whole of 13th April 1914 in searching for the cairn, but they could not find it.   MacMillan writes: "We scanned in vain the horizon for a cairn and continued to do so for some eight hours. . . . Tired and disappointed we trudged back to camp."[3]   Other explorers could scarcely be expected to spend so much time and trouble over Peary's record.

MacMillan gave up the search and proceeded with his more important quest for the mythical "Crocker Land."   When out on the sea-ice, however, he found that Peary's cape was farther west, and on returning to Axel Heiberg Land he saw a cairn "on the summit of a low, projecting point."   This was not, as Peary

[1] *My Attainment of the Pole*, p. 194.   For further reference to Dr Cook, see p. 177.

[2] *Ibid.*, p. 194.   Footnote, pp. 200–201.

[3] *Four Years in the White North*, p. 74.

supposed, the most northerly point of the land. With
much labour, which MacMillan does not attempt to
minimise, the record eventually was recovered. He
was then too tired to try for the second record, which
we presume was Cook's.

These particulars have been given because it could
be said that MacMillan did not find Cook's record,
Cook did not find Peary's record, and Peary did not
find Sverdrup's record, whereas MacMillan did find
Peary's record. It was well that he did, or we should
not have had this further proof of Peary's erroneous
orientation; and if he was wrong, it is necessary to
know this. MacMillan did not look for Cook's record
here, but he found one of his depots at the White
Mountain, not far away. Cook did not find Peary's
record, because Peary thought another headland was
the most northerly point of the land. For the same
reason Peary could not have found any record of
Sverdrup's, if he had left one, at Svartevoeg. As for
Sverdrup's cairn at Land's End, he said it was a small
one, and it would easily be drifted over with snow.
Probably, however, Peary thought some other headland
was the most westerly point of the land.

It was vital for MacMillan to find Peary's record;
he could not leave the district until he had done so,
because, if he failed to find it, the doubt that Peary
had ever reached here would become a certainty.
MacMillan had just performed the distasteful duty
of expunging "Crocker Land" from the map, and
would properly be jealous for the honour of his old
chief. His record was recovered by the merest
accident, as it was not where it should have been, on
the most northerly point of the land. Thus Peary
is tested against three other explorers, each of whom
had no hesitation in fixing on, or accepting, Svartevoeg
as the most northerly point, Cook and MacMillan
both confirming Sverdrup's survey. Peary thought
that his Cape Thomas Hubbard was the northernmost

point of the land. His photograph of it [1] proves that it was not Svartevoeg, for the outlines are too soft, and no vertical cliffs are seen. This is clear evidence of his inaccuracy and of his false orientation; he did not even know in what direction the North Pole lay! Had he started for it from here, as Dr Cook did, he would have set a N.N.W. course, thinking it was due north, and he would not have reached the Pole had he gone on for ever.

There is nothing worthy of attention during Peary's return from his western trip. He wrote the following on 10th July: "Out of my new domain and back into the known world again." [2] This was childish. His "domain" was fifty miles of frozen coastline, and the "known world" was more of the same, previously seen only by Aldrich of the Nares Expedition. Peary was unfortunate in having the Second *Fram* Expedition in a neighbouring district during the same four years as his *Windward* Expedition. His own feeble attempts at achieving world fame seemed to fall into the shade by contrast with the work of the Norwegians. Sverdrup discovered and made good maps of 100,000 square miles of land, besides doing much valuable scientific work. The linear miles of coast explored were 1750, against Peary's 250 miles, which were badly charted and with no scientific results, in the same period. Peary might well feel rather strongly about it, and he never forgot it.

Let us face the position, in 1906, from his standpoint. He had just suffered the most humiliating failure of his life. He had failed previously to achieve anything by his second North Greenland expedition, and he had failed to reach the Pole on the *Windward* Expedition. On his return in 1895 he had dragged in the meteoric stones to counterbalance and

[1] Opposite p. 199 of *Nearest the Pole*.
[2] *Ibid.*, p. 224.

divert attention from his ill success. He realised, in 1906, that the cleverest manipulation of his story would not enable him to claim the Pole, and the actual cause of failure accentuated this trouble. He could blame the blizzards, but he knew they were no more than contributory causes of his failure, and that the all-sufficient reason for this was his slow progress over the pack. He had not been able to travel at more than about *half* his estimated speed of ten miles a day, yet this had seemed a low enough estimate.

Thus, at the age of fifty, when he could hope for no further attempts, Peary was in a sad position. An expensive ship had been built specially for him; this was the fourth time he had failed; and for a great sledge traveller like himself to be unable to push out from 400 to 500 miles from his base; to be unable to exceed an average speed of five miles a day; and to be forced to turn back when 250 miles from land, was most humiliating.

Peary seems to have been the kind of man who would react to this position of affairs by a feeling of desperation. He would rouse himself to do something, anything, to distract attention from the main issue and to counteract its failure. He was skilful at this, having used the same stratagem before. Now he rose to the occasion, with no less than three items of diverting interest on his programme. The first item was the fifty miles of barren coast. If this was advertised enough it would contribute to his purpose. His second item was "Crocker Land," which no doubt he really saw, whatever or wherever it may have been. Lastly, he yielded to temptation and tried to jump the claim of Sverdrup to Axel Heiberg Land, trusting to luck that no busybody, with ridiculous notions of truth, would find out how little had been achieved by this costly expedition.

It is well to pause here and calmly review the situation. We stand on the threshold of Peary's culminating claim, that of having reached the North Pole. He must not be misjudged, nor, on the other hand, must anything that is untrue be extenuated or excused.

Accuracy had never been his strong point. His first reconnaissance in Greenland was useless because of the uncertainty of his position and of his height. The land he discovered across the inland ice was so badly charted as to be unrecognisable, and his Peary Channel was a fiction of his imagination. He made claims that simply were not true. His slipshod habits developed until he did not know the direction of the North Pole from the north of Axel Heiberg Land, and he made a mistake (shall we say?) in the date when he thought he first saw this land. His report of his journey beyond Storm Camp was most unsatisfactory; the whole of it could not be history, because his speed of 8 m.p.d. was inconsistent with the general purport of his story. The sum of the whole matter is, therefore, that his unsupported word was most unreliable. Should he ever, after 1906, make even modest claims on no better security than that of his own assertions, it would be necessary to receive them with considerable reserve. We are now to see how modest, or otherwise, were the claims he made.

SCHEDULE No. 4

1906.	Lat. N.		Geo. Miles.
Mar. 6	(82° 55′)	Left Pt. Moss; good going, then arduous; ideal day	(3·4)[1]
7	..	Heavy going; sledges damaged; ice active; fine	(3·4)
8	..	Better going, but ice in motion; more sledges broken; N.W.	(3·4)

[1] Mileage in brackets not given by Peary; average from latitudes.

SCHEDULE No. 4—(*continued*)

1906.	Lat. N.		Geo. Miles.
Mar. 9	..	Drifting E., but ice in motion; heavy N.W. and drift	(3·4)
10	..	Going fairly good; ice quieter; little wind; fine	(3·4)
11	..	Cache No. 1; cold; fine	(3·4)
12	..	(Scarcely mentioned); cold; fine	(3·4)
13	..	,,　　,,　　,,　　,,	(3·4)
14	..	(Altogether omitted)	(3·4)
15	..	Working supplies forward	(3·4)
16	..	(Not mentioned)	(3·4)
17	..	Land not as far away as wished; mixed going; fine	(3·4)
18	..	Land probably still in sight; probably fair going; very cold	(3·4)
19	..	..	(3·4)
20	..	(Not mentioned)	(3·4)
21	..	..	(3·4)
22	..	Cache No. 2; ice active; held up by fierce W. wind	o
23	..	Pressure and a channel; ice drifting E.	12
24	..	" Good march "; some danger on young ice	12
25	..	" Good march "; T.° –61° F.; misty, cold, calm	12
26	..	" A good long march " to Big Channel; T.° –60° F.; fine	12
27	..	Held up by Big Channel; T.° –66° F.	o
28	84° 38′, 74° W. var. 107½° W.	Obs.; held up by Big Channel; fine but misty	o
29	..	Held up by Big Channel; fine but misty	o
30	..	Held up by Big Channel; fine but misty	o
31	..	Held up by Big Channel; fine; wind S.S.W.	o

1906.	Lat. N.		Geo. Miles.
April 1	..	Held up by Big Channel; fine; N. airs	o
2	..	Cross Big Channel; colder; fine; N. airs	o
3	..	Heavy old ice; channels; biting wind N.W.; overcast	(8·5)
4	..	Heavy old ice; mixed going; biting wind N.W.; snow squalls	(8·5)
5	..	Going mostly bad; biting wind, N.W.; snow squalls	(8·5)
6	..	Ice in motion; blizzard began	(8·5)
7	..	*Storm Camp.* Held up by blizzard	o
8	..	,, ,, ,,	o
9	..	,, ,, ,,	o
10	..	,, ,, ,,	o
11	..	,, ,, ,,	o
12	85° 12', c. 62° W.	Obs.; surface improved; light W.S.W.; fine	o
13	..	Good going; speed 3 m.p.h.; wind S. of W.	30
14	(86° 12' reached)	Crossed 11 channels; half-gale with drift	30
15	..	Blizzard and channel at end of march; speed 2½ m.p.h.	(7·7)
16	..	(Not mentioned)	(7·7)
17	..	" Hell "	(7·7)
18	..	Ice improved; "travelled 10 hours"; near Cagni's record	(7·7)
19	..	(Not specifically mentioned)	(7·7)
20	..	Ice in motion; open channels; "forced march"	(7·7)
21	87° 6'	Observations	

CHAPTER VI

THE SECOND *ROOSEVELT* EXPEDITION

" I have known even great and highly-placed travellers to describe their sojourns in foreign lands, their hunting experiences, and their privations, in language more graphic than accurate."

EDGAR WALLACE.
Eve's Island.

1. SHORT OUTLINE OF EVENTS. 2. THE CRUCIAL PERIOD OF THE POLAR JOURNEY. 3. THE EVIDENCE BEFORE THE CONGRESSIONAL COMMITTEE. 4. PECULIARITIES OF THE RECORD.

1. IT is unnecessary to give more than the briefest outline of this expedition here, as a separate chapter, or at least a section, will be devoted to each important part of it. Thus the purpose of an introduction will be served, without repetition.

Peary set off for the Arctic, on his last expedition, in July 1908. He knew that he would never make another trip to the far north. His ship had been repaired and was splendidly equipped.

Eskimos and dogs were embarked from the Cape York district, on the way to Cape Sheridan; the same winter base, as in 1906, being reached early in September. The two *Roosevelt* Expeditions were very similar; there were only minor differences between them.

Depot laying to Cape Columbia, and hunting, occupied the autumn, as well as the moonlit days in winter. In March 1909 the journey across the pack-ice began, on a course that, apparently, was assumed to have been due north, true. The journey can be followed, day by day, on Schedule No. 5.[1]

[1] Pages 94–96.

MARCHES

RETURN   OUTWARD

⊙ NORTH POLE   90°N

10

←8→

- - - Camp Jesup 89°57′
Left April 7, 4 P.M.   →Arrived April 6, 10 A.M.   50′

Took Sounding

April 8   32   40′

                Left about 10 P.M.   30′

Slept a few   89°25′ April 5
hours   Arrived about 8.30 A.M. 20′

       28   10′

130

Lunch   88°57′   Left about 9 P.M.   89°
                April 4
                Arrived about 9 A.M.   50′

       25   40′

April 9   Left about 11 P.M.
       88°32′ April 3
                Arrived about 11 A.M.   30′

       20   20′

              Left soon after
       88°12′ April 2   midnight
              Arrived before noon   10′

       25   88°

                              50′

Arrived April 9, 87°47′ Left April 2, 1 A.M.-2 A.M
Evening   Bartlett returned
                    from here

PEARY'S RETURN FROM THE POLE TO BARTLETT'S LAST CAMP,
WITH HIS 'FINAL SPURT' OVER THE SAME DISTANCE.

(PLOTTED TO NATURAL SCALE. ALL MILES ARE GEOGRAPHICAL.)

facing p. 83.

One supporting party after another was sent back; Bartlett's party going the farthest north, the latitude stated being 87° 47′ N. From here Peary claimed to have reached the Pole, accompanied by his negro servant and four Eskimos. His return will be dealt with fully in a later chapter. The various parts of the trip must now be considered in detail.

2. *The Crucial Period of the Polar Journey.*—The accompanying diagram, plotted to scale from Peary's own data, represents the crucial period of the journey. One glance at it may satisfy most people. All responsible witnesses had been dismissed. No proof or disproof of Peary's assertions seemed possible. Yet a considerable amount of evidence can be brought to bear on this period of the journey, and some of this evidence appears conclusive.

No one is debarred from examining Peary's statements, and they do not all agree. This we shall see; but first we must quote his official record. This part of his journey was crucial because, while unwitnessed by another white man, Peary claims to have reached the Pole. Hence, his claim stands or falls by this portion of his effort. The period began with his northward advance from latitude 87° 47′ N., and ended with his return to this point. Special attention must be directed to his return from the Pole.

Peary wrote: "The North Pole was reached on April 6 at ten o'clock in the morning. I spent thirty hours at the Pole. . . . The six of us left the much desired 'ninety north' on April 7. . . . We returned from the Pole to Cape Columbia in only sixteen days." [1] He confirmed the former of these statements by saying: "About 4 o'clock in the afternoon of the 7th of April we turned our backs upon the camp at the North Pole. . . . Four hundred and thirteen nautical miles of ice floes and possibly open leads still lay between us and the north coast of Grant Land." [2] Once more we

[1] *The North Pole*, p. 7.   [2] *Ibid.*, p. 301.

read: "We turned our backs upon the Pole at about 4 o'clock of the afternoon of April 7." [1]

"The camp at the North Pole" was in latitude 89° 57′ N. It is clear, therefore:

(1) That Peary took his departure for the south from latitude 89° 57′ N. at 4 p.m. on 7th April.

(2) That he traversed "413 nautical miles of ice-floes and possibly open leads" "in only sixteen days." This point will be considered later.

With reference to the first of these statements, we read: "Friday, April 9, was a wild day. . . . The ice was raftering all about us. . . . When we camped that night, at 87° 47′, I wrote in my diary: 'From here to the Pole and back has been a glorious sprint.'" [2]

As 10th April began at midnight, and as Peary reached latitude 87° 47′ N. on 9th April, we have here the assertion, when coupled with Statement No. 1, that he sledged 130 minutes of latitude in *fifty-six hours or less. This distance is 149·6 English statute miles.*[3]

In his "First Account" Peary skipped very lightly over this part of his journey, merely saying: "Three marches brought us back to the igloos where the Captain turned back." The term "marches" may mean anything; and this statement failed to convey the fact that 150 miles *of latitude* were sledged in the phenomenal time of about two days.

Peary was fifty-three years of age at the time; he was accompanied by four Eskimos, and his negro servant who was forty-two years old; they were driving dog-sledges loaded with full rations for thirty-four days, in addition to the constant sledging and camping weights. The character of the ice will be considered in due course.

The distance travelled was more than 150 miles. It will have been noticed that this was only the latitude, or straight line, distance in a north and south

[1] *The North Pole*, p. 302.   [2] *Ibid.*, pp. 305, 306.
[3] Compare E. S. Balch, *The North Pole and Bradley Land*, p. 13.

TYPES OF PACK ICE: I.

facing p. 84

direction. It is scarcely necessary to remark that, anywhere on the surface of the earth, the distance actually walked exceeds that of an air-line between the termini by a considerable amount. Thirty *per cent.* is a common, if approximate, addition for deviations from a theoretical straight course. Travellers over the Arctic pack-ice frequently have deviated more than this. There are four causes of deviation on the pack:

(1) Vertical obstructions, such as pressure ridges.

(2) Horizontal obstructions, such as channels of open water.

(3) The drift of the ice, carrying the traveller off his course.

(4) Faulty navigation.

Peary admitted the first three of these, without making any addition to his distances on account of them. It will be seen in a later chapter that his methods of navigation were inadequate. His allowance for deviations, before his journey in 1906, was 25 *per cent.*[1] Subsequent experience of the pack-ice, apparently, caused him to increase this estimate, for his excellent assistant in 1909, George Borup, wrote: "We calculated thirteen miles to every ten miles of northing" on the onward journey.[2] This is no more than would be expected; but it makes the distance travelled, in less than fifty-six hours, 194 *statute miles*.

The character of the ice over which this had to be done is of sufficient importance to require a separate chapter. We must notice at once, however, that there is now positive evidence on this, independently of Peary. Commander Byrd, who flew over the North Pole, wrote that: "In the vicinity of the Pole the ice is slightly rougher than farther south, and is everywhere criss-crossed with pressure ridges."[3] Captain Amundsen, at "about 136 miles from the Pole on the

---

[1] See p. 55.   [2] *A Tenderfoot with Peary*, p. 174.
[3] *The Independent* (Boston), 12th January 1926.

European side, found very rough, hummocky ice and no large, smooth floes."[1]

Amundsen wrote: "We had reached 88° 30' N. latitude when we landed";[2] but the exact position, given on another page, is latitude 87° 43' N. and 10° 20' W.[3] There appears to have been rapid movement of the pack; certainly it would have been atrocious for sledging, though the season for this was over, as it was the end of May. The position of the two seaplanes, very approximately, was 150 miles from that given by Peary for Bartlett's last camp; and both were about the same distance from the Pole.

This evidence is of definite, though limited, value. The pack-ice, being in motion, will vary in character, in the polar area, as elsewhere. The photographs of the ice at the Pole, taken from the *Norge*, show the pack in such an advanced stage of disintegration as to be most unsuitable for sledging;[4] but this was on 12th May 1926, or a few weeks later in the season than it is safe to travel over this ice. In spite of these limitations, the fact remains that the only independent evidence we have as to the condition of the ice at the Pole clearly proves it to be no better there than elsewhere on the Arctic Ocean. The polar pack usually is a bad sledging surface.

If the distance travelled in 2¼ days was no more than 180 miles, which would be a little less than a 25 per cent. allowance for deviations, Peary's party would have had to march for forty-five hours, or longer, at not less than four miles an hour, leaving less than eleven hours, or about five hours on each day, for rest and food.

Peary says that he travelled 36 geographical (41½

---

[1] *The Polar Regions*, Dr Rudmose Brown, p. 59.

[2] *My Polar Flight*, p. 48.

[3] *Ibid.*, p. 37.

[4] See *Problems of Polar Research*, p. 94; *National Geographic Magazine*, August 1927, pp. 208–210.

statute) miles in straight lines around the Pole.[1]
With the above allowance for deviations, but none
for any movement of the surface or for any other
reason, he marched 51 miles during the thirty hours
he was there. He had averaged 37 statute m.p.d.
for the previous five days, since dismissing the last
of his witnesses.

These statistics are given below in tabular form.
The sledging surface is assumed, in these figures, to
have been stationary; no addition has been made for
the drifting of the ice.

TABLE No. 1

PEARY'S SLEDGING SPEEDS WHEN NORTH OF BARTLETT'S
LAST CAMP

(To the nearest whole number)

	Consecutive days.	Statute Miles.			
		Of Latitude.		On Route.[2]	
		Distance	av. p.d.	Distance	av. p.d.
Lat. 87° 47′ N. to lat. 89° 57′ N. . .	5	150	30	187	37
Travelling about the Pole . . .	1	41	41	51	51
Lat. 89° 57′ N. to lat. 87° 47′ N. . .	2	150	75	187	93
Total of above (2nd–9th April incl.) .	8	341	43	425	53

*Unless Peary and his party averaged over 50 statute
m.p.d. for eight consecutive days over the pack-ice he
did not reach the North Pole.*

It will be necessary to consider Peary's sledging
performances with some thoroughness a little later;

[1] *The North Pole*, pp. 289, 290.
[2] Twenty-five per cent. added for deviations.

but the contrast between the above speeds and what he had previously accomplished, as well as that between the character of the surfaces, demands a glance before we pass on.

The polar pack was so much harder for sledging than any other ice Peary travelled over that his speed, prior to 1909, had been no more than *from one-third to one-fourth* his usual rate in other places. He only once made, as we saw, a journey of 250 miles with loaded sledges (from Cape D'Urville to Fort Conger) at 28 m.p.d. His next best speed, over this route, had been 24 m.p.d. His speed over the pack for 251 miles, in 1906, had been 6 m.p.d. In 1909 his *witnessed* speed for the 289 miles to Bartlett's turning-point was 10½ m.p.d., or a trifle less than his own original estimate of 11½ (10 geo.) m.p.d. We have only his word for the 400 miles over this surface at 50 m.p.d.; and we are to see that, a few years later, he contradicted his own statement.

Before doing so, let us turn again to that most devoted follower of his, George Borup. This splendid young Yale athlete nearly worshipped Peary, and was most interested in sledging speeds; but he never said one word about his hero beating all other records. The two highest speeds given in his interesting little book [1] are those of an Eskimo, and of himself with MacMillan. The Eskimo, Seegloo, marched fifty-seven miles over the pack in two days, and Borup exults over this fine performance, which averaged 37 m.p.d. for these days, over the well-beaten trail. Had Borup known that Peary averaged this high speed for about three weeks there would have been no holding him in!

He and MacMillan did little less than Seegloo for a much greater distance, though not on the pack. They marched "about 270 sea miles" in eight marches on nine days, from Cape Morris Jesup to the ship, after

[1] *A Tenderfoot with Peary.*

Peary's return from his polar journey. This averaged 30 m.p.d. and 33·7 p.m. When they told Peary, he said: "Well, well, you've beaten my old record all to pieces." [1]

Peary's *latitudes* alone, apart from deviations, were nearly as much as this for 800 miles, if he reached the Pole.[2] Why did he say nothing about it? Mac-Millan and Borup were younger men, who could be expected to accomplish higher speeds than their leader of fifty-three years, and Peary did not dispute this. Would he not have said, had he beaten the young men's record: "Well, I guess your old Boss had to do better than that to reach the Pole," or words to that effect? Why did he say he had been to the Pole and yet try to hide the speed that alone could have given him success?

3. *Peary's Evidence before a Congressional Committee.*—*The Congressional Record* of the United States House of Representatives is the American equivalent of the British Hansard. Its issues for January and February 1916 contain a verbatim report of the evidence given by Peary and others before the Committee on Naval Affairs in 1910 and 1911. In the course of this evidence the following conversation took place:—

Mr Englebright. What was your best day's travel on your Arctic trip either going or coming?

Capt. Peary. The best day's travel was on the second march on the return from the Pole.

Mr Englebright. How far did you go?

Capt. Peary. Fifty geographical miles, estimated.

Mr Butler. How many hours were required to cover that march of fifty miles?

Capt. Peary. I cannot tell you. I made no entry in my diary for two days, for the 7th and 8th of April, and I do not know what the times were.[3]

---

[1] *A Tenderfoot with Peary*, p. 259.
[2] This will be shown in Chapter IX.
[3] *The Congressional Record*, 12th February 1916, p. 2828.

He admitted that there was pressure ice to be crossed on that march. "On Peary's official 'physical test' he covered fifty miles (18th and 19th December 1910) in fourteen hours and eleven minutes, with a night's rest between each twenty-five miles. This test was made over the proverbially good roads of Washington, D.C., with no load." [1]

It may suffice, at present, to note the following:—

(1) Peary said in *The North Pole* that he did 150 miles of latitude, or about 180 miles of travel, on the first two days of his return from the Pole. His statement to the Naval Committee does not merely contradict this, it does much more, as we shall see. Had his next best day's travel been only one mile shorter than the fifty minutes ($57\frac{1}{2}$ miles) he mentioned, he must have been at least fifty miles short of the Pole. He had written, with reference to his nearness to that point: "No one except the most ignorant will have any doubt but what, at some time, I had passed close to the precise point, and had, perhaps, actually passed over it." [2]

Any man of fifty-three years who had walked either fifty-seven or ninety miles in one day, over the Arctic pack and clad in furs, would know which of these distances he had done; and any traveller who said he did not know which distance he accomplished, probably did neither. Unless the longer distance was averaged on two consecutive days, Peary did not reach the Pole. This is not opinion, it is fact.

(2) In *The North Pole* Peary said his "best day's travel" was his *first* march on leaving the Pole, on 7th to 8th April. To the Committee he said his best day was his *second*, 8th to 9th April.

(3) His physical test proved him capable of walking no more than 25 m.p.d. for two days, over good roads and travelling light. If he reached the Pole he

[1] *The Congressional Record*, p. 2801.
[2] *The North Pole*, footnote, p. 295.

averaged 50 m.p.d. for eight days, over ice floes and in heavy clothing.

(4) He clearly intimates that he did not ride on his sledges,[1] and he did not use ski.

4. *Other Peculiarities of the Record.*—We have seen, in previous chapters, that Peary's word, unfortunately, was not reliable; yet he deliberately dismissed all credible witnesses at a point about 150 miles short of the Pole. His own unreliable word, therefore, must bear the whole weight of his claim to have attained his goal.

The general character of his story is not in accordance with the conditions that are known to exist on the polar pack. Peary represented his success as having been achieved much more easily than was possible. It would have been a Herculean task for a much younger and stronger man; so hard, indeed, that any explorer who accomplished it would be thankful if he returned to land, anywhere, and at any time, alive, if not in the best of health. Peary had made several previous attempts, but on none of them had he been able to control his return with any precision. Each attempt had been a dire struggle with the pack, and in 1906 it had been a race with death.

Dr A. C. Benson said that Tennyson turned the rough old Arthurian knights into polished Victorian gentlemen. In like manner, Peary presents a desperate encounter with the fiercest forces of nature as a drawing-room or Sunday-school story. In all his previous dealings with the polar pack he had come off, not only second best, but very badly; whereas his last trip is of little more interest than a railway journey. There are no rugged facts in the record. This complete difference in the character of the last attempt from all the others could not be due entirely to the special kindliness of the elements in 1909.

[1] *The North Pole*, pp. 193–194, 250–251. "Tramping," mentioned on p. 199.

We shall see, in later chapters, that there are
glaring inconsistencies in Peary's account of the unwitnessed portion of his journey. He complains of
shortness of sleep, when many hours every day are
unaccounted for. Prodigious distances are sledged
without any sleep. The movement of the pack never
caused him inconvenience or delay.

We must now decide upon the right course to
pursue. It is above all things necessary to preserve
a cool and impartial judgment. It would be unfair
to the memory of a great pioneer to leave the matter
here. The best of men make some mistakes; we
little know how many escape detection. On the
other hand, truth must be served. We dare not
attempt to excuse any form of deception.

We cannot do wrong, probably, to begin by sub-
jecting Peary's record to a candid review. This may
teach us much. It will then be necessary to consider
carefully the character of the surface over which he
had to sledge. When we have done this, we shall be
in a position to deal more fully with his speeds and
distances, as well as with other particulars that will
arise. Peary's methods of navigation will demand
our attention; comparisons can be made with other
polar explorers; and lastly, we may be able to form
an estimate of the explorer and his work. The fact
that his claim to have reached the North Pole was
accepted, apparently without examination, by many
learned institutions, makes it essential for our work
to be done as thoroughly as possible.

The authorities for Peary's expedition of 1909
appear to be as follows:—

(1) Peary's work, *The North Pole; Its Discovery
in* 1909, *etc.*, published by the Frederick A. Stokes
Co. The copy used was produced in September
1910, so that any corrections should have been made.
There were one or two earlier editions. The book
contains Mr Grosvenor's map, also dated 1910.

(2) *The Geographical Journal*, vol. xxxvi, No. 2, August 1910, which contains Peary's lecture at the Albert Hall on 4th May 1910.

(3) *The Bulletin of the American Geographical Society*, vol. xli, No. 9, September 1909. This gives a brief summary of the First Account of both Peary and Cook.

(4) *The National Geographic Magazine*, vol. xx, No. 10, October 1909, which gives the First Accounts of both Peary and Cook, with a note that the records of the explorers had not then been examined.

(5) *The Geographical Journal*, vol. xxxiv, No. 4, October 1909. This summarises the First Accounts of both explorers, adding one or two brief comments and a map.

The first of these, although a popular account, appears to be the only detailed official record that Peary ever published. There is nothing of any great importance in the other accounts that is omitted from the book. One or two slight variations will be mentioned, but more frequently the language used in 1 and 2 is identical. We have never been given, what is of the greatest consequence, a copy of the actual journal or sledging diary. Peary's book necessarily has to be used throughout the present inquiry.

[SCHEDULE.

SCHEDULE No. 5. PEARY'S POLAR JOURNEY, 1909 [1]

Date 1909.	Notes, Ice Conditions, Weather, etc.	Minutes of Lat.
Feb. 15	Bartlett left Cape Sheridan ⎫	
22	Peary left Cape Sheridan ⎬	90
28	Bartlett and Borup left Cape Columbia ⎭	
Mar. 1	Lat. 82° 7′ N. ; Peary left Cape Columbia ;	0
	rough pressure ; half-gale E. Drift to W.	10
2	Water ; held up ; 96 f. ; rough pressure ; half-gale E. Drift to W.	(12) [2]
3	Water ; rough pressure ; active ; half-gale E. Drift to W.	(12)
4	Water ; held up ; active ; wind to W.	(12)
5	Water ; held up ; "Big Lead," lat. 83° 53′ N. ; wind to W.	0
6	Water ; held up ; "Big Lead"	0
7	,, ,, ,,	0
8	,, ,, ,,	0
9	,, ,, ,,	0
10	,, ,, ,,	0
11	Water ; crossed 7 channels and 84th parallel ; active ; calm ; clear.	12
12	Water ; crossed cracks and narrow channels ; calm ; clear	12
13	Five miles rough, then better ; calm ; sun	12
14	c. 84° 29′ ; Dr Goodsell returns ; no march ; wind W.	0
15	Water ; 825 f. ; MacMillan returns ; "penetrating E. wind"	(7⅓)
16	Water stopped progress ; ice active	(7⅓)
17	Water stopped progress ; ice active ; a sledge broken ; reach 84° 51′	(7⅓)
18 [3]	Marvin sent to try and pioneer longer marches	17
19	Reach 85° 23′ ; fine ; sun	15

[1] The accuracy of this schedule cannot be guaranteed. The compiler, however, wishes joy to anyone who tries to correct it from Peary's record.

[2] Distances in brackets are averages, not given by Peary.

[3] This day is not mentioned in Peary's record ; but there seem to be fewer difficulties, by assuming that his first 19th should have been the 18th.

Date 1909.	Notes, *Ice Conditions, Weather, etc.*	*Minutes of Lat.*
Mar. 20	Borup returns ; 310 f.	o
21	Water ; $\overset{\cdot}{700}$ f. ; N. wind ; fine ; sun	10
22	Mixed going	15
23	Water ; 85° 48′, 1st obs. before march	15
24	86° 3′ ; Cp. Nansen reached ; Marvin's depot left	c. 15
25	Water ; " good going " ; W. blizzard	20
26	Water ; 86° 38′ before march ; 2nd obs. ; Marvin returns ; Cp. Abruzzi ; fine	15
27	Track of foxes seen ; very rough ; biting N.E. wind	12
28	Water ; c. 87° 12′ ; active ; biting N.E. wind	12
29	Water ; open sea ; $\overset{\cdot}{1260}$ f. ; active	o
30	Water ; better going ; active ; N.W. wind	20
31	Water ; fairly good going ; strong N. wind	20
April 1	87° 47′, 3rd obs. ; BARTLETT RETURNS ; strong N. wind	o
2	Water ; final spurt begun ; some pressure ; strong N. wind	25
3	Water ; final spurt ; some pressure ; calm	20
3–4	Final spurt ; little pressure	25
4–5	89° 25′, 4th obs. ; good going ; wind S.E.	28
5–6	NORTH POLE ; 89° 57′, 5th obs. ; Cp. Jesup ; good going	32
6–7	At NORTH POLE, taking obs. and travelling about	36
7–8	Return began at 4 p.m. on 7th ; $\overset{\cdot}{1500}$ f.	85
9	REACHED LATITUDE 87° 47′ ; N.N.E. gale	45
10		20
11	Recent fox tracks	32
12	Cp. Abruzzi reached	27
13	Cp. Nansen reached ; fresh S.W. wind	20
14	Calm ; sun	15
15	Recent bear track	30
16–17		25
18	Fine ; warm	17
18–19		22
20		24

SCHEDULE No. 5. PEARY'S POLAR JOURNEY, 1909—(*continued*)

Date 1909.	Notes, Ice Conditions, Weather, etc.	Minutes of Lat.
Apr. 20–21	"Big Lead" recrossed on 21st, MAIN TRACK BACK TO HERE	12
21–22	ONLY BARTLETT'S TRAIL FROM "BIG LEAD"	(22½)
22–23	REACHED CAPE COLUMBIA 6 a.m. 23rd	(22½)
23	Resting at Cape Columbia	0
24	„ „ „	0
25	"Reached Cape Hecla in one march"	45
26	"Reached Cape Sheridan in one march"	45

CHAPTER VII

PEARY'S BOOK, *THE NORTH POLE*,[1] REVIEWED

" If he seldom reaches supreme excellence, he rarely sinks into dullness."
Dr Johnson.
The Lives of the Poets.

" Criticism applied to life implies at least a semblance of satire."
The Times Literary Supplement.

1. Introductory. 2. The Style of the Book. 3. The Text. 4. The Subject-matter.

1. This is a remarkable book; it has, indeed, no parallel among works of its class. The leading explorers have long established the excellent custom of presenting their records in an appropriately dignified form, without the sacrifice of any feature that would prove interesting to readers of normal intelligence. The explorer's journal usually forms the basis, and frequently nearly the whole, of the book. No ulterior object on the part of an author has ever been suspected, in a somewhat extensive acquaintance with this class of literature, previously to reading the work before us. The immediate purpose of other books has been to give accurate and lucid accounts of the course of events, and this has fully satisfied their readers, as it appears to have satisfied their writers. Great explorers, with the natural modesty of conscious merit, conceal themselves as much as possible behind the work they strive to do and the excellencies of their associates.

There is nothing even remotely akin to all this in the book we are considering. The peculiar mentality of its author, for an explorer, is seen by a glance at

[1] Fred. A. Stokes Co., 1910.

each of the two frontispieces which embellish the opening pages. The first of these depicts, in vivid colours, "The Five Flags at the Pole," each banner uplifted by an Eskimo. The "Pole" is a pyramidal pressure ridge, natural or artificial, in front of which the group is suitably displayed. The second frontispiece, also in colours, is a "Portrait of Robert E. Peary in his actual North Polar costume"; he is armed with a formidable spear, and clad in the heavy furs in which he walked his 150 miles in two days away from the "Pole" already depicted.

We are back in the nursery. The appeal is that of a child-mind to child-minds. Had not Peary been honoured by learned societies, his claim, so presented, could not have been taken seriously. The book has no appearance of being an authoritative work; and this in spite of it being almost our sole authority for the expedition on which Peary claimed to have reached the Pole.

One of the strongest contrasts with other works of this class is seen in its apparently secret purpose of creating an "atmosphere." Here is no plain and straightforward record of work done. The decorations are the principal features, and their evident object seems to be that of leading the reader's mind along prescribed channels. Uncritical readers, naturally, will follow the course marked out for them, and so be led into the trap of accepting statements that could not be true.

The most objectionable feature of the book is its glorification of Peary. One charming instance of unconscious egoism must be given. He said that, if he lost his ship, it would be "Good-bye to my life's dream and probably to some of my companions." [1]

The type used in the book is large and clear, and the pages have wide margins. These recommendations also help out the amount of matter, which is little for the size of the volume and for the ostensible

[1] Page 78.

importance of the expedition. The total contents are about 100,000 words.

This is merely introductory. The book has merits as well as defects; but the first thought of a reader familiar with polar literature, on taking it up, is its complete divergence from the accustomed forms. Most polar books are intended for the general public; they are attractively produced and well illustrated. This book is unique in humiliating a noble subject.

2. *Style.*—Literary style is a matter of personal taste and opinion. Peary's mode of expression may be described in general, and inoffensively, as journalistic. Occasionally it is bombastic. Those who are attracted by a somewhat inflated and flamboyant manner of writing will most appreciate Admiral Peary's efforts. Its appeal is to the gallery, not to the stalls. The simple dignity we look for in this class of writing is replaced by pomposity, and the explorer's diary by a story that is sometimes very poor. And yet, from the viewpoint of Peary and his admirers, the book, with some exceptions, may be considered well written. It is seldom dull; on the contrary, it is usually "snappy" and bright. The descriptive powers of its author, especially when depicting natural scenery, are moderately good, though these powers are used, to a large extent, for the purpose of padding. Thus an interesting book is compiled, that leaves as little space as possible for the main event; examples of this will be given.

The introductory matter received the closest attention, and its style was carefully polished; but the author's judgment, in the book as a whole, was much at fault. He failed to see that his main purpose should have been to bring out, in high relief, his actual journey to the Pole. This was the great event for which all the rest of the book should have been written. Everything prior to his setting out from Cape Sheridan was merely introductory to the main act, as all that followed his return to the ship could be no more than epilogue.

Peary was oblivious of this, as he was of the immense extra burden he imposed upon himself, as sole witness and chronicler of his own greatest feats, in electing to have no other white man with him during the culminating period of the journey. Strange to say, this is the worst portion of the record; and as the crucial moment approaches, the story deteriorates. It is not necessary to be a literary critic in order to see these defects in the story. No educated reader could fail to notice them.

The story, up to a point, is well told, except for the number and length of its digressions; then the trouble begins. The audience is conducted, with great *éclat*, some distance out on the drifting ice floes, when the guide shows signs of nervousness. He pulls himself together for a time, but his mighty speeches and sparkling wit desert him. We lose confidence in his leadership. He gets confused about his dates, distances, and direction. At last we reach the end of the transition, and find ourselves wondering if we are not reading a piece of fiction.

There is little evidence in this book of any æsthetic sense in the author. He admitted that he had no time for scenic effects.[1] He was too seriously impressed with his own importance, and too mightily engrossed by his own generalship, for absorbing and depicting the genius of the pack. There are no nature notes, and there is no true artistry here.

Peary dwells little upon the pains or pleasures of Pole-seeking. His affected contempt of danger leads him, occasionally, into a braggart style, as if he were reckless of his life. This was far from the truth, although he was no coward. Courage most undoubtedly he possessed, but he made as certain as

[1] *Op. cit.*, p. 283.

money, foresight, and experience could make it that no accident should happen.

Commander Green says that Peary did not get on well with the public. This could not have been altogether Peary's fault, for his writing evidently was designed to please the masses. His style, at its best, is lively and picturesque; but it varies considerably, and parts of it are more after the manner of a commercial report than a record of an exploration. He puts all his stock into his shop-window, and tries to display all his knowledge to the greatest advantage. His book appears to be thoroughly censored, and bears little resemblance to the faithful pictures of travel presented by other explorers.

3. *Text.*—On turning to the text of this narrative, on which we must make a few remarks, we notice, first, that had it been a mediæval document we should have said that the text was occasionally corrupt. One or two examples of this may suffice.

It would appear that, on the outward journey across the pack, the main body of the expedition did not travel on 14th March, but "Henson got away early to the north with his pioneer division." [1] Twenty-four hours later "Bartlett and Marvin started off with the pickaxes." [2] There is no explanation of why *two* pioneer parties were sent on ahead, and this is the only occasion when it is mentioned. The account of the 15th has the appearance of forgetfulness that Henson had gone north the day before, but this is not the main point.

It is more important to notice that no distances are given on the 15th, 16th, 17th, and 18th of March, from which it is evident that progress was slow. The latitudes work out at $5\frac{1}{2}$ miles as the average for each of these four days; this is according to the text of the book, but if we turn to p. 237 we find "Monday, 15th March" mentioned. On p. 240, "in the morning"

[1] *Op. cit.*, p. 235.   [2] *Op. cit.*, p. 237.

must refer to the 16th, and the "next march" to the 16th is the 17th. On p. 241, "after a short sleep" might bring them to the 18th, or it could still have been the 17th. But after telling us of Marvin's good march of seventeen miles, Peary writes: "At the end of this march on the evening of the 19th"; thus an inconvenient day has been unceremoniously consigned to oblivion. So much for what Peary says; but if we *assume* that on p. 241 the date 19th is an error, and that it should read 18th, the account will fit in very well. For after speaking of the evening, on the next page he writes of the 19th as if he had not mentioned it before. Page 143 seems to confirm this hypothesis, for there he says that they did fifteen miles, whereas on p. 241 he had already told us that they did seventeen miles on that day.

This seems to be an example of what critics term composite authorship: that two independent writers composed the original accounts, from which our present version has been compiled by a third and later hand. We are told that on the 19th March they travelled both seventeen and fifteen miles, and the 18th is not mentioned. If, however, we may so far presume as to tamper with the text in the manner suggested, we may assume that they did seventeen miles on the 18th and fifteen miles on the 19th. This would increase the average on the 15th, 16th, and 17th, on which days no distances are given, from $5\frac{1}{2}$ to $7\frac{1}{3}$ miles a day. Unfortunately this hypothesis seems to leave one day too many, which a twelve hours' rest will not account for, so confusion must remain the worse confounded.

Another similar example will be found on pp. 247 and 252, the details of which would be tedious. We may notice, however, that on p. 7 "the 84th parallel was crossed on 18th March," and on p. 235 this happened on the 11th. The latter is correct and the mistake, in part, is quite simple. The 85th and not the 84th parallel would have been crossed on 18th March if a march was made on that day, though there is evidence that the expedition was held up then, and this day is not mentioned in the record of the journey. The story is very confused about this time; but there seem to be fewer difficulties on the theory that the first of the two 19ths of March should have been the 18th, and this we have assumed.

Peary wrote on his first 19th that "the end of the next march . . . would be five marches from where MacMillan and the doctor turned back." [1] Had this day been the real 19th March, the five marches, including this one, would take us back to the 16th. Peary had been quite clear that Dr Goodsell returned on the 14th and MacMillan on the 15th.[2] If the first 19th was the 18th, it was five marches to MacMillan's return, though it was six to the Doctor's. But enough of these errors.

Even Mr Balch, who began by supporting Peary, admitted that the "text is somewhat involved." We have seen the truth of this. Peary has left posterity to flounder in a textual morass where, frequently, there is no foothold. Controversy may arise as to the correct meaning of many passages. There is no straightforward record of events. The claim to have reached the Pole rests upon a most infirm basis.

4. *Subject-matter.*—The events described are of such interest that we must cruise steadily through most of the chapters and make our observations *en route*, leaving special points to be dealt with later.

Peary is introduced to the reading public by his friend, Mr G. H. Grosvenor. His main object, in his sketch of Arctic history with which the book opens, is to try and make the world believe that Peary was the crown and culmination of all the unsuccessful efforts of his predecessors, most of whom were not

[1] *Op. cit.*, p. 241.
[2] *Op. cit.*, pp. 235, 237, and Schedule No. 5.

Americans.   Nearly as much space is devoted to the
hero's broken leg as to the whole of Nansen's epoch-
making *Fram* expedition.

This *résumé* of Arctic exploration is well written,
though not always quite correct in matters of fact.
Captain Kellett discovered Wrangell Island in 1849;
Commander de Long did not see it until 1867. Peary
did not show the probable insularity of Greenland on
his crossing of the inland ice, but in 1900. These,
however, are trifling defects in an able essay.

More serious are the "brilliancy of results" claimed
for Peary's Greenland expeditions, which actually accomplished very little of permanent value; and "winds
of unusual fury" did not rob Peary of the Pole in 1906,[1]
though this was the excuse for failure. Nansen's
crossing of Greenland is compared unfavourably with
Peary's crossing; whereas the former was not only
the greater feat but had more important results.
Much of this chapter is empty flattery.

Peary properly opens his own account of the
expedition with a chapter on his plan of campaign,
in which he admits that authorities differed, after
1906, as to whether it was possible for him to reach
the Pole.   He then gives in full his "Published Statement," the main points of which are dealt with elsewhere in the present work.   The principal purpose of
this chapter, apparently, was to continue the laying of
the psychological snare begun by Mr Grosvenor.   The
success of *The North Pole* depended upon its readers
being led into the frame of mind that, later on, would
believe anything of its hero.   Rhetorical paint is laid
on thicker towards the end of the chapter, which
culminates in the alleged conquest of the Pole.

Chapter II opens with the inaccuracy that Peary
undertook, in 1886, "*entirely alone*, a summer trip to
Greenland" (our italics).[2] Surely he could not plead

---

[1] *Op. cit.*, p. 31 ; see p. 239.
[2] *Op. cit.*, p. 11.

that he had forgotten the existence of the companion
he had spoken of as "my friend Christian Maigaard."[1]
There was not glory enough for two. Peary could
say that he made all his preparations unaided; and
this appears to have been his conception of truth.

This chapter, like the previous one, is well planned;
but Peary seems to be posing on a pedestal from which
he condescends to tell us, quite amiably, though
imperiously, how he prepared for his triumph. He
ignored the awkward fact that there were four Poles,
and that two of them were geographic. There was
only one Pole for Peary!

Perhaps the most purple passage occurs on p. 15:
"When I gathered myself together and faced the
situation squarely, I realised that the project was
something too big to die; that it never, in the great
scheme of things, would be allowed to fall through."
It must be a tremendous uplift to feel that even
Providence cannot do without one.

Apart from this, the chapter seems normal; so
also is Chapter III, which includes the little com-
pliments paid to Peary by President Roosevelt. Peary
never left out anything of this kind, and introduced
the President as "the biggest man America has ever
produced." This enhanced Roosevelt's few, well-
chosen words, which he was officially obliged to say,
and would please one-half of the United States at
the expense of the other half.

Every feature that the vessel passed on its northward voyage along the coast was, if possible, described
in considerable detail, and all this helped to make a
nice, interesting book. In writing of the ship and
equipment, the pianola comes in for a paragraph;
and we are regaled with an inventory of the pictures
on his cabin walls and the flags that cheered him
onward.

Chapter IV takes us, in leisurely fashion, as far as

[1] *Northward over the Great Ice*, vol. i, p. 7.

Cape York, in the Whale Sound district. A good deal of not uninteresting small talk fills up the pages. This chapter is also padded with pages of valueless "remarks," such as "My dream . . . should I succeed?" etc., etc.

Peary then started on his Eskimos, whom he seriously overworked, from the literary standpoint, during the remainder of the book. We have no need to discuss the use of the backward races on expeditions; we are concerned with the way Peary used them, not for sledging, but for filling his book with entertaining though incidental, if not irrelevant, matter. The means by which an explorer gains his ends may or may not be worth writing about, but if they are, they should be treated in a manner quite subservient to the main purpose.

Three complete chapters, V–VII, are devoted to this side-issue. Their titles will nearly suffice us: "Welcome from the Eskimos," ten pages; "An Arctic Oasis," ten pages; "Odd Customs of an Odd People," nine pages. There is some repetition here. Nearly all this matter should have been compressed into one short chapter. The object of these long digressions, as we have seen, is to leave as little space as possible for the record of the actual journey to the Pole, while making the book as interesting as possible to the man in the street. The defect remains, that the story of the expedition is interrupted on p. 42 and is not resumed for thirty pages.

The title of Chapter VIII, "Getting Recruits," shows that the Eskimos are not finished with yet, though they are not unduly oppressive here. We find, however, the usual magnification of *minutiæ* and the spinning out of very feeble threads to inordinate lengths. The reader is conducted towards his main object with painful steps and slow. No excuse is missed to stop and gossip on the way.

The next chapter is concerned entirely with walrus.

Its greater part was written by George Borup. This was an excellent notion for making up a book without touching on its purpose. Walrus, like Eskimos, were connected with the North Pole as penguins and ponies were related to Scott's journey to the South Pole. Hence, four whole chapters could be composed of them, and this helped Peary to say as little as possible, when it would be dangerous to say a word too much. A page or two about walrus, in a short chapter on Eskimos, would have satisfied an explorer who was desirous of conducting his readers to his greatest exploit.

Chapters X–XII, and part of Chapter XIII, lie open to the same objection, but not in the same degree. The struggle with the ice of Kennedy and Robeson Channels was a vital part of the record, though only of how the expedition reached its base. It was natural that Peary should fall into his anecdotage at the sight of his old haunts, on the way to Cape Sheridan; but he might have spared us several pages of this, such as his feelings on revisiting Greely's old camping ground, and how the successful navigation of the ice-blocked channels was due to his perfect knowledge of the conditions. He was fully prepared, according to his own account, for every emergency that could possibly arise, and he knew precisely what to do, to save himself, if the vessel were lost.

The limbs of the story are longer, more numerous, and more bulky, than those of an octopus; while its body is sadly attenuated. One chapter on the navigation of the channels would have been better; but it would have reduced the size of the book, unless we had been told more of the actual journey to the Pole.

One whole page (104–105) is copied verbatim from *Nearest the Pole.*[1] The author, evidently, was more pleased with this specimen of his handiwork than many of his readers probably will be.

[1] Page 45.

Chapters XIII and XIV, taking them as a whole, are more satisfactory. They contain a good description of the last phase of the struggle with the ice, the reaching of Cape Sheridan, the establishment of the base and other matters of moment. Chapter XV, occupied with " the autumn work," requires no comment.

The next chapter and a half give an account of the hunting, another excellent excuse for expanding a limb to monstrous proportions; and then we come to Chapter XVIII, " The Long Night." This chapter and the next two can be mentioned together; they are quite good. Peary will be heartily commended, towards the end of this book, on his winter *régime*, which these chapters of *The North Pole* describe, and bring the history of the expedition to the threshold of the polar journey.

Peary is seen at his best during the final preparations. One cannot sufficiently regret that his character seemed to be warped in one important feature. The picture, skilfully drawn by himself, of the gnarled veteran lingering on the *Roosevelt* for a whole day, after every party had been sent forward to Cape Columbia, is impressive, as it was intended to be. In "perfect quiet and rest" the Commander ticked over in his mind every detail of the journey he would begin on the morrow. He then had "a few hours in which to look the situation squarely in the face" before his last sleep on the ship. Did he then, one may wonder, conceive the thought of claiming success whatever might happen? He had arranged to be the sole witness of his culminating effort.

Two chapters on sledging and the conditions on his route are next interpolated. They will not be considered here, as these subjects will receive particular attention in later chapters.[1] We must notice, however, that Peary's glaciology has never been systema-

[1] See Chapters VIII and XI.

tised, and is most unlikely to have any effect on the
progress of this science.   His practical remarks are very
different, for he was a man of action and not a scientist.

Chapter XXIII is suitably entitled: "Off across
the Frozen Sea *at Last*" (our italics).   Its opening
words are: "The work of the expedition . . . began
with Bartlett's departure from the *Roosevelt.*" [1]
Twenty-two chapters out of thirty-five, and more than
two-thirds of the total number of pages, are devoted
to matters that "were merely preliminary," or vale
dictory.   Only one hundred pages are given to the
great journey.   Yet this journey, if it actually took
place as recorded, was the most wonderful of its kind
in human history.   Peary's aversion to writing much
about the main purpose of his expedition is seen even
more clearly in the brevity of his descriptions when
he comes to the crucial parts of the journey, after
Bartlett's dismissal.

The chapter we are considering begins with a needless recapitulation of all the preliminaries; and no
remark is too trivial to make if there is the slightest
excuse for dragging it in.   There is some actual
repetition.   Apart from these defects, the story proceeds apace, and the chapter ends with the first day
on the pack-ice.

Chapter XXIV covers more than a week, from 2nd
to 10th March.   On 3rd March Bartlett's pioneer
trail was found a mile and a half to the west; so there
had been this amount of drift, *plus* the drift, if any, of
the floes Peary was on, in a very short time.   During
the night of 3rd to 4th March the wind went right
round to the west.   Peary's "gnawing torment ' at
being held up for a week by his "Big Lead" is the most
enlightening comment on his sledging system, especially in relation to his "best way of crossing leads."
The channel was only a quarter of a mile wide when
the expedition reached it.

[1] *The North Pole*, p. 213.

Chapter XXV carries the record to 15th March, a period of five days. A verbatim copy of a letter addressed to Marvin, who was in the rear, was considered of sufficient importance to be given; or it was an excuse for padding, of which there had not been so much in recent chapters. At the end of this chapter and the beginning of the next there is some confusion as to the date.

Up to this point there has been no evidence that Peary was not writing history. In Chapter XXVI, however, an element of romance appears to creep in, and causes no little disorder. There is, undoubtedly, a *substratum* of fact; but the text, as we have seen, is corrupt. As Peary was not a literary man, his introduction of fiction seems incongruous, as the result is neither a correct chronicle nor a plausible story, for in neither could a whole day be forgotten without damage to the writer's prestige.

When this journey is plotted, or written in diary form, as in Schedule No. 5,[1] the opening pages of this chapter are seen to reveal a state of mental confusion on the part of the writer.

Chapter XXVII begins: "Up to this time no observations had been taken." [2] We need only notice here that there was a high improbability that Peary was anywhere near the meridian of Cape Columbia; and it is impossible to say how many miles he had actually travelled. Had he never deviated from his meridian, except for the picking of his trail, he would have travelled about 240 miles. He started his journey before the Arctic sunrise. There was no need to do so, for he would have returned to land before the pack broke up, at the speed he gives, had he waited for two or three weeks, as he did in 1906. He felt it necessary, perhaps, to avoid observations for position as far as possible. His bitterness against Nansen probably was due to Nansen's exposure of his slipshod

---

[1] See pp. 94-96.   [2] *The North Pole*, p. 248.

observations in Greenland. His observations on the
pack, in 1906, seriously restricted his story of the
journey he made that year, and contradicted his
account of the "dash" from Storm Camp. He was
determined to have a free hand for his description of
the last journey, and would have eliminated astronomical observations entirely had he been able to
claim the Pole without them. Knowing this was impossible, he cut them down to a minimum by starting
so early that none could be taken for his first 240 miles
of travel.[1]

This chapter covers the four days, 23rd to 26th
March, between Marvin's first and second observations, and appears to be a more straightforward record
than its predecessor. There can be no doubt that Peary,
on this journey, surpassed Cagni's highest latitude.
How much farther he went is more liable to conjecture,
but Chapter XXVIII gives us some information.

When Marvin turned back from latitude 86° 38' N.,
Peary proceeded with Bartlett as pioneer, Henson and
the Eskimos, a total of nine men, with sixty dogs and
seven sledges. Bartlett was a much stronger man than
Peary, and was doing his best to reach as high a latitude
as possible before his dismissal; yet $17\frac{1}{4}$ statute miles
of northing formed his limit on 26th March. The
next march was harder; it was so hard that even
Bartlett's energy failed to achieve fourteen miles, and
he was worn out and discouraged at the end of the
day. The same distance was done on the 28th when,
after six hours' travel, open water stopped progress.

The value of this information is seen when these
marches are compared with those Peary claims to have
made after Bartlett returned. This fine pioneer was
thirty-three years of age and in the prime of his
strength, yet he could not average more than
16 m.p.d. over the ice in these high latitudes. Peary,

---

[1] He could have used the stars; but this part of the subject is
fully dealt with in Chapter X of the present book.

a weaker man, twenty years older than Bartlett, gives
us six marches, to and around the Pole, when he had
to do his own pioneering, that average over 28 m.p.d.[1]
It is certain that he could not have nearly doubled
Bartlett's average, and it is ridiculous to suppose that
he could have returned from the Pole to Bartlett's
last camp at *more than four times Bartlett's average*, or
at 65 geo. m.p.d.

During the whole of 29th March the expedition
was held up by open water. The pack closed up early
on the 30th, when a lake of level ice, six or seven miles
across, helped towards the total of twenty miles for
the day. The next march, Bartlett's last, was made
against a strong headwind that Peary admitted lost
them "miles of distance." Under these circumstances
it is difficult to believe that another twenty miles were
made good. Peary said that "had it been clear"
they would have done twenty-five miles. This, of
course, was merely hypothetical.

Bartlett was dismissed on 1st April and reached the
Roosevelt on the 24th.[2] His distance was about
380 miles, and his average speed about 15·8 m.p.d.
Peary stepped ashore at 6 a.m. on the 23rd, and would
have been at his ship on the 25th if he had not remained
for two days at Cape Columbia. It has been suggested
that he waited here because he was afraid of overtaking
Bartlett, and this is probable. Had Peary not spent,
according to his story, thirty hours at the Pole, he
would have overtaken him. Bartlett had not made a
tardy return; his march was a fine performance, almost
comparable to Cagni's speed over the pack. The relatively aged Peary said he travelled 400 miles farther in
twenty-five, than Bartlett travelled in twenty-four, days.
As he had more than double Bartlett's distance to travel
he had to move at more than double Bartlett's speed, for
the same time, in order to have reached the Pole.

[1] All these miles are minutes of latitude.
[2] *Op. cit.*, p. 325.

On turning our attention back to 31st March, the day on which Bartlett's last outward march was made, we find that the wind blew "violently" from the north all night. The result was seen next day, 1st April, when Bartlett got his latitude of 87° 47′ N. He had walked "five or six miles to the north in order to make sure of reaching the 88th parallel." [1]   Peary adds: "Our latitude was the direct result of the northerly wind of the last two days; . . . we had travelled fully twelve miles more than his observations showed in the last five marches, but had lost them by the crushing up of the young ice in our rear and the closing of leads," caused by the north wind. [2]

This passage is ambiguous.   Were the twelve miles lost in two days, or in five?   In spite of the latter part of the statement, added to represent the southerly drift as being comparatively slow, it is clear that the twelve miles were lost in two days only, because the north wind had blown for only the two days, as stated in the earlier part of the passage.   It had "blown violently from the north all night" of the 31st "and still continued." [3]   On the night of the 28th to 29th the drift of the ice on the northern side at a lead was to the *east*.   This confirms the fact that the southerly movement was restricted to the 30th and 31st.

The importance of accuracy here is seen when we realise that a drift of 6 m.p.d. had been going on. This is a very high rate, though not much more than half the 11 m.p.d. Peary recorded in 1906.   The north wind that caused this rapid southerly drift prevented Bartlett from reaching latitude 88° N., and if it were to continue would seriously handicap Peary in his effort to reach the Pole.   It had one good result, however, in closing the channels to the south, and thus making safer the first part of the return to land.

The only theory that appears to fit the facts is that

[1] *Op. cit.*, pp. 266–267.   [2] *Op. cit.*, p. 268.
[3] *Op. cit.*, p. 266.

Peary made up his mind not to lose touch with Bartlett's returning trail. As long as the wind kept in the north he would be safe, but an easterly or westerly slant would soon disrupt the tracks. Peary did not know what winds would blow during the next fortnight, and this was the least time in which he could have reached the Pole and returned to Bartlett's camp, a latitude distance of 300 miles. It seems clear, therefore, that he had decided to anchor himself to Bartlett's trail, which was his only link with land and life. To return to its northern end, after travelling 150 miles away from it, would have been a miracle, on those drifting floes, only equalled by the miracle of walking this distance in two days. We shall return to this matter a little later.[1]

Chapter XXX gives a short description of events on 1st to 3rd April. The first page and a half are devoted to Peary's reasons for taking Henson to the Pole, leaving six and a half pages for the record of three crucial days. The style of writing here is high-flown and rhetorical, to such an extent, indeed, that at least one statement is untrue. This occurs in the following passage: "The years seemed to drop from me, and I felt as I had felt in those days fifteen years before, when I headed my little party across the great ice-cap of Greenland, leaving 20 and 25 miles behind my snowshoes day after day, and on a spurt stretching it to 30 or 40." [2]

Peary ought not to have written this. In the first place, it was an attempt to mislead his readers into supposing that the polar pack was as good a sledging surface as the inland ice. We shall see, more fully in the next chapter, that it was not. Peary's average in Greenland was from 10 to 20 m.p.d., whereas on the pack, until his last journey, his average had been from 5 to 8 m.p.d. He makes an untrue and unfair comparison to prepare the right atmosphere for the miraculous marches he is soon to mention.

[1] See pp. 160–161.   [2] *Op. cit.*, p. 275.

In the second place, he exaggerated the daily distances he had travelled in Greenland. We have seen that his fastest crossing of the ice-cap was his return journey in 1895, and that he was justly proud of his average of 20·7 m.p.d. for the 500 miles of that journey. On the outward trip of that year his speed undoubtedly was slower than this, if only because he was careful not to give exact particulars of it, though he mentions three days on which he did 22, 28, and 30 miles. These are the greatest daily distances recorded, with one exception; this was on 3rd August 1892, when 35 miles were covered, *downhill*.

Peary insinuates in *The North Pole* that he had averaged from 20 to 25 m.p.d. in Greenland. This he never did for more than three days, and he never sledged as much as 40 miles in a day on the inland ice. He would not have failed to record it had he done so. He knew he had never done more than 35 miles in a day, and that only once, down a hill, on a good surface; but he had much "taller stories" than this to tell very shortly, and was merely leading up to them. He accomplished, as we know, not only 40, but 70 or 80 miles in a day once or twice *with light sledges*, and under exceptionally favourable circumstances; though not with loads, nor on the inland ice. He expected to take thirty days, which would average about 17 m.p.d. for his last journey over the ice-cap,[1] a proof that his outward journey of that year was not faster than this. Actually he made his return, as we have seen, in five days less than this.

Another injudicious statement, made at this time, was: "My food and fuel supplies were ample for 40 days." [2] This should be considered in relation to the further statement that his party was not hungry on the return to Cape Columbia.[3] The latter assertion is no surprise, because only twenty-two days (1st to

---

[1] *Northward over the Great Ice*, vol. ii, p. 457.
[2] *The North Pole*, p. 273.   [3] *Ibid.*, p. 317.

23rd April) were said to have been occupied in the remainder of the journey to land. The former statement was another of those slips of the pen that helps us towards the truth.

Peary was provisioned for forty days, at least, on parting from Bartlett. He added that, by eating dog, his party could manage to exist "for fifty days." This would be in such an eventuality as being held up by open wate.·. As the distance he had to travel was about 600 miles, the rate of progress was worked out at about 15 m.p.d. This would have been a splendid performance at Peary's age and under the conditions he had to contend with. If he had not returned to land in less than about forty days, we could not have doubted that he had reached the Pole. Had he taken longer than this, and especially had he reached land to the east or to the west of Cape Columbia, his claim would have been even more credible. In order to return in about half the time he was provisioned for, his speed had to be about double his estimate, or about 30 m.p.d.

We are not informed what was done with all the surplus food with which he left Bartlett in latitude 87° 47′ N. Nearly half the total amount was not required. The dogs could account for much of it, no doubt, but as unnecessary weights were not likely to be carried back to land, a great deal of it must have been dumped into the sea.

The fact that his provisions were based on a speed of 15 m.p.d. proves that he expected to average no less than this, but not much more. Sledge travellers are obliged to estimate their loads very carefully. Had Peary felt safe in forecasting a higher speed, he would have taken food for less than forty days, in order to save the dogs. His return to land in about half his estimated time is good evidence that he did not go the whole distance he was provisioned for. All his previous estimates of speed on the polar pack had been too optimistic, and we have no reason for believing that this is the one great exception.

Chapters XXX–XXXIII are referred to at some length in other parts of this book. There are only a few points, not dealt with elsewhere, that we need notice here.

Brief as is the space allotted to the crucial period of the expedition, many of these scant pages are filled with irrelevant remarks, and with references to matters that had very slight connection with the important work in hand. Thus, on p. 278, two paragraphs are devoted to Peary's meditations upon the moon; and nearly half a page is given to his recollections of the return in 1906.[1]

Chapter XXXI, however, could not very well contain much padding; for there are only six pages on which to describe the last three days of the outward journey. As Peary says that his party was making an average of "about" twenty-six minutes of latitude a day after Bartlett's dismissal,[2] we should have been glad to learn how it was done. This was thirty statute miles a day apart from deviations from the course, which must have added a further seven miles. Bartlett had not been able to average much more than half this speed. Peary realised this, and filled one of these six pages with a dissertation on the high efficiency of picked men; but he took care not to give his actual distances travelled in statute miles. Bartlett, the most efficient sledger on the expedition, was not one of the picked men, though he was undoubtedly faster, as Cagni was faster for long distances, than Peary. Six men form a large, and not a small, sledging unit to maintain an average of 37 m.p.d. for five consecutive days, and then to double that speed on the return. The return journey is dealt with elsewhere.

Four pages of Chapter XXXIV are concerned with the loss of Marvin, leaving five pages for the general

[1] On p. 281.   [2] Page 286.

narrative. Of these, the sweetest morsel to Peary was the entry, which he quotes, from his diary. In this he wrote: "My life work is accomplished. . . . I have now the last great geographical prize for the credit of the United States. This work is the finish, the cap and climax of nearly four hundred years of effort, loss of life, and expenditure of fortunes by the civilised nations of the world. . . ." [1]

He eliminated the South Pole, near which Shackleton turned back this same year, and other far greater geographical prizes than his North Pole. Even when allowance is made for patriotic fervour, we cannot forbear to notice that this vain boasting was associated with the kind of record we are now considering. Peary proceeds: "Our return from the Pole was accomplished in sixteen marches." These, for the distance he gives from the Pole to Cape Columbia, or 413 minutes of latitude, average less than 26 m.p.d. Even this speed would have appeared impossible if put in the statute miles we are accustomed to, as 29·7 m.p.d. for over a fortnight would be more than a party of six men could be expected to do on the Arctic pack. But the actual distance travelled was about 590 miles, which in "sixteen marches," that were also sixteen days, would require *an average speed of 37 m.p.d.* For any man of fifty-three years to pretend that he could walk at this rate over the drifting pack-ice of the Arctic Ocean is grotesque, and reduces Peary's self-esteem to its proper level.

The last chapter, XXXV, need not detain us. Of the book as a whole we have seen how inconsistent the story is. It is not a clear account of a journey to the Pole. The very text of the narrative is involved. We do not complain of these imperfections, for it is the author of such a book who is the sufferer. If he thought that, amid his own confusion, he could make good his escape from detection, he was greatly

[1] *Op. cit.*, p. 316.

mistaken.   As he deliberately prevented any corro-
boration of his story, he must be content to be judged
by it as it stands.   Instead of being a straightforward
account of his doings, it is in some parts ambiguous,
in other parts contradictory, and is obscure and
secretive almost throughout.   Some of Peary's statements are so incredible that they could not be accepted
unless supported by the most undoubted proofs;
other statements no proofs could establish.   All proof
or disproof, Peary decided, should be impossible.   By
his own choice, therefore, he left his claim to have
reached the North Pole unproved, but with evidence
amounting to proof that he could not have attained
his goal.

CHAPTER VIII

THE POLAR PACK ON PEARY'S ROUTES [1]

" The history of the pack-ice was one of continual, unceasing change. The field itself was never at rest."

J. M. WORDIE.
The Natural History of the Pack Ice.

1. A COMPARISON WITH THE INLAND ICE OF GREENLAND. 2. THE CHARACTER OF THE PACK: OPEN CHANNELS. 3. PRESSURE RIDGES AND PEARY'S SPEED. 4. THE MOVEMENT OF THE PACK PRIOR TO 1909. 5. THE MOVEMENT OF THE PACK IN 1909. 6. CONCLUDING REMARKS.

1. IT is now necessary to delve more deeply into the subject, and the first step must be that of making a somewhat exhaustive examination of the data relative to the sledging conditions that Peary met with to the north of Grant Land, especially from Cape Columbia. His claim to have set up new sledging records, apart from the 180 miles in two days, will not seem so extraordinary if the surface over which he travelled was exceptionally favourable. It will be advantageous to introduce this branch of the subject by a glance at the conditions Peary found on the inland ice of Greenland. A fair comparison of the two sledging surfaces can be made, leading to deductions of no little pertinence.

We can begin by eliminating the atmospheric conditions, as being approximately common to the ice-cap and the pack. It will be seen in Schedule No. 1 that in 1892 there were seven days' blizzard out of a total of sixty days; and in 1895 only one day was lost out of twenty-four days. On the pack, one day out of sixteen was lost by a gale in 1902, and seven days were

[1] This chapter necessarily is somewhat technical.

TYPES OF PACK ICE : II.

lost out of forty-seven in 1906. The gales on the ocean ice-floes were worse than those experienced on the inland ice; and they had a danger, impossible in Greenland, of driving the floating camp off the course, and perhaps to destruction.

There is, in Greenland, the effect of altitude to be considered; but sledging on the high plateaux of Greenland and Antarctica has affected explorers very little. This fact is so well known that there is no need to cite the evidence for it. Peary suffered no more than the slightest inconvenience from the height.

The decisive factor is *the sledging surface*. This is similar on the plateau of Greenland to that of Antarctica. Captain Amundsen, the only traveller to the South Pole who used dogs for the whole journey, found the surface excellent, and did his 20 to 25 m.p.d. continually over it. Peary wrote of the inland ice of Greenland: "The character of the snow" was such that "our broad-runner sledge and our snowshoes enabled us to skim along on its surface without undue exertion";[1] and again: "The same perfect snow surface."[2] It was not always "perfect"; soft and deep snow sometimes made progress hard, as it does everywhere in the polar regions, including the pack-ice.

Of the four single, or two double, journeys made over the inland ice, only one single journey, the last, was fast enough for Peary to give us his speed. Of this 500-miles journey in 1895 he wrote: "We had crossed from moraine to moraine in $24\frac{1}{4}$ days, making in that time 25 marches of 20·1 miles. This does not seem like the performance of exhausted men. Yet nowhere else in all the Arctic regions but on the Greenland ice-cap could we have travelled the distance we did in our condition."[1] They had just experienced a difficult and strenuous time. His party consisted of

[1] *Northward over the Great Ice*, vol. ii, p. 527.
[2] *Ibid.*, vol. i, p. 360.

three men, his two companions being much younger than himself; and they could travel faster than the party of six men who went north of Bartlett's last camp in 1909. Yet Peary wrote, in 1895: "June 15th and 16th. We made the same distance as during the preceding four marches, *i.e.* between twenty and twenty-one miles. This is our limit." [1] Again, in his remarks after the journey, he said: "Throughout the entire journey we pressed on to the utmost of our ability, making every yard we could in every march, and when our limit was reached, hastily pitched our tents. . . . We could feel the last mile or two of each march dragging the life and vital force out of us." [2] The above average of 20·1 m.p.m., for the distance of 500 miles, was 20·7 m.p.d. We must note, for future reference, that this average speed was clearly Peary's limit at the age of thirty-nine, with two younger companions; and that this excellent performance was made over a surface so good that Peary did not think so high a speed could have been made anywhere "else in all the Arctic regions." The character of the pack-ice on his routes to the North Pole must now be established.

2. *The Character of the Pack: Open Channels.*— We saw in Chapter II that the fundamental fact relative to the ice of the Arctic Ocean was its perpetual motion: as summed up by a recent authority, "All the polar pack has drifted and is drifting." [3] We saw also that, while the *cause* of this motion was the wind, its *effects* were mainly two: the formation of open channels, and of pressure ridges. The character of the pack-ice, as a whole, consists of areas of more level ice together with these two features. We have now to inquire more particularly as to its condition on Peary's routes.

Peary himself has provided us with most of the

---

[1] *Northward over the Great Ice*, vol. ii, p. 515.
[2] *Ibid.*, vol. ii, p. 519.
[3] *Geographical Journal*, July 1928, p. 80.

data we require. Only one other party has journeyed more than a very few miles north from Grant Land; this party being under the command of Lieut. Markham of the Nares Expedition in 1876. Markham turned back in latitude 83° 20′ N., or less than twenty miles farther north than Cape Columbia; his transport equipment being unsuitable to the conditions. His description of the ice was verified by Peary. Beyond Markham's turning-point we have the statements of airmen. It is necessary, unfortunately, to consider how far Peary's descriptions may be regarded as trustworthy. We may accept them safely whenever he was accompanied by other white men, but his orientation must be regarded as very approximate. We have, in addition to Peary, his biographer, Commander Green, and his assistant, Mr Borup, both of whom can give evidence on the subject.

Peary *nearly* always represented his track between land and the Pole as being the roughest sledging surface in the world, as probably it was. He gives a " sample " of it opposite p. 156 of his *Nearest the Pole*, and other examples opposite pp. 216, 217, 224, 225, 233, and 240 of *The North Pole*. These agree with his descriptions, and explain, as they were intended to explain, the slow progress that we have seen he made, before his last expedition.

The exceptional circumstances under which Peary did *not* represent his surfaces as being extremely rough, are remarkable. This happened, apart from one day in 1909, *only when he was accompanied by no credible witnesses*. The improvement in the sledging conditions, on both his last expeditions, was such a fortunate coincidence, and the mathematical chances of it occurring precisely where it did were so remote, that we must see if any other evidence can be found to support it.

The evidence of Nansen and Cagni is not as specific as we could wish, though it has its value. They were hundreds of miles distant from Peary's routes, but this is not necessarily of much importance. Cagni's turning-point was about the same distance from the Franz Josef Archipelago as Bartlett's last camp was from Grant Land; though, again, the archipelago does not affect the pack as Grant Land and Greenland affect it. The local conditions were by no means the same in the two districts. Still, Nansen and Cagni found the floes more level as they went farther north; but, beyond the level areas, they crossed plenty of rough ice, and this extended to the north of their turning-points.

The seasons vary considerably in the condition of the ice and the amount of open water at a given time. Nansen found the channels troublesome before the end of April 1895, in about latitude 85° N., as he journeyed south.[1] He had a beautiful summer. To the north of this latitude, Cagni, in 1900, crossed wide expanses of level ice on his way north. This level ice, on his return, came down to at least latitude 83° N., and the open water increased until he was fighting for life against the complete disintegration of the pack, as well as against a current that threatened to carry his party out to sea. Cagni met with a colder season than Nansen. The pack tends to break up everywhere and, apparently, in every year as summer advances.

Peary's information, as given on his last expedition, has been tabulated in Schedule No. 6.

He began to have trouble with open channels on his second day out from Cape Columbia, and they gave him no peace for eleven consecutive days, on six of which he was held up by his "Big Lead." Near the end of this period the channels had become mere cracks. After only one more march he had three or four more consecutive days on which the channels were troublesome. This brought him to about latitude 85° N., where he had four days of freedom from

[1] *Farthest North*, vol. ii, p. 151 and following pages.

SCHEDULE No. 6. SOME STATISTICS OF PEARY'S OCEANIC
JOURNEY IN 1909

		Percentage of Days.
Number of days from land to Pole	37	..
Number of days on which held up for whole day	10	27
Number of days on which held up for part of days	14	36
Number of days on which channels were crossed	over 17	over 46
Number of days on which troubled with channels	24	64
Number of channels crossed	over 25	..
Number of days on which pack was active	9	24
Number of days on which going was very rough	11	30
Number of days on which channels or rough going were experienced	35	94
Fine days	22	59
Days of cutting winds	6	16
Days of bad weather, apart from cutting winds	7	18
Days of blizzard	3	8
Days on which *minus* temperatures are recorded	26	70
Dull, misty, and cloudy days	4	10

open water. He then had one day's trouble, not very
serious, followed by three or four days on which he
met with no channels. By that time he had reached,
he said, his last bad patch, a little south of the 87th
parallel, which lasted for two or three days. From
there to what he claimed to be the polar area he said
he had no serious difficulty with open water. This is
not surprising, as he never had any difficulties after
the dismissal of his white companions. He crossed
four channels, according to his account, in three
consecutive days, as far north as between latitudes
87° 47′ N. and 89° N.; and his last channel was one
hundred yards wide, or about the width of the River
Severn at Worcester. Thus he was never free from this
trouble for very long, though he considered that he

had been "very fortunate with the leads." [1] He had trouble with them on two days out of every three on the outward journey. We have no reliable data for considering the return.

Here is one serious cause of delay that did not exist on the inland ice. Had Peary been thirty-nine instead of fifty-three years of age when he made his last attempt to reach the Pole, and if he had been accompanied by no more than two companions, as physically fit as Lee and Henson were in 1895, his speed for about 500 miles over the pack-ice must have been less than the 20·7 m.p.d. that he had done in Greenland. This follows from the time lost in crossing channels, and waiting for them to close or freeze over. Any party of six men will travel slower than a three-man unit, so that it is certain, from what we know already, that Peary's polar party of 1909, after leaving Bartlett, *could not have averaged as much as 20 m.p.d. for any considerable distance*. We have yet to consider, however, the pressure ridges and the drifting of the floes.

3. *Pressure Ridges and Peary's Speed.*—We have gathered a certain amount of information in earlier chapters as to the character of the pack, described by Peary on his journeys over it, prior to 1909. The slowness of his progress, of itself, is sufficient indication of the difficulties and delays that he met with. The speed of his last expedition, as far as Bartlett went, was the highest Peary had ever done, averaging nine minutes of latitude a day. We must examine the account of this part of the journey.

The diary of the sledging surface, given on the next page, shows concisely, though incompletely, the sledging conditions, without referring, for the most part, to open water, the particulars of which are given elsewhere. The ice, as far as the big channel, lived up to its reputation of being one of the roughest tracks, for

[1] *The North Pole*, p. 284.

SCHEDULE No. 7. DIARY OF SLEDGING SURFACES ON PEARY'S
LAST JOURNEY OVER THE PACK ICE

1909.	
Mar. 1	A " crazy zone " for several miles ; then very uneven ; sledges smashed.
2	" Much the same. . . . Rough and trying."
3	Crossed moving pressure.
4	" Not quite so rough."
5 6 7 8 9 10	At " Big Lead."
11	(No notes on the ice, which probably was fairly good.)
12	" An unbroken series of old floes."
13	" Going . . . fairly good. . . . For 5 miles we zigzagged through . . . very rough ice."
14	" Fairly good " over old floes.
15	Fairly good at first, then ice became active and broke up.
16	Channels shorten march.
17	" A broad zone of rough rubble ice " ; sledges damaged.
18	" At first . . . very rough ice, then . . . more level," but " decidedly rough."
19	" At first over heavy and much-raftered ice, then . . . more level," as before.
20	(No march.)
21	A sledge broken, so probably rough.
22	" At first tortuous " and extremely rough. " Then . . . large and level floes."
23	Trouble with open water.
24	" Heavy going. . . . Pressure ridges." A sledge damaged.
25	Good going.
26	Good going for $\frac{3}{4}$ of distance. Then " a rugged and trying surface . . . again deflected to W."
27	" Broken and raftered ice. . . . More rubble . . . a maze of small pieces. . . . Crazy road."
28	" Better going."
29	(Held up by open water.)
30	Crossed lake of young ice. Better surface.
31	" Fairly good."

(The record after this date is unreliable.)

its length, ever crossed by sledges. The next 2½ marches were over better surfaces. Then the party "zigzagged through a zone of very rough ice."[1] The next march was similar, until the ice became active again, and this caused a short journey on 16th March. The next march and a half were over very bad surfaces, followed by a half-march when they were better. On the 19th there was "heavy pressure to cross at first"; and when the surface became more level, Peary warns us that, when he says this, "the reader must understand that what is regarded as a level surface on the polar ice might be considered decidedly rough going anywhere else."[2]

No march seems to have been made by Peary on the 20th. The condition of the ice is not mentioned on the 21st, but as a sledge was broken, it was probably rather rough on that day. On 22nd March many deviations were necessary to elude heavy pressure, until a better surface was reached, later on the march. Open water was the trouble on the following day; and then, on the 24th, came "some pretty heavy going," with "heavy pressure ridges," enclosing more level floes. Nearly two marches were next made over better surfaces, but the latter part of the second march was very bad. They were "again deflected to the west some distance," and had "a rugged and trying surface to travel over."[3] "The first three-quarters" of this march of the 26th were remarkable: "The trail was fortunately in a straight line." This is the only occasion when "a straight line" is mentioned, showing how the trail usually twisted from side to side. The severe conditions of the evening before continued all next day, which "was by far the hardest for some days. At first there was a continuation of the broken and raftered ice, sharp and jagged, that at times seemed almost to cut through our sealskin kamiks and hareskin stockings, to pierce our feet. Then we struck heavy rubble ice

[1] *The North Pole*, p. 234.   [2] *Op. cit.*, p. 243.   [3] *Op. cit.*, p. 256.

covered with deep snow, through which we had literally to plough our way, lifting and steadying the sledges until our muscles ached." [1]

The camp at the end of this day was "in a maze of small pieces of very heavy old floes raftered in every direction"; and Bartlett's "men and dogs were tired out and temporarily discouraged by the heart-racking work of making a road." This was as far north as latitude 87° N. The surface here was so bad that Peary took 100 lbs. off "the loads of Bartlett's sledges," to help them in "pioneering in this rough going." [2] We must notice that twelve miles of this work exhausted even Bartlett's great strength.

The next day, 28th March, another twelve miles were covered in six hours over Bartlett's trail; and Peary wrote of this as being "a good rate," which it was. Active ice and open water then caused more than a day's delay. On the 30th, the lake of young ice, already mentioned, was crossed. The north wind was losing them "miles of distance" on the 31st, but this was more than compensated for, Peary said, by closing the channels. The twenty miles recorded on this day and on the 30th may have been done. As the remainder of the journey is so incredible we cannot examine it in detail.

From Cape Columbia to latitude 87° 47′ N., during thirty-one days, Peary had "good going" on no more than one whole day, 25th March. One day is not mentioned in Peary's record. On three days there are no remarks on the sledging surface, so probably they were neither very good nor very bad. On no other whole day, when untroubled by open water, was the surface better than "fairly good," and this was true only of two or three days. About three-quarters of one other day was described as "good." Only twenty-one marches were made during this period, and on two of these days we have no notes on the going. If, there-

[1] *Op. cit.*, p. 257. [2] *Op. cit.*, pp. 257–258.

fore, some allowance is made for parts of days when the surface was better, on about 90 *per cent.* of the marches the going was not good. The average speed alone tells the tale, for it was only, as we have seen, nine minutes of latitude a day.

We now know more precisely the character of the ice on Peary's last route, to within 133 minutes of the Pole. We cannot accept his account of what lay to the north of latitude 87° 47′ N., but we must notice his general statements that include the whole of his route to the Pole.

He wrote: "There is no land between Cape Columbia and the North Pole, and no smooth and very little level ice." [1] This does not imply any sudden change to the north of Bartlett's last camp. Nor does the fact that he could not use a sledgemeter for registering his distances, as he did "on the inland ice of Greenland. . . . This could not possibly be used on the ice of the polar sea, as it would be smashed to pieces in the rough going." [2] This evidence is further supported by his excellent photograph entitled "Typical view of the ice of the Arctic Ocean, north of Grant Land." [3] The proportion of level ice seen here, on the best line that could be taken across the pack, is not more than about 20 *to* 25 *per cent.*

The best evidence we have as to the character of the ice in the more immediate area of the Pole is that already given, of Commander Byrd and Captain Amundsen. The former described it as "slightly rougher than farther south," and the latter found the same condition at a similar distance from the Pole as Bartlett's last camp.

We can now form a somewhat more definite estimate of Peary's possible speed, after dismissing Bartlett. We have seen that his physical limit, at the age of thirty-nine and over a good sledging surface, was 20·7 m.p.d.; and that the delays caused by open

[1] *The North Pole*, p. 194.   [2] *Ibid.*, p. 211.   [3] Opposite p. 209.

water in the pack must have made 20 m.p.d. for several hundreds of miles, in 1909, impossible. This certainly would have been his limit had there been no pressure ridges and had the sledging surface been fixed. A further reduction must now be made for the roughness of the surface, and the estimate again shall be as conservative as possible. From one to two miles a day would be the least delay that would be caused by the inequalities of the ice. We shall be quite safe, therefore, in assuming that Peary could not average, for any great distance, more than 19 m.p.d.

A practical illustration of the difference between the sledging conditions on the inland ice of Greenland and over the Polar pack is seen in the very different type of sledge that Peary used for each. The sledges used on the ice-cap were very light, weighing 48 lb., with ski runners, and were most suitable for a smooth surface; while those used on the pack were extremely heavy, and built up of massive timbers, to withstand rough usage. The former do not appear to be described, as are the latter;[1] but the photographs of each speak for themselves.[2] No one could doubt that the sledging conditions on the inland ice were much better than on the pack.

4. *The Movement of the Ice prior to* 1909.—Our consideration of the ice conditions Peary found on his journey in 1902 left us in no doubt that "the activity of the pack was his greatest difficulty."[3] Cape Hecla and Point Moss are so near to Cape Columbia that there is no difference in the character of the ice to the north of these capes. Moreover, Peary crossed the meridian of Cape Columbia twice in 1906; his course then, as far north as beyond latitude 85° N., being approximately the same as in 1909. As the records of

[1] *Op. cit.,* p. 135.
[2] *Northward over the Great Ice,* vol. i, pp. 2, 15, 16, and *The North Pole,* p. 123.
[3] See p. 48.

the earlier journeys over the pack may be, to some extent, more reliable than the account of the last expedition, we must now follow Peary's references to the movement of the ice on his journey in 1906.

He left Point Moss on 6th March. A strong N.W. wind set the pack in motion on the 8th and 9th, and on the latter day Peary wrote: "The floes upon which my advanced loads were placed yesterday drifted a mile or more to the south-east, and the trail disrupted for a long distance." [1] We are told shortly after: "We were steadily drifting eastward." About five days are then eliminated from the record, and two more days are scarcely mentioned. No reference is made to the drifting of the pack until 22nd March, a fierce wind having arisen on the 21st and stirred up the ice. On the 23rd "the northern ice in every instance had shifted to the eastward." [2] The next two days have nothing to our purpose. The march of the 26th brought Peary to his big channel, which extended "east and west across our course. . . . The northern ice was slowly moving west." [3] He does not comment on this direction being the opposite of the previous movements, nor does he give the direction of the wind, but probably it was from the east. The drift of the northern ice to the west continued throughout the 27th and 28th.

The difference between absolute and relative motion of the sides of a channel is never mentioned, though it is obvious that both sides may be in motion. It is even possible that the apparent westerly movement of the northern ice was due to its drifting to the east more slowly than the southern side on which Peary stood. This may not have happened during the delay at the big channel, from 27th March to 2nd April 1906, because observations on the 28th showed "we were somewhat farther west than I had intended," though this was "owing to the constant tendency of

[1] *Nearest the Pole*, p. 106.   [2] *Ibid.*, p. 111.   [3] *Ibid.*, p. 115.

Henson and his party to turn to the left." [1] Nothing
is said about the possibility of the camp having drifted
west during the time, nearly two days, Peary had been
there.

His statements then are as follows: "An easterly
movement of the northern ice during the night" of
31st March to 1st April "had opened a place some
200 feet wide on the northern side of the lead which
effectually barred crossing. The set of the current
was still to the west." [2]

What are we to understand from these apparently
contradictory statements? The reversal in the direction of the drift of the northern ice is supported by
the fact that, on 31st March, the wind is said to have
been "S.S.W. true"; but it is difficult to understand
what is meant by the current being "still to the west."
Peary had a theory that this big channel was a tidal
crack, and there may be nothing to gain by attempting
to elucidate his meaning.

On 3rd April, the day after crossing the channel,
the wind came from the north, but backed into the
west and gradually worked up to a full gale, which held
the party up for six days, dying down in the S.W.
on the 12th. Peary expected that the pack "was
moving eastward as one mass," [3] and his observations
on the 12th showed that he had been driven from
about longitude 74° W. to about 62° W., or approximately seventy miles eastward, in less than a week.
This, if reliable, may be taken as the highest rate of
drift on record in the Arctic pack-ice, being $11\frac{1}{2}$ m.p.d.

The next mention of drifting is on 18th to 19th
April, when a number of "cracks and narrow leads"
were crossed; they were "uniformly at right angles to
our course, and the ice on the northern side was
moving more rapidly eastward than that on the
southern." [4] Peary naturally assumed that the whole

[1] *Nearest the Pole*, p. 117.   [2] *Ibid.*, p. 118.
[3] *Ibid.*, p. 127.   [4] *Ibid.*, p. 133.

pack was moving east, as no doubt it was then. The landward ice must always tend to retard the movement of the more southerly parts of the pack. The wind, from the 12th to the 21st, "had blown with greater or less force, but without interruption, from a little south of true west." [1]   We cannot be sure of his orientation.

Peary turned back on 21st April, and the next day the trail was faulted by lateral drift; but the igloos of Storm Camp were found in due course. This camp had drifted another seventy miles to the east, according to the chart, while Peary had been to the north of it, or from 13th April to about the end of the month. As no dates are given after the 21st we can only estimate, very approximately, the rate of this part of the drift. Nine days were taken on the northward trek from Storm Camp. As the outward trail was picked up, apparently, for a great part of the return, we may assume, perhaps, that this camp was reached again in about a week, or, to be definite, let us say on 28th April. This would indicate a drift of 4 m.p.d. from the 13th. We are on such uncertain ground here, however, that it will be safer to be satisfied with the qualitative fact that Storm Camp lay on Peary's route from his farthest north to Cape Neumeyer in Greenland.

The last reference to the movement of the pack on this journey is during the time when Peary was waiting to recross his big channel to the south. He then wrote: "Here we remained, drifting steadily eastward, watching the lead slowly widen, as it had done on the upward march." [2]   We have no proof that the ice was drifting eastward at that time, as there is no mention of longitude observations being taken. Peary assumed that the movement in this direction, which he had proved a few weeks earlier, still continued. This may, or may not, have been true. A northerly and southerly movement, however, was taking place, and this caused

[1] *Nearest the Pole*, p. 139.   [2] *Ibid.*, p. 144.

the opening and closing of channels that extended east and west.

In 1906, as in 1902, the movement of the pack was Peary's greatest difficulty. To such an extent was this true in 1906 that the existence of his party was seriously endangered by the amount of the drift from west to east. All Peary's experience, prior to 1909, showed that the ice to the north of Grant Land and Greenland was in constant, and often very rapid, motion. The direction and the rate of movement would vary from time to time; but it would be useless for anyone to affirm, after the foregoing evidence, that the ice between Cape Columbia and the North Geographic Pole would be found almost stationary.

5. *The Movement of the Pack in* 1909.—Had Peary said, in 1909, that his route from Cape Columbia to the Pole was motionless, he would have flatly contradicted all his previous evidence on the subject. He did not say this, but he insinuated it in two ways: by marking his route on his chart as a straight line from land to the Pole, and by travelling only, so it appears, the latitude distance.

Peary often contradicted himself; and he did so over particulars that were vital to his claim to have reached the Pole. We have seen how he stated, at one time, that he walked over 150 miles in two days, and at another time that his best day was 50 miles on one of those days. We now find that the distance he said he marched, to the Pole and back to Cape Columbia, was the distance that would have been made over an immovable surface; while he gives ample evidence that his sledging surface was seldom still! His distance, also, allowed nothing for deviations, from any cause.

We have considered this evidence from his earlier journeys; we now turn to that from his last journey, with the warning that, in 1909, we meet with conflicting statements, some of which must be untrue.

We are told, however, that between Cape Columbia
and the Pole the following winds blew:

On 7 (almost certainly on 8) days strong winds from
E. and N.E.

On 4 (probably on 6) days strong winds from N.

On 3 (probably on other) days strong winds from W.

On 2 (possibly on 7) days it was calm.

On 1 day, 5th April, the wind was south.

The journey is said to have taken thirty-seven days,
on more than fourteen of which the motive power was
at work that could not fail to have blown Peary off his
course, or backwards, not only, or so much, during his
marching hours, as all the time he was in camp.   Many
of these winds were strong, and would cause a drift of
more than 2 m.p.d.; but on this moderate estimate,
the ten days of easterly and westerly winds would
drive him twenty miles, altogether, off his course.   He
had no means of knowing this, as he took no observations for longitude.

Peary based his claim to have reached the Pole on
his ability to travel 413 geographical miles in the time
he stated; [1] he never spoke of any extra distance due to
the drifting of his sledging surface, nor did he acknowledge deviations of any kind.   Yet he wrote: "The ice
of the polar sea is not an immovable surface," and
spoke of "the constant movement of the ice during the
brief summer." [2]

Peary's whole theory of his return from the Pole
depends upon the pack having been almost rigid after
Bartlett's return.   Peary admits that the trail was
occasionally faulted; but when within sight of land he
wrote: "So far we had seemed to bear a charm which
protected us from all difficulties and dangers . . . at
no single lead had we been delayed more than a couple
of hours." [3]   This is the only example on record of
any traveller, including himself, possessing a mystic
"charm" potent enough to tame the polar pack.

[1] *The North Pole*, p. 193.   [2] *Ibid.*, p. 195.   [3] *Ibid.*, p. 312.

We must not forget, on the one hand, that the ice conditions vary considerably from one year to another; but neither is it possible to forget, on the other hand, that the most fundamental fact relative to the pack is its mobility.   While 1906 may have been a more windy season than 1909, we know that Peary experienced winds, some of them strong winds, during nearly half his outward journey in the latter year.   We must remember, also, that he undoubtedly told the truth in 1902, and as far as Storm Camp in 1906.

The fact, then, of the almost constant movement of the ice on Peary's route of 1909 is undoubted.   As to the *rate* of the drift, the evidence is that it is higher between Grant Land and the North Pole than in other parts of the Arctic Ocean.   Dr Nansen, our greatest authority on this subject, tells us that his movement in the *Fram* was usually at the rate of one or two miles a day; he became jubilant when a distance of thirteen minutes was covered in six days,[1] which extended to fifteen minutes in eight days.   Occasionally we find as much as 4 m.p.d. recorded,[2] and once "about five minutes a day."[3]

The maximum rate of drift on Peary's route of 1906 was over 10 m.p.d., or twice Nansen's maximum. The highest rate recorded by Peary in 1909 was twelve miles in two days.[4]   This was in a southerly direction and appears to have been only estimated; but, with the 10 m.p.d. of 1906, it is sufficient, if reliable, to show that the drift over Peary's portion of the pack was much more rapid than over Nansen's route in the *Fram*. This matter is further considered elsewhere.

As to the *direction* of the drift in 1909, we have a scientific report to enlighten us.   Appendix I of *The North Pole* was written by Mr R. A. Harris, of the Coast and Geodetic Survey, Washington.   In this we read that Peary "found an eastward drifting of the ice

[1] *Farthest North*, vol. ii, p. 53, footnote.
[2] *Ibid.*, vol. i, pp. 265, 393.   [3] *Ibid.*, vol. i, p. 268.   [4] See p. 113.

due to westerly or north-westerly winds. Moreover, along the line of separation between two icefields the northern field had a greater eastward motion than had the field to the south of the line." [1]

We must be content, at present, to note this assertion, as it will be necessary to devote future sections to Peary's return over his outward track (when the alleged eastward drift is of vital importance) and to the direction of the currents. The winds, in 1909, moved the ice in other directions, as well as eastward.

In saying, before he set out, "My course will be more west of north than before," etc., Peary showed that he expected to travel along the hypotenuse of a triangle, from Cape Columbia to the Pole, the base of which was the Columbia meridian. He would know, from this, that the extra distance he must travel, due to his sledging surface not being rigid, would depend upon the rate of the adverse drift. If a transverse drift of only two miles a day was assumed for one month, more than sixty miles, or approximately 15 per cent., would be added to the length of the journey.

We have seen that the drift was said to have been more frequently from west to east than in any other direction. Unless it was from south to north, which is never mentioned,[2] some distance must have been added each day, whatever its direction, to the length of the journey. We find, however, to our amazement, that Peary claimed to have reached the Pole by travelling only the latitude distance, or along the base, instead of the hypotenuse, of the triangle mentioned. In other words, his distance travelled assumed a rigid, instead of a drifting, surface.

The result would be the same if the pack drifted, as it did, to some extent, alternately east and west. We have then to imagine a series of small triangles,

[1] *The North Pole*, p. 337.
[2] A southerly wind is recorded on one day in 1909.

on each side of the Columbia meridian, and along the
hypotenuse of each Peary must have travelled, in order
to keep his course. Hence, from the drift alone,
Peary was short of the distance to the Pole by the
amount, unknown, that he was carried transversely
or backwards. He claimed to have reached the Pole
without travelling the distance to it.

6. *Concluding Remarks.*—Commander Green gives
corroborative evidence as to the rough and difficult
nature of the polar pack on Peary's route.[1] He writes:
"The great northern pack is in a constant state of
motion. Sledges on it out of sight of land can never
be quite sure which way they are drifting" without
astronomical observations.[2] He gives the distance
from Cape Hecla to the Pole as 490 miles, and then
proceeds: "But this 490 miles is over the most frightful
going that it is possible to imagine. Pressures of wind
and tide are continually driving the main 40-foot-thick
pack against the land and shoals that surround the sea.
In this way mountainous ice-ridges are formed. . . .
The surface of the sea ice is a vast, tumbled plain of ice
fragments, some of which are the size of a small house."[3]
Peary's biographer repeats his hero's refrain that the
going improved at a considerable distance from land;[4]
but he, in common with the rest of the world, has only
Peary's word for this, and we have seen that, unfortunately, Peary's word is unreliable. The evidence
is that, even if there is some truth in this, the sledging
conditions are no better between latitudes 87° and
90° N. on Peary's route than Cagni and Nansen found
them at somewhat lower latitudes, on their routes.
As large land-masses have the greatest effect in disturbing the pack, the best conditions on Peary's route
probably are worse than the average on the other two
routes. The ice is more disturbed, for many miles to

[1] See *Peary the Man*, p. 231.   [2] *Ibid.*, p. 8.
[3] *Ibid.*, pp. 251–252.
[4] *Ibid.*, pp. 255, 300, 301, 302.

the north of Grant Land and Greenland, than anywhere else at an equal distance from the Pole. It may
well improve farther from land, and yet be a very bad,
indeed the worst, sledging surface.

Peary's routes lay across the most congested part
of the pack that lies round the Pole. This follows
from the fact that he set out from the greatest land-
masses. The northern coasts of Grant Land and
Greenland inexorably prevent the ice from spreading
southward. The North-east Passage has been made,
and vessels annually coast the Arctic shore of Alaska,
but it is inconceivable that any ship could be navigated
along the north coasts of Grant Land and Greenland.
The ice here is so tightly packed that the highest
pressure ridges ever recorded attest the conflict
between rock and pack.

If we may assume, tentatively, that the *prevailing*
drift of the ice in this locality is from west to east,[1]
we shall see that the southern portion of the pack will
impinge against the coastal ice. This trends north-
east and narrows the space through which the pack
must pass. Northward lies the mighty mass of a
thousand miles of sea ice, while southward lies the
land. Thus a species of funnel is formed, that becomes
narrower towards the east, until it opens again beyond
Cape Morris Jesup. The pack, forced into this funnel
by the prevailing winds, is crushed up. In order to
accommodate itself to less horizontal space it is
necessarily pressed up vertically into the highest
ridges known.

This theory would also account for the exceptional
rate of drift recorded by Peary. When a fluid passes
through a smaller channel, its velocity increases.
Hence the 11 m.p.d. reported in 1906. All Peary's
attempts to reach the Pole were made across this
"funnel," where the worst sledging conditions round
the Pole are found.

[1] But see Chapter XIII, Sec. 2.

There is not a scrap of evidence to support Peary's
assertions that the surface of the pack, north of
latitude 87° 47′ N., suddenly and permanently improved all the rest of the way to the Pole. On no
other journey over the pack has its most northerly
section been of such a completely different character
from that in lower latitudes. It is very remarkable, not
to say suspicious, that this improvement should occur
precisely when and where it was wanted. We may
be quite sure that, nowhere on the Arctic Ocean, has
there ever been such a progressive improvement in the
going, extending for over 150 miles.

The character of the pack-ice is now known well
enough to be confident that it is universally hetero-
geneous. Wherever an explorer proceeded alone, and
turned back, pressure ridges would be found, and as
summer advanced, open water would increase. Pressure
is seen, indeed, in the photographs Peary professed to
have taken at the Pole; and the evidence of Commander
Byrd is conclusive that the pressure at the Pole may
be worse than farther south. Yet when Peary left
Bartlett he never referred to the labour of breaking
his own trail, though he had to do his own pioneering.

From Cape Columbia to Bartlett's last camp
channels were crossed on two days out of every three,
and freedom from trouble by pressure ridges appears
on only three or four days out of thirty-one. In 1902
and 1906 the movement of the ice caused the greatest
difficulties. It would have been remarkable if the
character of the pack had radically altered in 1909. It
is characteristic of Peary, however, that his data shows
the ice to have been much the same as before, while all
his unwitnessed performances intimate and demand
conditions almost entirely different.

The Pole was reached, on paper, by psychological
suggestion. Certain conceptions were injected into
the public mind. Peary's biographer treads the same
roseate path. He shows how all credible witnesses

were sent well away. Then, how an atmosphere of exhilaration is created around the hero and his gallant party. Next, all difficulties vanish like smoke; and at least twenty years, when Bartlett's back is turned, drop from Peary's age. "Pressure ridges continued to dwindle. A sledge broke but was quickly repaired. Both dogs and men were sensing victory now. Marches lengthened out to 25 and 30 miles a day. . . . The going still improved. . . ." [1]

All this is false glamour. Had we been told that "the marches lengthened out" to 37 and 45 miles a day, the effect would have been spoiled; but they did, in statute miles of distance travelled, if Peary's figures were correct. So the minutes of latitude are rigidly adhered to. Thirty geographical miles of latitude could not be done by walking less than about 45 statute miles. Why were all deviations and drift omitted? There is not one mile added for either of them, from Cape Columbia to the Pole. Peary could not have reached the Pole by doing only the distance he gives; he would have been over a hundred miles short of it. But his claim would not have been credited for one moment had his actual distance travelled, over this moving surface, been admitted.

Unbounded confidence, even when almost devoid of other qualities, too often wins its way in this world. Yet the red line of Peary's route, dead straight across the drifting pack, should have made people take notice. Peary had condescended to assimilate his previous narratives, for the most part, to the laws of nature, by marking his routes with wavy lines that allowed, also, for a drift from west to east. His final line is a pontifical pronouncement that the polar pack, during his final journey, was nearly as solid as rock.

As this conclusion is in almost direct opposition to the fundamental fact of the pack's continual movement, we need have no hesitation in concluding our

[1] *Peary the Man*, p. 302.

previous estimates of Peary's highest possible speed.
We found that, had the ice been fixed, this could not
have exceeded 19 m.p.d. for his unwitnessed distance.
In order to be as moderate as, if not more moderate
than, circumstances would permit, only one mile a
day will be deducted for the drifting of the ice. Peary
would gain much by returning over his outward trail,
a particular that will be developed in the next chapter.
Let us assume, therefore, that it was possible for him
to have averaged 18 m.p.d. for the 600 miles from
latitude 87° 47′ N. to the Pole and back to land. This
would have been a splendid performance for any man
of fifty-three years of age, and is only 2·7 m.p.d. less
than he averaged for 500 miles in Greenland at the age
of thirty-nine. *His claim to have reached the Pole
depends upon nearly double this speed having been
maintained.*

CHAPTER IX

FURTHER CONSIDERATION OF THE LAST POLAR JOURNEY

" O grant me such a mighty fish,
I pray, that even I,
In telling of it afterwards,
Shall have no need to lie."

The Fisherman's Prayer.

1. The Unwitnessed Distances. 2. Comparison with Amundsen. 3. The Retracing of the Outward Trail. 4. Barlett's Certificate of Latitude 87° 47′ N.

1. THE claim to have reached the North Pole was presented to the world in such a manner that the truth was not immediately apparent. By a kind of trick, the minutes of latitude were used alone and without exception; no reference was made to the distance actually travelled; and there was a tacit assumption that the pack-ice was motionless, and that pressure ridges and channels never caused any deviation from the meridian of Cape Columbia.

Peary was sharp enough to see that he would not be believed if he claimed to have walked more than about 25 m.p.d., and he found it necessary to produce elaborate explanations of how he could do this "extraordinary speed," as he frankly admitted it to be, over that surface. What he did not see, unless he was prepared to risk the exposure, was that the truth must be found out sooner or later; that he could not have reached the Pole from Bartlett's last camp and have returned to land in the time he stated, unless he had averaged much more than 25 m.p.d., which represented only his latitude distance; and that the speed he

TYPES OF PACK ICE : III.

facing p. 144

acknowledged, and which he admitted was "extra-ordinary," must have left him over a hundred miles short of the Pole.

Avoiding the use of the statute mile was part of the stratagem. Everyone knows, with some accuracy, how many statute miles can be walked in an hour, in a day, and perhaps in a week or longer, but the geographical mile, or minute of latitude, is not well known. Hence, in order to judge Peary's claim, these minutes must be reduced to statute miles.

In spite of the fact that no one could walk to the Pole without greatly exceeding, in miles of travel, the latitude distance, we could almost be content to let Peary's own figures speak for themselves, merely by putting them into our accustomed English miles, and computing his average speeds therefrom, thus:

The latitude distance from Pole to
    land as given by Peary . . 413 minutes,
becomes .   .   .   .   . 475 stat. miles.

As this was done in sixteen days, the average speed was not 25 but over 29½ (and nearly 30) m.p.d. *of latitude*. This is not, let us repeat, the distance travelled, as there are no allowances for deviations from the course. These, naturally, are often mentioned and are implied, when there was pressure to cross, a channel to cause a detour, or lateral drift, when not actually referred to. The following are a few references to them:

Page 223.   Bartlett's trail was a mile and a half to
             the west.
 ,, 234.   "Zigzagging" mentioned.
 ,, 238.   A deviation to the west.
 ,, 247.   "The going was tortuous."
 ,, 250.   "Obliged to climb over heavy pressure
             ridges."
 ,, 256.   "Again deflected to the west."

Henson wrote: "The course from the land to the Pole was not direct and due north, for we followed the

10

lines of least resistance, and frequently found ourselves going due east or west, in order to detour around pressure ridges, floe bergs, and leads." [1]

George Borup amply confirms this, as far as he went (latitude 85° 23′ N.). He gives a photograph of a rough and sinuous trail, labelled: "Rough going. We guessed and groped, north, ever north, with many a twist and turn." [2]

Adding 25 per cent. for these deviations, we find *it was about* 590 *statute miles and not* 413 *geographical miles* from Cape Columbia to the Pole, and *Peary must have averaged over* 37 *m.p.d.* for the whole of his return.

We need not concern ourselves greatly with the outward journey, south of latitude 87° 47′ N., where the last competent witness was dismissed, because everything up to that point may have been intended to bear the responsibility of Peary's unwitnessed claims. It cannot possibly do so; the change is far too sudden and complete. Peary's unwitnessed speed is said, at first, to have been double the previous rate of progress (it was more); and later, as we have seen, it rose to five and six times that speed. We have not yet, however, given our undivided attention to his total unwitnessed distances.

The distance Peary gives from Cape Columbia to the Pole, as we have noticed, is 413 minutes. This appears to make the latitude of the cape 83° 7′ N., which is General Greely's figure,[3] and that of the Admiralty chart. There is always uncertainty about Peary's facts and figures, and hours may be spent in attempting to arrive at any satisfactory conclusion with regard to them. His daily marches, which are only given in minutes of latitude, appear to total 419 geographical miles, though any student may make a different sum. The polar camp was said to have

---

[1] *A Negro Explorer at the North Pole*, p. 111.
[2] *A Tenderfoot with Peary*, opposite p. 141.
[3] *Three Years of Arctic Service*, vol. i, p. 331.

been in 89° 57′ N. latitude, and the only latitude of Cape Columbia that Peary gives is "about latitude 83°." [1] Instead of one plain statement, therefore, we have to do the best we can with the following:

Minutes.[2]

1. The correct latitude distance, 83° 7′ to 89° 57′ N.   410
2. The correct latitude of Cape Columbia, 83° 7′ to 90° N.   413
3. Peary's latitude of Cape Columbia, 83° to Cape Jesup, 89° 57′ N.   .   .   417
4. Peary's latitude of Cape Columbia, 83°, to 90° N.   420

Nine miles may have been lost by southerly drift. The Canadian Government maps show Cape Columbia at about latitude 83° 2′ N.

Peary's biographer gives the distance from Cape Hecla to the Pole at 490 miles. These miles were evidently statute, as the exact distance is 494½ miles; the latitude of this cape being 82° 50′ N., or 17 minutes farther from the Pole than Cape Columbia. Taking this distance, which is 19½ statute miles, from Commander Green's 490 miles, leaves 470½ miles, which is a good check on the 475 miles that is the equivalent of 413 minutes of latitude.

In writing of his return at 25 minutes (nearly 30 statute miles) of latitude a day, Peary draws a veil over his previous statements, that he had walked at least 41 miles about the Pole on the day before he left it, and that he had averaged from 30 to 37 m.p.d. for the five previous days. His total unwitnessed latitude distance (including his polar peregrinations), strangely enough, amounts to precisely "the number of the beast," or six hundred, three score, and six

---

[1] *The North Pole*, p. 216.

[2] It will be convenient to use the term " minutes " for all geographical miles, and reserve the term " miles " for statute miles.

statute miles. As he says he walked this distance in
twenty-two days, his average is more than 30 m.p.d.;
but this 666 miles is much less than anyone would have
to walk if they visited Peary's latitudes, and if the pack
had been stationary. Latitude distance is a theoretical
measurement necessarily exceeded in practice. A well-
known example will make this clear.

Captain Scott's course, from his Corner Camp on
the Ross Barrier to the South Pole, deviated from a
straight line considerably less than any course over the
polar pack must do, between Grant Land and the
North Pole. As Corner Camp lay in latitude 78° 3' S.,
Scott's latitude distance from here to the Pole was
717 minutes. His actual mileage, as registered by his
sledgemeters, was 854 minutes between these points.
His route-miles, therefore, exceeded his latitude distance by 137 minutes, or over 16 per cent. Peary's
allowance, prior to 1909, was approximately 25 per
cent., but as he evidently found this insufficient,
Borup informs us that, in 1909, it was 30 per cent.

Attention must be drawn to this, because it is a
vital point in the judgment of Peary's claim. When
he presented it to the world, *he eliminated the whole
30 per cent. of miles actually travelled, in order to make
it acceptable.* This allowance was not excessive for the
polar pack. Scott's journey was made over fixed
surfaces; but let us suppose, so as to give Peary
every possible advantage, that his unwitnessed route-
miles were only 20 per cent. more than his latitudes.
Table No. 2 (next page) is the result.

Does this make Peary's claim to have reached the
Pole any more credible? Why did he try to hide his
actual mileage, and make the impossible claim of having
travelled only the theoretical distance? Why, also,
was he so restless about even this? He returned to it,
time after time, like an escaped criminal haunting the
scene of his crime.[1]

[1] See pp. 7, 303–306, 316 of *The North Pole.*

TABLE No. 2. PEARY'S UNWITNESSED DISTANCES

	St. Miles.	Days.	Av. m.p.d.
Lat. 87° 47' to lat. 89° 57' N. .	180	5	36
At the Pole	41	1	41
Lat. 89° 57' to lat. 87° 47' N. .	180	2	90
Total of above . . .	401	8	50
From the Pole to Cape Columbia	529	16	33
Total unwitnessed distance .	799	23 marches	34 m.p. mar.

A quotation from Peary's letter to the Secretary of
the United States Navy has been given, in which, before
1906, he expected to reach the Pole from land and
return "in about 100 days or a little more, an average
travel of about 10 m.p.d." In other words, he expected to travel 1000 miles, "or a little more," to
compass the latitude distance of twice 400 miles, or a
little more. This was quite reasonable and correct.
He knew that his route-miles would exceed the latitude
distance by approximately 25 per cent. In order
to make himself world famous, the miles actually
travelled had to be reduced by this amount; and the
world acclaimed him the "Conqueror of the Pole"
when, from his own account, he was over 100 miles
short of it.

He was very careful how he mentioned his total
distance, and he appeared to do so only twice.[1] On the
first occasion he wrote of travelling "nearly a thousand
miles with dog sledges over the ice of the polar pack";
but it is by no means certain, as usual with Peary, that
he meant what he said, for he proceeded to add that
the distance from the ship to Cape Columbia was
"ninety miles in a north-westerly direction," and in
the next paragraph he wrote: "From Cape Columbia

[1] See *The North Pole*, p. 193.

we were to go straight north over the ice of the Polar Sea—four hundred and thirteen geographical miles." These distances total 1006 miles from the *Roosevelt* to the Pole and back again; and this probably was the "thousand miles" we have just seen that he referred to.

What else could it be? As the latitude distance from Cape Columbia to the Pole was 413 miles, this double journey would be only 826 miles "over the ice of the polar pack." Did he intend this to be "nearly a thousand miles"? He could not have referred to route-miles, for these amounted to at least 570 miles each way over the pack, and the double journey would be *much more than*, instead of "nearly," a thousand miles.

The second reference to the distance is merely parenthetical: ". . . all the way to the Pole and back (some nine hundred odd miles)."[1] No doubt he was thinking of the approximate length of the double journey.

We must leave this with the remark that, in order to be perfectly fair to Peary, we must not expect him to be precise in the use of language. He was not that type of man. As we must find out the truth, however, at least in its broad outlines, it is necessary to inquire, very often, what exactly he intended to convey.

The authenticated, or witnessed, speed to Bartlett's turning-point stands out in vivid contrast to Peary's unwitnessed speeds. The 285 minutes occupied 31 days of about 9 m.p.d. The whole outward journey to the Pole works out at an average of 11½ m.p.d., while Captain Scott averaged 10 m.p.d., without dogs, for his 717 minutes from Corner Camp to the South Pole. It is interesting to note that the speed of Peary's last expedition, until the dismissal of Bartlett, was not very much more than that of 1906.

2. *Comparison with Amundsen.*—When the truth of the last section is seen, there seems little need for

1 *The North Pole*, p. 206.

further treatment of this branch of the subject; but there are two reasons for still pursuing it. The first reason is that Peary's claim to have reached the North Pole stands or falls by his sledging alone; and, secondly, the world as a whole yet believes that he attained the Pole. He was a great, a lifelong, sledge traveller. Because of this, his claim was accepted entirely without question. Only a few geographical students have discovered the miraculous speeds and distances that the claim to the Pole involved.

Sledging speed depends mainly upon two prime factors: the efficiency of the transport system, and the quality of the surface over which the journey is made. Captain Amundsen is acknowledged by the leading polar authorities to have been the most efficient sledge traveller of modern times. His transport system, as used in Antarctica, was greatly superior to Peary's transport, as we shall see more fully in another chapter. Dr H. R. Mill wrote, with his usual discrimination, that Amundsen's raid on the South Pole "was the finest polar journey in history." [1]

This raid was made over three kinds of surface, of which only two, the Ross Barrier and the Plateau, will concern us. The latter is similar to the inland ice of Greenland. The surface of the Ross Barrier is almost ideal for dog-sledging, while no delusions are possible as to the very different character of the Arctic pack, especially on Peary's route to the North Pole. The pack, on that route, is about as bad, as the Barrier is good, for sledging. Yet note the following comparison.

It happened that both Amundsen and Peary recorded two exceptional and consecutive days' sledging. The former explorer, on the excellent Barrier surface, and with very light loads, on letting his dogs show what they could do when they really tried, accomplished 122 miles in the two days. This may be accepted as perfectly true. It was distance actually travelled.

[1] *Nature*, 6th October 1928, p. 516.

Peary claims to have done 150 miles of latitude, probably 180 statute miles of travel, with heavy loads, in about the same time, on 7th to 9th April 1909. Should he require the benefit of the extra six hours (for his time may have been 2¼ days), his distance was yet 160 miles in the forty-eight hours. He said his surface here was good for the polar pack, but it was worse than the Barrier. Amundsen's best single day was one of the days just mentioned, 15th February 1911, on which 71 statute miles were covered. Peary's best day appears to have been 7th to 8th April 1909, with 97 statute miles! This comparison may well be carried a little further.

Peary says he had eight consecutive days on which his average was much higher, for the same period, than on any other part of his journey. This period included his absence from Bartlett's last camp. Amundsen's eight consecutive best days' travel can be taken from an unbroken series of twenty days, when he returned across the Barrier at the rate of thirty-four minutes on one day and seventeen on the next, with the regularity of clockwork. This averages 29 statute miles a day. Amundsen previously had eight consecutive days, during his outward crossing of the Barrier, on which he drove at 26½ m.p.d.

We have seen that Peary's average for the eight days, 2nd to 9th April, was 43 m.p.d. of latitude, or 53 statute m.p.d. of travel. Thus his claim to the Pole involved more than a week's sledging, over a very bad surface, at nearly double the speed of Amundsen's best week over an excellent surface.

Peary's total unwitnessed distance, of about 800 statute miles, was supposed to have been done in twenty-three marches, of twenty-one consecutive days, at nearly 34 statute m.p.d., and then two days' rest before averaging 45 m.p.d. for the last two days. The whole averaged 34 statute m.p.m. Amundsen's highest rate for a similar period was his return across the Barrier, already mentioned, with the last three days on the glacier. This averaged 27½ m.p.d. The above will be seen more clearly as follows:—

TABLE No. 3.   PEARY'S AND AMUNDSEN'S SPEEDS COMPARED
(Statute miles)

	1 *day.*	2 *days.*	8 *days.*	21 *days.*
			m.p.d.	*m.p.d.*
Peary, bad surface, inferior equipment . . .	{ 97 loaded	160 loaded	53	34
Amundsen, good surface, superior equipment . .	{ 71 light	122 light	29	27½
Peary's excess over Amundsen	26	58	24	6½

3. *The Retracing of the Outward Trail.*—Peary attributed the high speed of his return journey to the retracing of the main outward track of the expedition for seven-eighths of the distance from the Pole to land. The distance retraced was 370 minutes, or 425 statute miles of latitude, and it requires our serious consideration.

We have seen that the ice on his route appears to have been rougher and more active than that on Nansen's and Cagni's outward journeys; and that the drift of the pack, between Cape Columbia and the Pole, was found by Peary, prior to 1909, to be mainly at right angles to his course. We have now to notice how he deals with this.

He wrote: "In view of the striking manner in which the final event bore out the prophecies I had made, it may be of interest to compare in some detail the plan. . . ." [1] About three pages of this are given, of which we are concerned now only with the following: "Leaving the land, my course will be more west of north than before, in order to counteract or allow for

[1] *The North Pole*, p. 3.

the easterly set of the ice between the north coast of Grant Land and the Pole, discovered on my last expedition." [1] He expected to "do voluntarily what I did involuntarily last time; that is, retreat upon the north coast of Greenland (a course diagonally *with* the set of the ice) instead of attempting to come back to the north coast of Grant Land diagonally *against* the set of the ice." [2]

Peary was quite certain that there was a west to east current across his route; so that a traveller setting out from the North Pole along the meridian of Cape Columbia, if he walked in a straight line, would step ashore somewhere on the coast of Greenland. This would mean a lateral drift of about 150–200 miles.

To provide for this drift, depots were laid on the Greenland coast; and in the event of any reversal in the direction of the drift, they were laid also on the coast of Grant Land, to the west of Cape Columbia. This procedure, on the evidence of lateral drift that Peary believed he had, was strictly correct. The polar party might well be in dire need of supplies on its return to land. We have now to notice the sequel.

We read: "It will be noted in this comparison" of his prophecy with its fulfilment, "that practically the only feature of the plan from which essential deviation was made was in returning to Cape Columbia on the coast of Grant Land instead of farther eastward to the northern coast of Greenland as I had done in 1906. This change was made for excellent reasons, which will be made clear in their proper place." [3]

The only place where this promise appears to be fulfilled, and it is nowhere "made clear," is on p. 304, where we are reminded that, in 1906, "strong winds carried the ice upon which we travelled far to the eastward of our upward course," and then these words

[1] *The North Pole*, p. 4.   [2] *Ibid.*, pp. 4–5.
[3] *Ibid.*, pp. 7–8.

are added: "This time, however, we met with no such misfortune. For the most part we found the trail renewed by our supporting parties easily recognisable, and in most cases in good condition."

This seems too good to be true, and is not a convincing manner of showing that all his previous experience of the ice-drift was falsified in 1909. No one could question the truthfulness of Peary's 1902 record. He then said that he hurried his departure from his northernmost point, in latitude 84° 17′ N., "in order to utilise as much of our tracks as possible before they were obliterated."[1] The last of the four conclusions that we drew from his attempt of this year[2] was the great difficulty he experienced, on his return, through the faulting of his outward trail.

That 1902 was not an exceptional season was seen in 1906, with its transverse drift of 11 m.p.d. The latter year may have been exceptional, and 1909 *may* have been exceptionally calm, but the facts do not seem to support this theory. We are faced, in the account of the last expedition, with the factor, a most important one, of Peary's unreliability; and we must proceed with due caution in any attempt to find out the truth. Let us begin by quoting an important passage on the subject.

"Although the 'Big Lead' was frozen over, we found that Bartlett on his return had lost the main trail here and did not find it again. For the rest of the ice journey, therefore, we were compelled to follow the single trail made by Bartlett instead of our well-beaten outward trail. I could not complain. We had kept the beaten road back to within some fifty miles of the land."[3]

We must make sure that we do not misunderstand this passage, for it deals with a matter of no little

[1] *Nearest the Pole*, pp. 344–345.
[2] At the end of Chapter III ; see p. 49.
[3] *The North Pole*, p. 314.

moment. Peary's statement is that he returned from
the Pole over the main "outward trail" of the expedition for about 425 miles of latitude, or over 500 route-
miles. This brought him to his big channel, which
he says was then "some fifty miles" from land. (On
the outward journey this channel was forty-five miles
from Cape Columbia.) From here to the land, on
his return, he found only Bartlett's trail.

A glance at Schedule No. 5 will show that, on the
outward journey, the ice was in rapid motion to the
north of the "Big Lead" on 11th March. Peary is
quite clear about this in his book.[1] He is equally clear
that the ice was active on the 15th, when "the wind
had shifted again to the east and was very penetrating."[2]
This would tend to drive the ice to the west, a movement of the pack which appears to have continued for
five days and nights, the ice grinding and rumbling
while in camp. Even after the 19th there was much
motion in the ice, especially on the 28th and 30th
March.

Peary admitted that the northerly winds of the
30th and 31st March drove him about twelve miles
to the south.[3] Hence the easterly and westerly winds
could not fail to move the pack at right angles to his
course, especially as no land existed in these directions,
as it did to the south, to arrest the drift.

Lateral motion of the ice is virtually proved by the
fact that only one depot was left on the outward
journey to be picked up on the return. This was on
24th March, for Marvin to pick up two days later,
which he did. Had Peary thought there would be no
transverse drift, all the stores would not have been,
as alleged, carried all the way to the Pole and back
again. Commander Green writes of this as follows:
"Food could not be left behind on the ice because of
the continual movement."[4] This could only be east

[1] *The North Pole*, pp. 232–233.   [2] *Ibid.*, p. 237.
[3] *Ibid.*, p. 265.   [4] *Peary the Man*, p. 302.

and west movement, as a north or south drift would
not prevent depots being left; but east and west
movement *must* fault the trail.

In spite of all this evidence, Peary only once admits
lateral movement of the pack. This was on the night
of 28th March, when the ice cracked right through the
camp, and we read: "Bartlett's igloo was moving
east." [1] This alone would be sufficient to fault the
trail for a returning party, though Bartlett, on his
return, might be able to knit the main trail together
again. [2]

Peary twice mentions that there was "no lateral
movement" of the sides of the big channel on the
outward journey; though this is not of much consequence in relation to the difficulty we are at present
trying to solve. What is of consequence is Borup's
evidence, which, as we saw in Chapter VI, is positive
as to lateral drift. He says that when poor Marvin
turned back from latitude 86° 38′ N. he found that
"the trail was badly faulted." [3] Borup himself, who
returned from latitude 85° 23′ N., refers to the faulting
of the trail several times, and writes of his return:
"We were extremely anxious to get to land, to hold
the trail before a wind wrecked it beyond repair.
Besides a prolonged gale might have blown us over to
the Greenland coast." [4]

Borup followed the outward trail on the return
from his first trip north, he said, "to where the young
ice had been on the outward trip. The place was
unrecognisable, being a tangle of pressure ridges mixed
up with a small remnant of young ice. . . . We beat
it for dear life, and on reaching *terra firma*, in the shape
of old ice, we found the trail gone—no signs of it
anywhere. Now the question was, had the wind blown
the ice on the northern side of the lead to the westward farther than that on the landward side, or *vice*

---

[1] *The North Pole*, p. 260.   [2] See Chapter XI, Sec. 5.
[3] *A Tenderfoot with Peary*, p. 202.   [4] *Ibid.*, p. 182.

versa? In a hurried consultation the huskies decided the trail was east of us, so we set out in that direction. After going for a couple of hours we hit our old trail, and saw at once that the main party had passed the day before." [1]

Peary's plan for his return was to do two of the outward marches every day. This was based on the grand assumption that the trail had not been faulted; and an unbroken trail depended upon hundreds of miles of pack-ice either remaining at rest or moving *en masse* for several weeks.

The great difficulty about Peary's account is that he distinctly says he followed the "well-beaten *outward* trail" from the Pole to the "Big Lead" on his return, and that this seems impossible.

Ample evidence could be brought to show that the pack between the big channel and the land had considerable lateral movement while Peary was north of it. Thus Borup, on returning from his first trip north, says: "We saw that, instead of being opposite Columbia, the trail had been blown away to the westward, and that we'd hit the coastline near the middle of Markham Bay," [2] twenty miles to the west. There would be no difference, in all probability, between the movement of ice north and south of the big channel. No offshore current has been proved to exist; but, on the other hand, the land-adhering ice would tend to retard any drift, lateral to Peary's course, and this retardation would diminish with increased distance from land.

Here, then, is another dilemma, unless we feel justified in refusing to accept one of Peary's contradictory assertions. Will any glaciologist of repute believe that *the ice immediately to the north of the "Big Lead" remained perfectly stationary from* 11th *March to* 20th *April, or for a period of forty days?*

In spite of this, there seems no doubt that Peary

[1] *A Tenderfoot with Peary*, p. 153.   [2] *Ibid.*, p. 155.

did return over a great deal of the outward trail. He wrote on 11th April, when in about latitude 87° N.: "So far there had been no lateral east-and-west movement of the ice. This was the great, fortunate, natural feature of the home trip, and the principal reason why we had so little trouble." [1] It is sufficiently obvious that, had the trail been faulted to the north of Bartlett's last camp, 180 miles could not have been done in 2¼ days; but it appears to have been true that there was little lateral movement, from wherever Peary turned back, to his big channel.

His account of the return from latitude 87° 47′ N. bears all the semblance of reality. However remarkable this may be, it would seem that we ought to accept it. The old igloos and camp-sites are re-passed; a piece of broken sledge is seen; and his Eskimos recognise the igloos by their workmanship. We are told that the secret of this was the prevalence of northerly winds and calms. Above all, we have the early date at which Peary returned to Cape Columbia.

Not that the record of the return, even south of latitude 87° 47′ N., is free from mistakes, for Peary says that he was "very near the 87th parallel," [2] i.e. he was approaching it from the north, when actually he had passed it, and was five miles to the south of it. Again, the return does not agree with the outward journey, as seen in the remark that "we had covered Henson's three pioneer marches in 15½ hours of travel." [3] These marches were those of 15th to 17th March and totalled only twenty-two miles. He would not have given us his speed had he realised that it would work out at no more than 1½ m.p.h., for he must have averaged double this rate to have returned to Cape Columbia when he did.

We must repudiate all responsibility for trying to make the return agree with the outward journey, or any one part of Peary's book coincide with other parts—

[1] *The North Pole*, p. 307.   [2] *Ibid.*, p. 307.   [3] *Ibid.*, p. 312.

e.g. Marvin and Bartlett's trail was followed for about a day. "It was not until eleven that night (15th to 16th April) when we again picked up the main trail." [1] From this we learn that, while Peary had a "beaten road" to follow, he made a mistake in saying it was "our well-beaten *outward* trail." He also admitted one other breakage of the trail, on the 15th to 16th April, writing: "We found the trail badly faulted." [2] This was about half-way back, and was due to the only active ice mentioned during the return; but the old trail appears to have been soon found.

In this somewhat complicated problem that Peary has set for students to solve, we know:

(1) That he returned to Cape Columbia. We may accept his word for this;

(2) That he appears to have returned over the greater part of his outward trail;

(3) That he could not have reached the Pole.

We are forced, therefore, to the conclusion that he took care not to lose Bartlett's returning trail; though how far he went to the north of latitude 87° 47′ N. is more uncertain.

Commander Cagni tried to return to Cape Fligeley in his outward tracks. His party "travelled from 28 to 29 miles" on the first day homewards, which tired the party very much; [3] and "a degree towards the south in four days." [4] Cagni wrote, on the fourth day: "We definitely lost our former track." [5] The movement of the pack prevented him from retracing his steps more than sixty miles. The exact distance appears to have been less than this. The drift of the ice, which became so serious farther south, must have been very little during those four days, or else extensive areas were moving intact. Some evidence has been given to show that the movement of the pack on

---

[1] *The North Pole*, pp. 301–311.   [2] *Ibid.*, p. 319.
[3] *On the " Polar Star " in the Arctic Sea*, vol. ii, p. 496.
[4] *Ibid.*, p. 500.   [5] *Ibid.*, p. 499.

Peary's route was considerably greater than on the drift of the *Fram*. The maximum rate reported by Peary was double that recorded by Nansen. The *Fram* passed right across the line of Cagni's subsequent route. Had the ice conditions on Peary's and Cagni's routes been identical, Peary could not, one would suppose, have retraced his outward tracks for more than about sixty miles, and the Pole was nearly three times this distance beyond the north end of Bartlett's trail.

To write a fairy tale is easier than to travel at 30 m.p.d. for several weeks over the polar pack. No authentic record exists of any traveller "merely" having to retrace an outward track for 500 miles across the drifting ice floes, and all who understand the pack will deny the possibility of anyone doing it. Half this distance, or from Bartlett's last camp to the big channel, *may* have been possible.[1]

After stating that he returned from the Pole to Cape Columbia in sixteen days, Peary continued: "The extraordinary speed of the return journey is to be accounted for by the fact that we merely had to retrace our old trail instead of making a new one, and because we were fortunate in encountering no delays. Excellent conditions of ice and weather also contributed, not to mention the fact that the exhilaration of success lent wings to our sorely battered feet." [2]

After all his care in covering up the actual distance, Peary felt that explanations of the ease and speed of his return were necessary. Yet this was on his assumption that he had travelled at only 25·8 m.p.d. for 413 miles. His actual unwitnessed distance, if he reached the Pole, we have seen would be about 800 statute miles, and his average, 34 statute m.p.d. How much greater the need for explanations of this speed! The

---

[1] The knitting together of the broken trail by the supporting parties is mentioned in Chapter XI, Sec. 5.

[2] *The North Pole*, p. 7.

fact that he tried to explain the lower speed is eloquent; but it could not have brought him back from the Pole which, from the distance he himself gives, was far beyond his turning-point.

Consonant with this is his first explanation that he returned on his outward track; for this would have been impossible, to Cape Columbia, had he travelled 180 statute miles beyond Bartlett.

Peary's silence is as eloquent as his language. He gives no explanation of how he performed any of his miraculous feats. Had they been possible, and had he performed them, we should have been told all about them in the manner customary, not only with other explorers, but with Peary himself on previous journeys. He wrote only for those who knew nothing of the subject. When we wish to understand how he was able to retrace his outward trail, we are put off with high-flown verbiage, consisting of mere generalities that are most suspicious. All difficulties are swept aside with a magnificent gesture and a classical allusion; but raising an image of the fabled Mercury does not make 34 m.p.d. possible.

Peary's story of how he attained the North Pole, when submitted to a normal examination, becomes simply confusion. As, however, he returned to Cape Columbia, and as he could not have averaged more than 18 m.p.d. for 600 miles over the drifting pack, we can tell approximately how far he could have gone. Latitude 87° 47' N. is about 417 route-miles from land. Peary reached Cape Columbia, *in Bartlett's tracks*, twenty-two days after Bartlett turned back. This is remarkable, because at 18 m.p.d. the direct journey would occupy twenty-three days.

The theory that Peary quietly followed Bartlett back agrees with the information of which we can be certain, better than any other hypothesis. We know the character of the ice and the highest speed that Peary and his party were capable of making over it.

He has told us he returned over Bartlett's trail to Cape Columbia. This is sufficient to restrict him to a northern limit of somewhere about latitude 88° N.

4. *Bartlett's Certificate of Latitude 87° 47′ N.*—For many years one felt confidence in Captain Robert Bartlett, and so had no hesitation in believing that Peary reached the latitude of 87° 47′ N., where Bartlett was sent back. The evidence that came out, however, before the Congressional Committee, robs us of certainty even on this point. The evidence is as follows:

Peary exhibits "a certificate given me by Bartlett," an external proof that the latitude mentioned had been reached.

"MR ROBERTS (*after examining paper*). Are these figures in your handwriting.

CAPT. PEARY. In Bartlett's handwriting.

MR BUTLER. This was written away up at the point where Bartlett left you?

CAPT. PEARY. That is just as he wrote it in one of his notebooks, and he tore it out and gave it to me. He kept a copy."

Mr Helgesen [1] draws attention to Peary's evasion; there were many such during the inquiry.

"MR ROBERTS. When were those figures (*indicating*) inserted?

CAPT. PEARY. Immediately after the observations. The only thing that held Bartlett from starting on his return was the making of the observations, and the moment he had taken the observations and made the record he started back.

MR ROBERTS. Why did he use two pencils on that record?

CAPT. PEARY. That I cannot say.

MR ROBERTS. I should judge that evidently *that* was a different pencil (*indicating*); that looks like an indelible pencil.

[1] See Appendix.

Capt. Peary. Yes, Sir.

Mr Roberts. And this looks (*indicating*) like an ordinary lead pencil.

Capt. Peary. Bartlett can answer that question better than I.

Mr Dawson. Have you also the journal or log of your party?

Capt. Peary. I have.

Mr Roberts. Do you know whether or not Bartlett signed that (*indicating*) after making his observations, after putting down the figures?

Capt. Peary. Yes, Sir; I think he did.

Mr Roberts. It looks like a different pencil entirely.

Capt. Peary. Yes, Sir. That was signed at the time, and of course it was done after the observation was made.

Mr Roberts. It seems rather strange that he had such an assortment of pencils there—three pencils. Those entries were all contemporaneous; made the same day?

Capt. Peary. Yes, Sir." [1]

[1] *The Congressional Record*, 12th February 1916.

CHAPTER X

NAVIGATIONAL METHODS AND ASTRONOMICAL OBSERVATIONS [1]

" The history of Arctic discovery shows how the development of the human race has always been borne along by great illusions."
F. NANSEN.
In Northern Mists.

1. THE FIXING OF POSITION. 2. PEARY'S METHODS OF NAVIGATION. 3. THE ALLEGED OBSERVATIONS AT THE POLE.

1. IN order to locate any desired point, such as the North Pole, on an extended plain, like the Arctic pack-ice, there are two essentials: direction and distance. The point aimed at cannot be found unless both these factors are known; and the accuracy with which they are determined settles the accuracy of the location of the required point.

Four kinds of measurements and observations are necessary on a journey for this purpose, namely:—

(*a*) Measurements of the daily distances travelled.
(*b*) Observations of the latitude.
(*c*) Observations of the longitude.
(*d*) Observations of the variation of the compass.

Before glancing at these, it is important to understand the difficulty in fixing any position accurately by means of these observations.

Dr W. M. Smart, about five years ago, read a paper on "Navigation" before the British Association, at Liverpool. He showed how a small error in the dead reckoning led to a large error in the position; and he gave the example of a cruiser which got twenty miles

[1] This chapter is somewhat technical.

out of her position and ran on a beach, due to an unknown current. He said: "Navigation observations
involved an enormous amount of calculations." Errors
of ten and fifteen miles were quite common at sea,
even though the navigating officers in the Navy are the
most expert on the subject. From this, the difficulty
in fixing positions on the moving pack-ice may be
appreciated.

Mr E. S. Balch wrote on this: "It is extremely
difficult for travellers to take astronomical observations
in the vicinity of the North Pole"; [1] and Dr W. S.
Bruce said: "The getting of accurate longitude and
even latitude in these regions . . . is so difficult that
it is scarcely fair to say that a land does not exist
because it is not within a few miles of the assigned
position." [2]

(*a*) The daily distances must be measured carefully
to act as a check on the astronomical observations, with
which they should agree. These measurements of
distance are known as the Dead Reckoning, which is
commonly contracted to D.R. All the great Antarctic
explorers, Scott, Shackleton, Mawson, and Amundsen,
"logged" their D.R. by means of sledgemeters. These
instruments have been adopted for the express purpose
of obtaining accurate D.R. on polar journeys. They
are somewhat similar to the well-known speedometers
on motor cars, but are attached to a wheel on the rear
of the sledges.

Peary never used a sledgemeter on the Arctic pack,
saying it would have been smashed by the rough
surface; yet Nansen used one on a similar, if not the
same, surface. Peary wrote: "The distance which
we travelled day by day was at first determined by
dead reckoning, to be verified later by observations for
latitude. Dead reckoning was simply the compass
course for direction, and for distance the mean estimate

---

[1] *The North Pole and Bradley Land*, p. 27.
[2] *The Scottish Geographical Magazine*, 1912, vol. xxviii, p. 315.

of Bartlett, Marvin, and myself as to the length of the day's march." [1]

Marvin was sent back in latitude 86° 38′ N. and Bartlett in latitude 87° 47′ N. For the last 150 statute miles of latitude-distance Peary had no one to check his own estimate of what the D.R. should be. At the end of the first day after leaving Bartlett he wrote: "We travelled for ten hours without stopping, covering, I felt sure, thirty miles, though, to be conservative, I called it twenty-five." [2] His D.R. for this day, according to his own account, may have been five geographical miles in error. As he was five days travelling from Bartlett's last outward camp to the Pole, there was a possible error of twenty-five miles in a distance of 130 miles, or over 20 *per cent.*; yet he says nothing about any difference between his D.R. and the first observations he took, for latitude only, on this final spurt, in latitude 89° 25′ N.

Rear-Admiral E. R. G. R. Evans had to navigate Captain Scott's last supporting party a distance of 750 miles without a sledgemeter. "To be deprived of it in a wilderness of snow without landmarks," Mr Cherry-Garrard says, "adds enormously to the difficulties and anxieties of a sledge party." [3] Frequently there are several miles of difference in the estimates of two men, as to the daily distance marched; and this was so with the estimates of Admiral Evans, and Lashly, one of the members of his party.

(*b*) *Observations for Latitude.*—Peary's first latitude observations were taken after about 184 miles of latitude, or 230 route-miles, had been travelled. This gave 85° 48′ N. latitude. His next observation was in latitude 86° 38′ N.; both these were taken by Marvin. The third observation was taken by Bartlett in latitude 87° 47′ N.; and his last before reaching the Pole, by

[1] *The North Pole*, p. 24.
[2] *Ibid.*, p. 276.
[3] *The Worst Journey in the World*, vol. ii, p. 385.

Peary himself, in latitude 89° 25′ N. These four were latitude sights only and will be considered, as will his observations at the Pole, a little later. We may notice now, however, that as the latitude distance from land to the Pole was 475 statute miles, these observations average only one for every 118 miles. For the purpose of comparison with other explorers' observations, about 25 per cent. must be added to the latitude for deviations from the proper course, in order to find out the distance travelled. This would be 593 miles, with an average of one latitude observation for every 148 miles.

(*c, d*) *Observations for Longitude and Compass Variation.*—During the giving of Peary's evidence before the Congressional Committee, already mentioned, he said: "I took no observations for longitude at any time on the trip." He also admitted taking no observations for compass variation; but then he abruptly changed the subject, as he did more than once during the giving of his evidence. The following is an excerpt:

"Mr Englebright. In using a compass in the northern regions you use it with a calculated variation?

Capt. Peary. You use it, checking it by observations wherever you can. To give you an idea of what the variations are, here at Roosevelt (*indicating*) the variation is approximately 95° W. In other words, the north end of the needle points a little south of true west, and as you go west that increases.

Mr Englebright. Is not that all charted by the Coast Survey and by the maritime nations of the world?

Capt. Peary. They have the lines of certain variations, but, of course, the greater the number of observations, the more accurate the data.

Mr Englebright. Did you have such a chart with you?

Capt. Peary. No, Sir; I did not have such a chart.

MR DAWSON. Did you make any observations which would tend to throw any additional light on the variation of the needle?

CAPT. PEARY. I did not on this last expedition; I did on the previous ones, when I went along this coast (*indicating*). I should say that on this trip I had what is called a double team of dogs—twelve—and a light sledge. The usual team was eight dogs. . . ." [1]

Mr Congressman Helgesen well remarked: "Peary suddenly found it very convenient to change the subject abruptly." The Superintendent of the United States Naval Observatory stated that "the traveller from Cape Columbia to the North Pole might expect to find large changes in variation."

At the "Peary hearing," Mr Macon remarked: "Then you took no observations, longitude or otherwise, for a distance of 133 miles after you left Bartlett at 87° 47'?

CAPT. PEARY. No, Sir.

MR MACON. And without that you managed to make a straight course to the Pole without anything except conjecture or estimate to guide you. Is that it?

CAPT. PEARY. I leave the observations to answer that question. I am satisfied that I made that distance. . . ." [1]

On 25th February 1915 the Hon. Henry T. Helgesen made a speech in the House of Representatives, during the course of which he commented on Peary's navigational methods as follows:—

"Mr Peary also stated to the Congressional Committee that throughout a journey of 410 miles over the trackless expanse of the Arctic Ocean he made only three observations for latitude,[2] and these were made while the sun was at no time higher than eight degrees above the horizon, while an altitude of ten

---

[1] *The Congressional Record*, 12th February 1916.

[2] There appear to have been four of these observations.

degrees above the horizon is the lowest altitude at
which our Navy Department declares approximately
accurate results for latitude can be made. The three
observations made by Mr Peary for latitude were, of
course, valueless without the correlative observations
for longitude and for compass variation. The fact is
indisputable, therefore, that at no time after he left
the sight of land could Mr Peary have known his
position, since he claims to have travelled by compass,
yet did not know the direction in which his compass
needle pointed, neither did he know whether he was
travelling on the 70th or any other meridian, or at
right angles to both." [1]

Captain Scott, in addition to frequent observations
for latitude, took numerous longitude observations
also, for the very necessary purpose of keeping on the
meridian along which he was travelling to the South
Pole. When he, or Captain Amundsen, found that
they had diverged perceptibly from their meridians,
they took special sets of observations to correct their
positions.

2. *Peary's Methods of Navigation.*—Peary has told
us how he set his course; this was as follows: "Our
course was nearly, as the crow flies, due north across
floe after floe, pressure ridge after pressure ridge,
headed straight for some hummock or pinnacle of ice
which I had lined in with my compass." [2]

All polar navigators, geographers, and magneticians,
know the uncertainty of the compass within some
hundreds of miles of the magnetic polar area, such as
along Peary's route. Lieutenant Bowers, one of the
best navigators on Captain Scott's last expedition,
wrote: "Owing to the proximity of the Magnetic Pole
the pull on the needle is chiefly downwards. It is
forced into a horizontal position by a balancing weight
on the north side, so it is obvious that its directive

---

[1] *The Congressional Record,* 12th February 1916.
[2] *The North Pole,* p. 276.

power is greatly reduced. On the ship . . . we were absolutely unable to steer by the compass at all when off the region of the Magnetic Pole." [1]   Scott's parties, indeed, found the compass almost useless; and their journeys were made, similarly to Peary's journeys in the Arctic, near the magnetic meridian. *Peary had nothing but his practically useless compass to give him his direction.*

Captain Amundsen was a good navigator, and he flew over the North Pole. In praising Commander Byrd for performing the same feat, Amundsen draws special attention to "the difficulties involved in making accurate observations of position in those regions," that is, in the polar regions. He proceeds to say, and this is the main point of the quotation: "The magnetic compass is there very sluggish." [2]

Peary claimed to have found the Pole with nothing but a compass and four latitude observations. This would not be impossible, provided that progress were slow enough to permit the needle to settle; that this was done with sufficient frequency; that the distances were measured; and that the longitude on the drifting ice was known during the journey. These conditions Peary did not fulfil.

He seems to be quite candid about his simple method of navigation, but on the moving pack-ice it was hopeless. Dr Nansen, an accurate observer, took a large number of longitude observations on the pack, yet he had great difficulty in fixing his positions, mainly owing to the unknown direction and rate of drift of the ice. If navigation on the pack was not easy for him, how could Peary keep a course?

We are not told what course was set on leaving land. Peary intended to bear more to the west of north than on his journey in 1906, to allow for the prevailing drift of the ice towards the east, while

[1] *The Worst Journey in the World*, vol. i, p. 120.
[2] *My Life as an Explorer*, p. 171.

travelling on it for several weeks; but as a strong east wind was blowing when he left Cape Columbia, he may have set a N.N.E. course to counteract the westerly drift that this wind would cause. He would do his best, undoubtedly, to allow for all movement of the ice transverse to his course, for he had to keep, if possible, on the meridian of Cape Columbia. The whole theory of his journey is based on the assumption that he never diverged from this meridian. His difficulty was that, as he took no longitude observations, he could not know the rate of the drift; nor could he even be certain of its direction when out of sight of land.

If he diverged from his meridian he did not reach the Pole, for his distances and his chart permit of no divergence. On a zigzag course the distance travelled would be much greater than Peary recorded.

As long as land was in sight, or during the first few days, he could keep near the Columbia meridian, though not without travelling more than the latitude distance (which is all he says he travelled) because of the strong east wind. On losing sight of land, he could only judge whether he was being drifted to east or west of his meridian by the direction of the wind. This was most uncertain, and must have carried him off his course, though he had no means of knowing how far off it he was carried. The wind, during his outward journey, was in some quarter of east or west on at least ten days, and was moving the pack all the hours he was in camp. It is evident, from his failure to distinguish between absolute and relative movement of the sides of open channels, on his earlier journeys over the pack, that he was not sure whether he was being carried to east or west. It would be impossible for anyone who took no longitude observations, to be certain if the *apparent* motion of the far side of a channel was real, or only relative to the motion of the side on which the observer was standing. When the

fast, or land-adhering, ice was left behind, the whole
pack was in motion.

It is clear, therefore, that Peary would soon lose the
Columbia meridian.   Even on land, the best navigators
can only keep on their meridian by frequent observations for longitude, of which Peary took none.   Sir
Clements Markham justly observed that Peary's
"course was assumed to be due north (true).   Peary
refers to the meridian of Cape Columbia as if he had
never deviated from that meridian during the whole
journey.   Yet there is no record of the latitude and
longitude of Cape Columbia having been fixed, and no
mention of any observations for amplitude during the
whole journey.   Without such observations it would
not be possible to keep on the same meridian." [1]

Having only a rough bearing on the Magnetic Pole
from Cape Columbia, Peary was lost as soon as he left
his meridian.   He had no means of knowing where he
was.   If he assumed he was on his meridian when he
was miles to east or west of it, his compass bearings
would lead him farther astray; and not knowing his
longitude he could not correct his bearings, so that his
compass, apart from its unreliability in that region,
would be useless.   It was impossible for him to keep
his course on the Geographical Pole.

No astronomical observations of any kind were
taken until the twenty-third day after leaving land.
The expedition was then supposed to have travelled
about 230 miles; but as the distance was not measured,
it is impossible to say how far they had travelled.   The
latitude sights could do no more than place them on a
parallel which extended completely round the world.
The sledging surface had been moving continually for
over three weeks.   Yet the distances given by Peary,
as we have seen, admit of no deviation from the
Columbia meridian on which he had no means of
keeping!

[1] *The Lands of Silence*, p. 357.

Had Peary been a proper navigator, or had he been particular about reaching the Pole, his system of navigation would have been very different from the slipshod method he made use of. As he was a naval officer he got the credit of understanding navigation; but he was not a sailor, he was a civil engineering assistant, engaged on dockyard work, and never served in the navy at sea; still less was he a navigating officer.

His navigation always had been careless and inaccurate. Hence, he was quite the wrong type of man for a Pole seeker. Had he seriously intended to reach the Pole and prove to the world that he had done so, he would have taken at least two competent navigators for the whole of his journey, and no other companions were necessary. Dr Nansen showed the inaccuracy of the observations Peary took, in 1886, in Greenland. He got into trouble repeatedly, during his first crossing of the inland ice, by being off his course. It seems probable, from what we know of his methods of navigation, that he lost his big depot in 1894 because of his inability to fix its location accurately. Blizzards he had then, no doubt; but just as he could use the storm of 1906 as a specious excuse for not travelling faster, the blizzards in 1894 would cover up more than his depots. Even his biographer writes: "The *approximate* position of the big cache was reached"[1] (our italics). Peary completely lost his bearings when, in 1906, he was near the magnetic meridian, and he thought the North Pole lay to the north-west of Axel Heiberg Land.

Sir Ernest Shackleton said that the finding of one of his depots on the Ross Barrier, in Antarctica, was as difficult as picking up a buoy in the North Sea; but he and Captain Scott were navigators by profession, and neither of them ever missed a depot on an open plain. Yet neither of them was content with his own observations. Each was careful to take other navi-

[1] *Peary the Man*, p. 128.

gators in the polar party, and to keep them, as all honest and rational men would, for the vital part of his journey.

Many other examples could be given to illustrate what Peary ought to have done, but one more instance must suffice. Sir Aurel Stein's survey, in the featureless sand of the Takla-makan Desert, agreed with that of Ram Singh, his Indian surveyor, to within "about half a mile in longitude and less than a mile in latitude"; [1] Ram Singh having come 500 miles and Sir Aurel 120 miles. The contrast between good and bad navigation, on featureless plains, is unmistakable.

3. *The Alleged Astronomical Observations at the Pole.* —It may well appear to be waste of time seriously to consider the alleged observations of any man who, first, stated that he sledged over 150 miles in two days, and subsequently cut this down, so that he could not have been within fifty or more miles of where he claimed the observations to have been taken; and whose methods of "navigation" were so crude that he had no means of knowing where he was, when he had lost sight of land. Our examination of Peary's work, however, would not be complete if we ignored his observations; and copies of them were submitted to experts, who reported that they were quite correct. Observations that were otherwise would not, of course, have been submitted; but such observations are no proof that a traveller reached the point where they were said to have been taken. The figures can be constructed anywhere, as Captain Amundsen, and other supporters of Peary, have admitted. [2] To begin by assuming that an explorer has not forged his observations is most proper and pleasant; but some precaution should be taken, especially when dealing with men whose credentials are not above suspicion.

We have seen, in previous chapters, that from

[1] *The Sand-buried Ruins of Khotan,* pp. 283–284.
[2] See p. 4.

Peary's own statements he could not have reached the Pole. Hence, his alleged observations at that point are worthless. His *original* figures, with his instruments and journal, have never been examined by an unimpeachable authority. *Copies* of observations and other matters were sent out, as Dr Cook sent copies of his records to Copenhagen; and Peary's papers were no more proofs that he had reached the Pole than were Cook's papers.

Captain Hall having examined these observations technically,[1] we have only to compare them with those of other polar claimants, and to draw a few conclusions.

All reputable explorers, navigators, and students of the subject are agreed that isolated observations, made in one locality, at the end of a long journey, are of little value; but that their value is at once enhanced by a good series of observations taken with considerable frequency during the course of the journey. They should be like a ladder, the foot of which stands at the expedition's base, and which reaches the farthest point of the unknown by steps that are as regular as possible. Thus, observations taken at either of the Poles may be almost worthless, unless they are the culmination of a good series of navigational observations. The geographical position should be fixed every few days—preferably, indeed, every day—from the beginning of the journey; then the farthest point reached cannot be much in error. If no point is fixed during the journey, the inexactitude of the turning-point may be very great.

There have been four claimants to the North and South Geographical Poles. These, in chronological order, were Dr F. A. Cook and Admiral Peary for the North Pole; Captains Amundsen and Scott for the South Pole. We are able, therefore, to apply the comparative method of examination. The records of all

[1] See Appendix.

four claimants will be accepted, to begin with, at their
face value.

Some explanation for introducing Dr Cook's name
here may be expected; though it is mentioned only,
as Peary's name is mentioned, as a *claimant* to the
North Pole. One reason for not excluding Cook is
that his account of his farthest north was given to the
world a week before Peary's account of his farthest
north. This is a historical fact.[1] Furthermore, as
Peary's account of the conditions found at his farthest
north agreed with Cook's account of the same, Peary
either copied or confirmed Cook. There are difficulties in the latter's book, *My Attainment of the Pole*;
but it compares favourably with Peary's book *The North
Pole*. Another reason that may be given for including
Cook in a comparison that includes Peary is that more
than half Cook's polar journey has been verified by
subsequent explorers. It is not necessary, from these
statements, to conclude that Cook reached the North
Pole, for this is most improbable; but his claims
appear to have been less fantastic than Peary's.

Cook claimed to have reached the Pole on 21st
April 1908, after a journey of 546 miles from land. He
used a pedometer for dead reckoning and averaged
about 14 m.p.d., with two or three days of twenty miles
or a little over. He was accompanied only by two
Eskimos. He kept a daily meteorological record, and
took at least seven observations of the sun during the
outward journey, excluding those taken at his destina-
tion, or an average of one set of observations for every
seventy-eight miles. All these observations were for
longitude as well as for latitude, though, as his chronometer could not be checked, the value of his longitude
observations is uncertain. His D.R. seems to have
agreed fairly well with his latitude sights. On reaching
a point that he considered to be the Pole, he took
seven complete sets of observations, one every six

[1] See *The North Pole and Bradley Land*, E. S. Balch.

hours from noon on 21st April to midnight on the
22nd. His first observation gave latitude 89° 59′ 45″,
and his journal for that day recorded: "Long. 97° W.,
Bar. 28·83, Temp. 37·7,[1] Clouds Alt. St. 1, Wind 1,
Mag. S., Iceblink E., Water sky W." In giving his
corrections for instrumental error, he points out that
the corrections for refraction and ice-drift are not
known. He shrewdly observes also that "the value
of all such observations as proof of a polar success . . .
is open to such interpretation as the future may determine."[2] The altitude of the sun was on and off
twelve degrees, and a six-foot pole gave a twenty-eight-
foot shadow for twenty-four hours, which agrees with
this altitude. He moved camp four miles towards the
magnetic north, and spent forty-eight hours here,
noting down in his journal while there, and on the
journey, a surprising amount of scientific data. The
only particulars that concern us at present are the
following: he found the drift of the ice at his turning-
point to be in the direction of Greenland, and the
condition of its surface "nearly the same as it had been
continuously since leaving the 88th parallel. It was
slightly more active."[3] The ice, where he measured
it, was 16 feet thick, and the tallest pressure ridge
was 28 feet above the water.

Peary did not fix, for he had no means of fixing,
so much as a single position, from land to latitude
89° 57′ N., or for a distance of nearly 600 statute miles
travelled. There, he says, he took his first polar
observations at noon (Columbia meridian time) on
6th April 1909. His second observation could not be
taken at 6 p.m. as the sky was overcast, but having
moved on ten miles he got them at midnight. At
6 a.m. on the 7th he took his third sights, and at noon
his fourth and last. After giving these particulars he

---

[1] This was *minus* 37·7° F. There were no *plus* temperatures on
the journey.

[2] *My Attainment of the Pole*, p. 302.   [3] *Ibid.*, pp. 296, 310.

enlarges upon them considerably, in accordance with his custom, and then in a footnote he deals with the question as to how closely the Pole can be determined.

This note is an example of Peary's best work. From his own point of view he handles the subject well. His style is sufficiently pontifical, but he successfully evades, while appearing to settle, the crux of the matter. He says that the master of a ship is assumed to be able to calculate his position to "within about a mile." Peary being in the United States Navy, he got the credit of being able to fix the Pole as accurately as this. He professes to be much more modest, however, and allows for possible errors up to five, and even as much as ten, miles. He is careful not to inform the general public, for whom he writes, that no ship can sail within 500 miles of the Poles; and that, in the ordinary course of navigation, ships never get nearer to either of them than about a thousand miles. The result is that no mariner has to depend for his position on a noon observation with the sun only seven degrees above the horizon, which was its altitude at the North Pole when Peary professed to have been there, with all the difficulties and uncertainties resulting from its being so low. We shall return to this later.

He admits, perhaps unguardedly, that it is only by an extended series of observations that the Pole can be determined "within entirely satisfactory limits." Thus he can pose as a scientist before the unlearned; though he did not do so at his turning-point, where he spent no more than one day, without anyone to check his observations. He denied himself the extended series of observations that he knew to be vital, if his results were to be placed above dispute.

The two American explorers are in a class by themselves; each appears to be comparable to the other; while neither can compare with the two claimants to the South Pole, to whom we now turn.

Captain Amundsen and his four Norwegian companions arrived there at 3 p.m. (meridian of Framheim, in the Bay of Whales) on 14th December 1911, after a journey of 879 statute miles, as registered by sledge-meter, from his base. The following observations had been taken during the journey:

TABLE No. 4. AMUNDSEN'S NAVIGATIONAL OBSERVATIONS

Latitudes South

	Observations.	Dead Reckoning.
1	82°	82°, but 3½ m. to west in fog
2	83° 1′	83°
3	85° 36′	(Not given)
4	86° 21′	86° 23′ [1]
5	86° 47′	(Not given)
6	88° 16′	88° 16′
7	88° 47′	" To within a mile "
8	89° 15′	89° 15′
9	89° 30′	89° 29·5′
10	89° 37′	89° 38·5′

To these must be added the fixing of the depots in latitudes 80° and 81° S., making a series of twelve observations, or an average of one for every seventy-three route-miles. The full particulars of the navigation are not given; but we are told that they had four compasses, three sledgemeters, three artificial horizons, and two sextants. The leading sledge had aluminium, instead of iron, fittings and no sledgemeter, to avoid deflection of the steering compass. From this we gather that they steered by compass, which, at their great distance from the Magnetic Pole, would be their best method.

Every member of the Norwegian polar party appears to have been a navigator, and all five checked

[1] Amundsen wrote: " This did not agree very well " (*The South Pole*, vol. ii, p. 81).

the first set of observations at midnight after their arrival at the Pole. Amundsen writes: "The result at which we finally arrived was of great interest, as it clearly shows how unreliable and valueless a single observation like this is in these regions." [1] They found that they had gone out of their meridian, midnight giving a greater altitude than noon. The latitude came out at 89° 56′ S. Wisting, Hassel, and Bjaaland then set out on their ski to "encircle" the Pole, with radii of 12½ miles. Amundsen and Hanssen, in the meantime, took thirteen hourly observations (from 6 a.m. to 7 p.m. on the 15th), as the former writes, "to get our north and south line and latitude determined, so that we could find our position once more." The resulting latitude was about 89° 54′ 30″, and they were able to fix their meridian, so they moved on the remaining 5½ geographical miles, and set up their tent in time for noon observations on the 16th.

Sights were then taken "every hour throughout the whole twenty-four," until noon on the 17th, when "Hanssen and Bjaaland went out four geographical miles (seven kilometres) in the direction of the newly-found meridian." During the night of the 17th to 18th they began their return journey, after spending about three and a half days at the Pole. Altogether forty-two observations had been taken at the Pole, in addition to those taken during the journey. The sun's altitude at the Pole was somewhat over 23°. On the return of the expedition to Norway, these observations were submitted to the authority which had examined Dr Nansen's Arctic observations, and his verdict, in short, was that the camp at the Pole lay between latitudes 89° 57′ and 89° 59′ S., and the longitude must be between 30° and 75° E., and the probable position being approximately 60° E.

In Captain Scott's polar party it is certain that there were three navigators, and possibly there was a

[1] *The South Pole*, vol. ii, p. 125.

fourth, Captain Oates being the doubtful member. Bowers, who was a lieutenant in the Royal Indian Marine, generally took the observations,[1] and Dr Wilson, against his natural inclinations, had learnt navigation for the occasion. At least twenty-five latitude observations were taken during the outward journey of 908¼ miles, the distance being measured by sledgemeters. These observations, therefore, averaged one in every thirty-seven miles. Good as this is, in comparison with the next best polar journey, it is as nothing when we notice the navigation across the plateau. Here, in a distance of 341 miles, eighteen latitude observations were taken, or one in every 18·9 miles; thirteen of these were accompanied by observations for longitude, and nine times the variation of the compass was observed. This series of observations is so good that it must be reproduced in its entirety.[2]

Here is an example of how a polar journey ought to be conducted. Scott's observations are, of course, by far the best of the four we are considering; their accuracy, and those taken by Amundsen, were proved on the arrival of the British expedition at the South Pole, where the Norwegian records were found.

Scott's party reached latitude 89° 53' 37" S. on 17th January 1912 and then went on 6½ miles due south (true), where Bowers took a second observation. On the 18th they found that they were one mile beyond the Pole and three miles to the right, and on moving in the new direction, at about a mile and a half from their location of the Pole, they came to the Norwegian tent. Scott wrote: "Sights at lunch gave us half to three-quarters of a mile from the Pole. . . . There is no doubt that our predecessors have made thoroughly sure of their mark, and fully carried out their programme."[3]   Scott started back the same day,

---

[1] *Scott's Last Expedition*, vol. i, pp. 539, 543.
[2] See Table No. 5 on next page.
[3] *Scott's Last Expedition*, vol. i, p. 546.

TABLE No. 5. CAPTAIN SCOTT'S PLATEAU OBSERVATIONS

	Latitude S.	Longitude E.	Barometer.	Compass Variation.
1	85° 13′ 30″	161° 55′	22·3	175° 46′ E.
2	85° 22′ 1″	159° 31′	21·61	
3	85° 50′	159° 8′ 2″	21·22	
4	86° 2′	160° 26′	21·02	
5	86° 27′ 2″	161° 1·15′	20·64	179° 33′ E.
6	86° 55′ 47″	165° 5′ 48″	20·08	175° 40′ E.
7	87° 20′ 8″	160° 40′ 53″	10,250 [1]	180°
8	87° 32′	..	10,180	
9	87° 57′	159° 13′	10,320	
10	88° 7′	..	10,430	
11	88° 18′ 40″	157° 21′	10,570	179° 15′ W.
12	88° 25′	159° 17′ 45″	10,270	179° 55′ W.
13	88° 29′	159° 33′	10,540	180°
14	88° 52′			
15	88° 57′ 25″	160° 21′	10,270	179° 49′ W.
16	89° 20′ 53″	..	9,950	
17	89° 26′ 57″	160° 56′ 45″	9,920	179° E.
18	89° 53′ 37″	..	9,500	

and on his way wrote: "It is satisfactory to recall that these facts give absolute proof of both expeditions having reached the Pole, and placed the question of priority beyond discussion." [2]

The radical difference between the two pairs of polar expeditions was well expressed by Captain Scott when he wrote that the Norwegians had "made thoroughly sure of their mark." The fundamental weakness of both the American explorers was that they did not go to the trouble of making their mark sure. The north and south polar areas are in part similar to, and in part dissimilar from, each other. In both regions the sun makes a very small angle with the horizon; and it is on the horizon that the aberrations

[1] Scott changed here, giving the aneroid heights in feet instead of barometer readings.

[2] *Scott's Last Expedition*, vol. i, p. 563.

caused by the atmosphere are at their maximum. Refraction is not only a very great but a most uncertain, if not incalculable, cause of error. The uncertainty of all solar observations in these regions was vividly seen on Sir Ernest Shackleton's *Endurance* Expedition.

On 15th April 1915, one minute after the sun had set, it rose again "a semi-diameter clear above the western horizon." Again, seven days after it should have set for the winter, the sun appeared, on 8th May, at 11 a.m., disappeared at 11.15 a.m., rose again at 11.40 a.m., set at 1 p.m., rose at 1.10 p.m., and set lingeringly at 1.20 p.m. Sir Ernest added: "These curious phenomena were due to refraction, which amounted to 2° 37′ at 1.20 p.m. . . . We calculated that the refraction was two degrees above normal; in other words, the sun was visible 120 miles farther south than the refraction tables gave it any right to be."[1]

Scott stands apart from the other three polar claimants in that he found the Pole located when he reached it. Two of the other three, Amundsen and Cook, fully admit the uncertainty of such observations as are usually taken. Amundsen says, as already quoted, that a single observation, even with four navigators to check it, is "unreliable and valueless." Peary had four observations taken by one navigator, if he can be termed one. He stands absolutely alone in endeavouring to base his claim on such a futile foundation. This is a matter of great significance. Cook, quite properly, appeals to the sum-total of the records presented by the explorer. We have seen how much reliance can be placed upon Peary's records.

Every isolated observer lays his observations open to dispute because there is no possible check on mistakes. This liability to error makes all observations that are not checked by at least one other observer,

[1] *South*, pp. 45–49.

especially in these regions, of very little value. Captains Scott and Amundsen knew full well that observations at the Pole, taken by a single observer, would be rightly open to dispute; hence, they were equally careful to have several skilled navigators at the crucial point, in order amply to verify the sights. Amundsen probably took one or two more navigators than Scott, because the attainment of the Pole was the sole object of the Norwegian Expedition, whereas it was only one item, if an important one, on the British programme. Yet Scott instructed those of his staff, who were not professional navigators, in the science of navigation. Thus the southern observations never could be questioned.

The establishment of all observations above dispute was of far greater importance at the North Pole than at the South Pole, because of the circumstances peculiar to the Arctic, in addition to the difficulties common to both Poles.

As there is no land at the North Pole, all observations must be taken from a floating platform of ice, and no record can be left to be verified by subsequent explorers. Further, it was vital to the whole purpose of both the American explorers that their most northerly positions should be fixed, if it were possible, beyond all reasonable doubt; yet neither of them took even so much as a second navigator, and neither stayed more than two days at the Pole. In acting thus they were simply asking for all the trouble that has arisen in consequence of their own neglect. The only reason Peary ever gave for not taking a white companion, that he would allow no one else to share with him the glory of the achievement, is most reprehensible.

The errors of the individual observer are multiplied by the atmosphere, and can be eliminated only by a long series of sights. It is difficult for explorers to remain many days at the Poles; but if they wish their claims to be accepted they should not undertake these ventures unless they can do so fully equipped. The following table shows at a glance the navigational observations in their order of merit:

TABLE No. 6. NAVIGATIONAL OBSERVATIONS
(In order of merit)

Explorer.		Route Distance.	No. of Latitude Obs.	No. of Av. Miles for Lat. Obs.	No. of Longitude Obs.	Compass Variation.
		Miles Stat.				
Scott {	whole journey	{ 908 measured	25	37	13	9
	plateau	{ 341 measured	18	18	13	9
Amundsen . .		{ 879 measured	12	73	?	?
Cook . . .		{ 546 measured	7	78	7	?
Peary . . .		(Said to be 413 geo.) Actually about 593 st. Not measured	4	148	None	None

We can now summarise the astronomical observations at the Poles in the same order; adding only that Scott had no need to linger, or to take as many observations, at the South Pole as Amundsen.

It will be seen that Peary's observations are the worst of them all. It was not altogether his fault that the sun was so low, because he was obliged to return to land before the pack broke up. Still, the fact remains, that the value of the northern observations is yet further reduced, as compared with the southern observations, from the single circumstance of the lower altitudes of the sun. Scott and Amundsen

TABLE No. 7.   POLAR OBSERVATIONS

South Pole

Explorer.	Sun's Altitude.	Hours at Pole.	No. of Observers	No. of Observations.	Date.
Amundsen	23°	72	5	42	14th–18th Dec. 1911
Scott .	23°	48	3 or 4	4	16th–18th Jan. 1912

North Pole

Cook .	12°	48	1	7	21st–22nd Apr. 1908
Peary .	7°	30	1	4	6th–7th Apr. 1909

timed their arrival at the South Pole to coincide with the Summer Solstice. Peary's observations, however regarded, are the most unsatisfactory ones that have been taken at either of the Poles, even according to his own account. He stayed the shortest time and took the least number of observations, with the sun at its lowest declination.

Amundsen, even with four skilled navigators, had not been able to keep on his meridian, and it was necessary for him to fix it accurately. Peary never made any attempt to fix a north and south line. Again, even the excellent Norwegian observations could not fix the longitude, a few miles from the Pole, within 45°. At the mathematical Pole this does not matter; but the range of meridional uncertainty increases with the distance from the Pole. Peary entirely ignored the movement of his sledging surface, and never attempted to determine his compass variation. As he could not have been within fifty or more miles of the Pole, the uncertainty of his longitude must have been enormous. The position he attained never will be known.

The maximum culmination of the sun is very difficult to judge at the Poles; and the displacement of the periods of culmination amounted to as much as one hour and a half, with Amundsen, in latitude 89° 59′ S. Its apparent altitude at culmination, at the North Pole, was less than half that at the South Pole, owing to the difference in the dates, so that Peary's liability to error was much greater than Amundsen's or Scott's. Peary claims to have located the Pole to within five miles, if not to within one mile; but he could not possibly prove that no mistakes had been made, or indeed that the altitudes on which he based his calculations had been, in fact, observed. This depends entirely upon their reliability.

These claims to have attained the Poles cannot be judged on less than the fullest consideration of all the data the explorers bring back. The verdict of science must be that, apart from the journal and the navigational observations, those taken at the end of a long journey are of no particular value as proof of any position, unless they are checked by several observers over a long series of sights. Thus it was that when Cook's observations were submitted to the scrutiny of the University of Copenhagen they gave the only possible verdict: that such figures were no scientific proof of his attainment of the Pole. But, in the wretched controversy of that time, the equally certain verdict on Peary's observations was never sought; though, if his figures had been submitted to the same or any other independent authority, *no other verdict was possible*.

Neither Peary's nor Cook's observations could amount to positive proof that they had reached the North Pole, if only because a single observer can write down any altitude he pleases. The claims made by these two explorers required to be well substantiated by all their other records, and especially by their daily journals. We have carefully examined, in previous chapters, Admiral Peary's record of his journey; and we have found that it cannot support his claim to have reached the Pole. His claim has broken down because it is not substantiated by the detailed account he has presented. The reliability of his word has been destroyed by his own contradictions, as well as by the subsequent discoveries of other explorers, in spite of the fact that some of them admired while they corrected him.

CHAPTER XI

PEARY'S DISCOVERIES AND HIS SLEDGING

" The voyage of the ' Discovery' was not conducted in a spirit of pure adventure, but . . . we strove to add, and succeeded in adding, something to the sum of human knowledge."

CAPTAIN R. F. SCOTT.
The Voyage of the " Discovery."

1. PEARY'S PIONEERING. 2. HIS SLEDGING RECORD. 3. HIS SLEDGING SYSTEMS. 4. THE SIZE OF HIS UNITS. 5. SUPPORTING PARTIES.

1. IT has been our duty, in pursuit of truth, to place on record the unsatisfactory nature of Peary's geographical claims; but that is not the whole story. A more pleasant aspect of the subject now comes before us.

Human knowledge is greatly increased by geographical discovery, especially if a due proportion of the information brought back to civilisation is intensive as well as extensive. No normal person could spend the best years of life on the confines of unexplored regions without extending man's sway over nature to some extent.

To claim the discovery of a geographical Pole is to be guilty of a terminological absurdity, equivalent to that of discovering the Equator. The position of each can be located by navigators who have sufficient knowledge and skill; but these geographical features should be treated with proper respect.

Peary's failure to reach the North Pole cannot deprive him of the credit of discovering a fair amount of land, though he did not accumulate much information about it. Most of his exploratory work was of a very sketchy character. He was not a scientist, and

he seldom took out men who were qualified to conduct
the investigations that are the first essentials in new
countries. If he included a few students on his staff,
as he did on two or three of his expeditions, he was
careful *not* to permit them to accompany him to his
most distant points; though that is precisely what is
wanted, and what the great explorers always do.
Peary preferred to have Henson and the Eskimos as
his companions, in spite of the fact that all of them,
from the most important standpoints, were perfectly
useless.

The value of geographical discovery depends
entirely, in the first place, on the charting of the new
lands; and in the second place, upon the amount of
scientific data brought back. Accurate surveying is
the first essential, because no proper conception of
topographical conditions can be formed without good
maps; and all the other work that should be done by
explorers—meteorological, geological, magnetic, biological, and, in polar regions, glaciological—is based on
the local topography.

Peary failed in all this. He made rapid journeys
over unexplored countries without actually exploring
them. He was not, strictly speaking, an *explorer*.
He did nothing more than pioneer a way into the unknown, leaving after him little that was less ephemeral
than the wake of a ship. Other and more painstaking
explorers are bequeathed the labour of following him
everywhere, and doing the work he left undone.

Captain Amundsen, in his great journey to the
South Pole, has been criticised severely for the same
defect; and the criticism is just. What benefit is
there from travelling in new countries if little or no
information, of a reliable and serviceable nature, is
brought back from them? Peary and Amundsen were
alike in this: that they made spectacular journeys,
and received the same honours as other explorers who
really *explored*, and not merely passed through, new

lands.   It is unfair to the best explorer, who makes a
good survey of all his discoveries, and returns loaded
with scientific data, that the man who merely travels
at his highest speed, and has no time even for mapping,
should receive the same credit for visiting the same
amount of new land.

Little more can be asked from those who are only
pioneers, perhaps, than good maps of their discoveries,
accompanied by a few accurate notes on the principal
features of the countries that they alone have seen;
but this we are entitled to expect.   The mapping of
both Peary and Amundsen was deplorable.   Both of
them, also, did very little detailed exploration; though
Amundsen discovered much more land on his one
Antarctic expedition than Peary did all his life.

Peary made an attempt, on his First North Greenland Expedition, to collect a certain amount of scientific
data, and in this he was partially successful.   One of
his assistants, the unfortunate young Verhoeff, has
left some meteorological notes, extending from August
1891 to March 1892; he took also some tidal observations.   Dr F. A. Cook did some useful anthropological
work among the Eskimos.   Peary filled in the intervals
between his longer journeys by mapping Inglefield
Gulf and parts of Whale and Murchison Sounds.   He
discovered several glaciers and three meteoric stones,
one of the latter being the largest in the world.   He
was the first human being to look upon North-east
Greenland, but he made no proper survey of his discoveries there.   His chart of this locality was a mere
freehand sketch, that did not do him justice.

During the *Windward* Expedition he appeared to
do a great deal of surveying, though little use has been
made of it.   No maps have been issued of a large
enough size to see any detail upon them.   Their scale
is 80 geographical miles to the inch.   The district
surveyed was East Grinnell Land.[1]   Peary's dis-

---

[1] They accompany Peary's *Nearest the Pole.*

coveries on the north coasts of Greenland and Grant
Land were very roughly surveyed. Some tidal
measurements were made on these coasts on his
later expeditions, and a few soundings were taken in
the Arctic Ocean; but Peary's navigation was not good
enough to make the latter of much value, as there is
too much uncertainty about their positions.

The following figures necessarily are very approximate, because Peary's data are so uncertain:

TABLE No. 8. LAND DISCOVERED BY ADMIRAL PEARY

Year.	Locality.	Linear Miles.		
			Inland Ice.	Coastal.
1886	Greenland, inland ice . .	100 }	600	
1892	Greenland, inland ice . .	500 }		
	Greenland, north-east . .	30		} 130
	Greenland, Inglefield Gulf .	100		
1899	Grinnell Land . . .	150	? 100	? 50
1900	Greenland, north coast . .	140		} 240
1906	Grant Land, north coast .	100		
	Total . .	1120	? 700	? 420

The query as to the proportion of coastal survey
in Grinnell Land is due to the small scale of Peary's
map; but there is little doubt as to the total, for his
routes are clearly marked in red. Three-fifths of the
"land" he discovered is inland ice. Land lies beneath
the ice-cap, but it is a sterile waste, with nothing
to explore upon its surface, except by glaciologists.
Peary explored very little of the land he discovered.
Inglefield Gulf and McCormick Bay seem to have been
the only localities that were even moderately well
mapped; and only a trace of scientific work was done.

13

Such was the result of Peary's whole life as an explorer. It is commonly said that he spent twenty-three years in the Arctic; but about half this time he was doing his civil engineering work in the dock-yards, preparing for his next expedition, or returning from and lecturing upon his last venture. It will be seen that he was actually in the far north about ten years, spread out over twenty-three years:

	Years.	*Months.*
1886. Greenland, 6th June, to 6th September . . .		3
1891. Greenland, 23rd June, to about end August 1892 .	1	2
1893. Greenland, end July, to end August 1895 . . .	2	1
1896, 1897. Greenland, summer cruises . . about		1
1898. Etah, end July, to end August 1902	4	1
1905. Cape York, 7th August, to 26th September 1906 .	1	1
1908. Cape York, 1st August, to 26th August 1909 . .	1	1
Total . . .	9	10

Three and a half years were spent in Greenland, the remaining six years being devoted to (one is tempted to say "wasted over") vain attempts to reach a certain spot in the Arctic Ocean.

Peary led six expeditions to the Arctic, on the third and last of which no land was discovered. The two summer cruises to Greenland were not expeditions; their sole purpose being to transport the meteoric ironstone to the United States.

The only fair manner in which to judge the results of Peary's life, is to compare them with what his contemporaries have accomplished, as follows :—

TABLE No. 9.

LAND DISCOVERED BY RECENT POLAR EXPLORERS

Explorer.	Dates.	Number of Expeditions.	Approximate Linear Miles Discovered.	Scientific Results.
Peary . .	1886–1909	6	1120	Very poor
Scott . .	1901–1913	2	1635	Excellent
Shackleton .	1907–1916	2	1635	Excellent
Sverdrup .	1898–1902	1	1750	Very good
Amundsen .	1910–1912	1	1750	Poor
Mawson . .	1911–1914	1	1840	Excellent

This shows that Peary did not discover very much land, in comparison with other modern polar explorers and the number of expeditions; but this is by no means all.

The above table fails to bring out the full contrast; for the other explorers, except Amundsen, in addition to their discovery of new lands, carried out an immense amount of valuable work. They made good maps of all the land discovered, and they explored in some detail the more important parts of it. Geological, glaciological, biological, and other surveys were conducted by competent scientists, and frequently by men of the highest standing in their professions. All the British explorers took out *scientific* expeditions; Shackleton having twenty-two, Scott twenty-three, and Mawson twenty-nine trained scientists and technicians.[1] Their winter quarters were scientific stations, fully equipped with modern instruments and apparatus. Their meteorological, magnetic, and other work was of great importance. Dr Charcot's, Dr Bruce's, Dr Nordenskjöld's, and Professor Dry-

[1] If Shackleton's last expedition is included; he took out thirty scientists, etc.

galski's expeditions were equally good from the scientific standpoint, though they did not aspire to the discovery of vast tracts of land. Dr Nansen's First *Fram* Expedition and Captain Sverdrup's Second *Fram* Expedition in the Arctic were of a similar order.

While, therefore, Peary must have full credit for all he actually accomplished, it should be understood that he cannot rank with these other explorers just mentioned. He dissipated too much of his time Pole-seeking. Nor would his attainment of the North Pole have made the slightest difference in this respect. He would then have been a somewhat more successful pioneer than he was; but the difference between north latitudes 88° and 90° is not great, except in the difficulty of reaching them; and this was what Peary, no doubt, thought.

Anything more than a pioneer, and one who gave the world poor maps of his discoveries, Peary never was. He ranks with Amundsen, among his contemporaries; with those who yield to the call of the wild, for fame or for sheer adventure. All Peary's expeditions, like Amundsen's Antarctic expedition, were simply raids into the unknown. Such pioneers have their place; they are the irregular troops of geographical progress, but they can never, of themselves, win decisive victories over nature.

Peary was sedulously puffed, or "boosted" as Americans term it, until popularly supposed to have been a great explorer; but a slight paraphrase of a famous passage aptly gives us the needed corrective: "The writer evidently means to caution us against the practice of puffers, a class of people who have more than once talked the public into the most absurd errors, but who surely never played a more curious or a more difficult trick than when they passed Mr Robert" E. Peary "off upon the world as a great" explorer.

Peary's last journey over the polar pack, even if he

had attained the Pole, would have been of very little value.   It is waste of time and resources to make such journeys as this, unless accurate information is brought back.   Where is Peary's daily meteorological register? He kept none, and *estimated* even his temperatures. He did no biological work; and now, twenty years later, our two leading authorities on the subject cannot agree as to the amount of life beneath the ice! Where are his oceanographical reports?   They do not exist.   Peary missed a golden opportunity to carry on the work of Nansen.   Magnetic observations are particularly needed from the area he crossed; but he never took a magnetician on any expedition.   A glaciologist would have rejoiced at Peary's opportunity of studying the ice-phenomena, for the pack seems to be specially interesting on his routes.   He has given the world no reliable data on any subject.   He was obsessed with the fetish of reaching a certain point. He worked for himself, for his own fame, and paid the advancement of knowledge no more than the merest lip-service.   A glorious opportunity of reaping a rich harvest of substantial results was recklessly thrown away.

Sir Clements Markham "always deprecated the diverting of exploring energy to dashes for the Pole, if this be the sole object"; and he added, with no little discernment, "Since Nansen's discovery that the Pole is in an ice-covered sea there was no longer any special object to be attained in going there." [1]   Peary stirred up a kind of craze for this particular point, thinking he saw in it his pathway to fame; but it was not the most difficult point to reach on the Arctic Ocean.

Dr H. R. Mill said in April 1928, on the subject of allurements to scientists in the polar regions: "The attainment of the South Pole was a matter of no importance at all except as an inducement to heroic young men to go out and make investigations on their

[1] *The Lands of Silence*, p. 351.

way to it. It was one of the worst calamities that
could have happened that the South Pole was discovered
prematurely; it would have been better for geography
if expeditions had been kept going for another century
at least in the effort to reach the Pole." [1]

The attainment of the North Pole by Peary would
have been "a matter of no importance at all." We
may go as far as Dr Mill and say that the false report
that it had been reached was "one of the worst
calamities that could have happened." It certainly
robbed Captain Scott of the South Pole. Had Peary
announced that he had turned back from latitude
88° N., or wherever he got to, the *Fram* would have
made for Bering Strait instead of the Bay of Whales.
But we must not continue to pursue hypothetical
considerations.

Perhaps "heroic young men" will yet go and do
what Peary failed to accomplish. A properly led and
equipped expedition on the pack to the north of Grant
Land and Greenland could do much valuable work.
Should such an expedition be projected, the existence
of Bradley Land should be decided. If it were found,
it would form an excellent advanced base towards
Mr Stefansson's "Pole of Inaccessibility." The evidence seems to be that the ice to the north of Axel
Heiberg Land is a much better sledging surface than
that on Peary's routes. From Bradley Land, if it
exists, Dr Cook's Glacial Island should be sought, and,
if found, investigated; it may be a unique mass of
amphibious ice. In any event, this route to the North
Pole appears to offer decided advantages; and the
Cook controversy would finally be settled.

2. *Peary's Sledging Record.*—Schedule No. 8 is merely
a tabular arrangement of information given by Peary
himself. Its utility depends upon analysis, and this
will follow shortly; but a few explanatory remarks on
the statistics must first be made.

[1] *The Geographical Journal,* September 1928, p. 231.

Schedule No. 8. Peary's Sledging Record (from his own Data)

Date.	Journey.	Sledges.	Distance, Miles.	Days.	Av. Speed, m.p.d.
1892	First crossing, inland ice	Loaded	500	60	8·3
1895	Last crossing, inland ice	Light	502	24¼	20·7
1898	C. Wilkes to C. D'Urville	,,	c. 80 {	21½ hours	c. 80
1899	Ft. Conger to C. D'Urville ; riding	,,	250	11	22·7
	C. D'Urville to Ft. Conger ; riding	Loaded	250	10	25
	Ft. Conger to C. D'Urville ; riding	Light	250	6	42
	Trip to Whale Sound	,,	240 {	6 marches	40 p.mar.
1900	Etah to Ft. Conger	Loaded	342	24	14
	North from C. Jesup	?	c. 16	3½	c. 4½
	South to C. Jesup	?	c. 15	1 march	c. 15
1901	Ft. Conger to Payer Harbour	Light	300	20	15
1902	Payer Harbour to Ft. Conger	Loaded	300	14	21
	North from C. Hecla	,,	87 [1]	16	5·4
	South to C. Hecla	?	87	? 7	? 12
	Ft. Conger to Payer Harbour	Light	300	11	27
1906	North from Pt. Moss	Loaded	251	47	5·3
1909	Cape Columbia to lat. 87° 47′ N.	,,	289	31	9·3
	Lat. 87° 47′ to lat. 89° 57′ N.	,,	130	5	26
	Lat. 89° 57′ to lat. 87° 47′N.	,,	130	2	65
	Lat. 87° 47′ N. to Cape Columbia	?	289	13	22

The long march of 1898 was estimated by Peary at ninety miles; but the distance was seventy miles in a

[1] All distances on the pack-ice are minutes of latitude.

straight line, and he admitted, in later years, that he
had been wont seriously to overestimate his earlier
distances. All his mileage, except across Greenland,
was *estimated*, and we have seen how frequently the
estimates disagreed with the latitude observations.
The number of days occupied by the trip to Whale
Sound, in 1899, is not given; sixty to seventy miles
was the estimated distance on the last day of this
journey. It is perhaps questionable if the short
journey over the pack from Cape Jesup, in 1900, should
be given; but it is of interest as the first of its kind,
besides being of some little value in showing how little
Peary's speed over the pack increased, until he had
dismissed his witnesses.

Usually he gave the particulars of his journeys in
marches instead of days. This is of no moment when
one march is made every day; but on most long
journeys a few days are lost through blizzards, and, on
the pack, from open channels. It is useless to plead
that a party is capable of travelling several miles a day
faster than conditions permit. The only point that
matters is the speed actually made under the existing
conditions; and this necessitates only miles *per diem*
being considered. Peary's "System" involved waiting
for channels to close or freeze over, thus requiring
lon;er than if kayaks were used.

The value of the analysis given on the next page,
and of the comparisons with other sledge travellers, in
estimating Peary's accomplishments, is obvious; but
before commenting upon it, we must add a reference
to Sverdrup's and Rasmussen's sledging.

During the same four years that the *Windward*
Expedition was in the Arctic, Captain Sverdrup's
parties were sledging in the same district. The surfaces over which they travelled were about the same
as Peary's, apart from his first attacks on the polar
pack; but the Norwegian sledges were superior to
Peary's. Hence, Sverdrup's speed was somewhat

SCHEDULE No. 9. ANALYSIS OF PEARY'S AUTHENTIC SLEDGING
SPEEDS AND SOME COMPARISONS

1. JOURNEYS ON ICE OTHER THAN PACK-ICE

(a) *With Light Sledges*

		Distance, Miles.	Speed, m.p.d.
1899	Ft. Conger to C. D'Urville	250	22·7
	Ft. Conger to C. D'Urville	250	41·5
	Whale Sound trip	240	40 p. mar.
1901	Ft. Conger to Payer Harbour	300	15
1902	Ft. Conger to Payer Harbour	300	27

(b) *With Loaded Sledges*

1899	C. D'Urville to Ft. Conger	250	25
1900	Etah to Ft. Conger	342	14
1902	Payer Harbour to Ft. Conger	300	21
1912	*Rasmussen in Greenland*	628	36·6

2. JOURNEYS ON THE PACK-ICE, PRIOR TO 1ST APRIL 1909

1902	C. Hecla to lat. 84° 11′ N.	87	5·4
1906	Pt. Moss to lat. 86° 17′ N.	251	5·3
1909	C. Columbia to lat. 87° 47′ N.	289	9·3
	Six best consecutive days	92	15·3
1895	Nansen, from *Fram* to lat. 86° 14′ N.	165	6·6
	Nansen, lat. 86° 14′ to 82° 21′ N.	233	4·3
1900	Cagni. Main part of journey	601	6·3
	Cagni. Lat. 86° 34′ N. to 82° 30′ N.	244	13·5
	Cagni. Six best consecutive days	127·5	21·2

higher than Peary's, running from 20 to 25 m.p.d.
with full loads.[1] On some days, 29, 35, 37, 38, and 39
miles were covered with loaded sledges.[2] When the
sledges were running light, all distances up to eighty
miles in a day and a half were done. The accuracy of
Sverdrup's statements may be relied upon.

[1] See e.g. *New Land*, vol. i, p. 287.
[2] *Ibid.*, pp. 353, 281, 331, 120, 332.

In 1912 Messrs Rasmussen and Freuchen crossed Greenland, on a course roughly parallel, and very near, to Peary's route, at an average rate of 36·6 m.p.d. with full loads. The conditions of Rasmussen's and Peary's journeys were so similar that the comparison is perfectly fair, with the observation that a pioneer must always have the credit of breaking a new trail. Peary's last journey over the inland ice was a race with death, but his speed was only 20·7 m.p.d. with light loads.

We find, then, that Peary was not as fast as other sledge travellers, such as Sverdrup, Cagni, and Rasmussen. MacMillan also was faster than Peary; but there may be no need to extend this comparison further. Let us now turn to our analysis of the speeds over the polar pack.

The great difference between the pack-ice and other sledging surfaces should have been seen already. All Peary's witnessed speeds over the pack average about one-third of his rate elsewhere. He raised this to about one-half in 1909, and then spoilt everything by his unwitnessed claims of miraculous marches. That he thought better of this, and tried to reduce his best day from ninety to fifty miles, is good evidence that he did not even do the shorter distance. We must, therefore, eliminate his unwitnessed figures.

His best authentic speed, as far as latitude 87° 47′ N., in 1909, at last justified his original estimate of 10 m.p.d., as made to the Secretary of the United States Navy in 1905.[1] As Peary did not surpass, nor indeed equal, the speed of other sledge travellers off the pack, neither did he on that arduous surface; and the reason is not far to seek.

Sledging speed depends, not only upon the surface, but also upon the efficiency of the equipment. Peary's sledges and his system of dog-traction were relatively crude and absolutely unscientific, for they were simply improved Eskimo methods. His sledges were of solid

1 See p. 54.

beams and extremely heavy. It has been said that
they had 50 lb. of useless wood in them. Dr Nansen's
sledges and whole transport system, especially as used
by Sverdrup, Cagni, Amundsen, and Scott, were not
only much better than Peary's, but the best that have
ever been used. Amundsen's twelve-foot sledges
weighed 53 lb.;[1] and Scott's eleven-foot sledges only
40–47 lb.[2] Peary's sledges "averaged ninety-five
pounds" in weight.[3] The result was that nearly all
these other explorers drove faster than Peary. Cagni
may have had a somewhat better surface for the main
part of his splendid journey than that on Peary's
route; but against this must be set the excessively low
temperatures endured for several weeks; they were
the lowest recorded on any polar journey and were a
serious handicap. His equipment was excellent.

The comparison, therefore, of Cagni's 244 miles,
at an average of $13\frac{1}{2}$ m.p.d., with Peary's 289 miles,
nine years later, at only 9·3 m.p.d. does not seem
unfair to either of these explorers. It should be added
that Cagni's distance cannot be increased to the same
mileage as Peary's by extending the former a few days
longer, because of the disintegration of the pack. If
Cagni's previous two days are added, his distance
becomes 279 miles in twenty days; and the next day
before this, 22nd April 1900, being 18 miles, he did
297 miles at the fine average, for the polar pack, of
14·1 m.p.d.

Comment on the six best days of each explorer is
needless; but it should be pointed out that Cagni's
whole journey was the finest ever made over the Arctic
pack-ice. Peary has left no authentic distances to
compare with Cagni's 600 miles at over 6 m.p.d.;
though Peary *may* have done about 300 miles back to
Cape Columbia at approximately 18 m.p.d. Cagni's

[1] *The South Pole*, vol. i, p. 349.
[2] *The Voyage of the "Discovery*," vol. i, p. 424.
[3] *Secrets of Polar Travel*, p. 250.

transport system being superior to Peary's, it will be seen that the latter's unwitnessed claims of speed are highly improbable and most of them impossible.

SCHEDULE No. 10. APPROXIMATE DISTANCES SLEDGED BY
PEARY PERSONALLY [1]

Year.	Journey.	Miles.	Miles.	Miles.
1886	Reconnaissance in Greenland	200	..	..
1892	Around Inglefield Gulf	200	..	..
	To Navy Cliff and back	1200	..	..
	Around Inglefield Gulf	200	..	..
			1800	..
1894	Attempt on ice-cap journey	250	..	..
	In search of meteorites	c. 100	..	..
	Winter of 1894–1895	c. 200	..	..
			550	..
1895	To Navy Cliff and back	1200	..	..
			1200	..
1898	Autumn, estimated	500	—	3550
	Winter depot journeys	750	..	..
			1250	..
1899	Conger to ship, riding	250	..	..
	Ship to Conger, riding	250	..	..
	Greenland reconnaissance	50	..	..
	Conger to ship	250	..	..
	Surveying, etc.	c. 200	..	..
	Whale Sound trip	240	..	..
	Various short trips	120	..	..
			1360	..
1900	Etah to Conger	c. 350	..	..
	Conger to Cape Jesup	c. 350	..	..
	On sea ice	c. 30	..	..
	C. Jesup to east and back	200	..	..
	C. Jesup to Conger	c. 350	..	..
	To Lake Hazen and back	200	..	..
			1480	..
1901	To Lincoln Bay and back	c. 80	..	..
	Payer Harbour	300	..	..
	Etah, etc.	200	..	..
			580	..

[1] It is impossible to get the distances accurately from Peary's maps.

Year.	Journey.	Miles.	Miles.	Miles.
1902	To Conger	300	..	..
	C. Hecla and back	200	..	..
	C. Hecla to lat. 84° 17′ and back	226	..	..
	Conger to ship	300	..	..
			1026	..
1906	C. Sheridan to Pt. Moss	60		5696
	Pt. Moss to lat. ? 87° 6′ N.	? 326	..	..
	? 87° 6′ N. to C. Neumeyer	? 320	..	..
	C. Neumeyer to C. Sheridan	c. 150	..	..
	Western journey	c. 660	..	..
			1516	..
1909	Probably about	..	1000	..
				2516
				11762
	Add 10 per cent.			1176
				12938

Probably about 13,000 miles, in ten years.

3. *Peary's Sledging Systems.*—When Peary first threw himself into Arctic sledging he instituted a system that appears to have had a high efficiency, and by means of which he made two journeys, each of these as long as a journey to the North Pole from Cape Sheridan. This system may be described briefly as consisting in a simplified outfit. The weight of the heaviest sledge was cut down to 48 lb.; and Peary correctly argued that the greatest speed was only to be attained by the smallest party. A fleet of sledges, like a naval squadron, must set its pace by that of its slowest unit.

In 1892, when Peary left his supporting party about 120 miles out, he continued his journey with one companion and thirteen dogs, and he completed therewith a distance of 1200 miles. In 1895 he began a journey of 1250 miles, with two companions and seventeen dogs. As he became acquainted with the sledging conditions of the polar pack on the one hand, and with wealthy supporters on the other hand, he completely changed his original system. No doubt he needed more dog and man power on the pack than on the inland ice; but he also found that an impressive organisation had only one disadvantage, when compared with a more modest one—it was slower.

The first of Peary's "Essentials of Success," as he entitles one of the chapters in his last book,[1] was his so-called "Peary System." He described it as consisting of fourteen parts, only one of which, the use of Eskimos, could be called his own. No less than ten of these parts are quite general, and some of them are universal. Two of them are rather ridiculous. The first of these is "To know by long experience the best way to cross wide leads of open water."[2] Peary never did cross them; he waited for them to close or to freeze over. Water can be crossed properly in no other way than by boat or canoe, and he never carried these, as Nansen and Cagni did. The other ridiculous part of this advertised "System" is printed in italics. The gist of it is "to return by the same route followed on the upward march." This assumes a rigid sledging surface, while the pack is ever moving; but this point has been dealt with.

The pioneer party is not included as part of this peculiar system; but Peary wrote: "The pioneer party is original with my expeditions."[3] It is true that pioneers, as an institution, may not have been used by any previous explorer; nevertheless, H.R.H. the Duke of the Abruzzi has the credit of first suggesting them. This he did as a result of Commander Cagni's great journey in 1902. As there was a copy of the Prince's book[4] on the *Roosevelt*,[5] it is evident

[1] Chapter XXII of *The North Pole*.
[2] *The North Pole*, p. 202.
[3] *Ibid.*, p. 204.   [4] On the "*Polar Star*" in the *Arctic Sea*.
[5] *The North Pole*, p. 180.

that Peary copied His Royal Highness without acknowledgment, as he copied other suggestions also.

In the course of his "Observations with regard to any future expedition towards the North Pole," the Prince advocated Peary's route, and wrote: "Several men must be employed to clear the way wherever it may be necessary." [1] This was the result of Cagni's experience on the pack. He said: "I had also observed how necessary it always was to send forward at least two men to prepare the way." [2] The Prince intimates that, at 10 m.p.d., "if they did not reach the Pole, they would at least come very near it, and then, returning to 84° latitude, land on the north coast of Greenland." This advice Peary took three years after the Duke's book was published, or in 1906; though the Greenland coast was not then furnished with the depots suggested.

4. *The Size of Peary's Sledging Units.*—The smaller the unit, in polar sledging, the greater the efficiency. This is axiomatic; but as safety must be considered also, there should never be less than two men on polar journeys. Navigation, usually, is of sufficient importance to require a check on the possibility of individual mistakes, and the usefulness of the work may be doubled by having two men instead of one. Peary was one of a unit of two on his first reconnaissance in Greenland, though the usefulness of the trip is problematical; and, again, he made his first crossing of the inland ice, in 1892, accompanied only by one companion.

Units of three men, probably, are the ideal. Some speed is lost, in comparison with smaller units, but this is more than compensated for by the increased safety and usefulness of the party. In case of emergency, for which provision should be made, a smaller unit than one of three men is handicapped. Two men can save the life of one, when one man would be unable

[1] *On the "Polar Star,"* vol. i, p. 274.　　[2] *Ibid.,* vol. ii, p. 392.

to do so, and two lives might be lost instead of none. This unit has the weighty support of Sir Douglas Mawson, who used it throughout his great Antarctic expedition of 1911–1914.

Peary agreed with these principles in theory, and practised them, wherever possible, on all his journeys, except his last. In 1895 he had planned for three parties to do independent work across the ice-cap, in two units of three, and one unit of two, men. This would have necessitated eight men making the main journey. Only three actually went. On his next important journey, that along the north coast of Greenland in 1900, he started with two supporting sledges. He sent back one of them, with two Eskimos, at the Black Horn Cliffs, and dismissed another pair later; leaving himself, Henson, and one Eskimo as the unit for the main part of the journey.

His attempt to reach the Pole in 1902 was a good example of his sledging system, as applied to long journeys. Payer Harbour was left with fourteen sledges, and Fort Conger with nine. Near Cape Hecla three more Eskimos were sent back, leaving Peary with Henson and four Eskimos. On, apparently, the seventh day from land, two more Eskimos were dismissed and the unit of four went forward. The exceptionally rough going of the polar pack was paid the compliment of the extra man, and no doubt more strength was needed. We have seen, however, that the speed was slower.

On this attempt, Peary learnt that special measures would have to be taken in order to meet the unusual difficulties of the pack-ice. The result was that his next attempt in 1906 was fortified with a pioneer party and numerous supports, in addition to his base being on the coast of the Arctic Ocean. This did not increase his rate of progress as much as expected. The great storm left him, as he complained, with eight mouths to feed. He could not cut down this number and, of course, the progress of so large a party was not fast. The mystery of his claim to have got it along sixty minutes in two days has been mentioned.

Peary was able to carry out his plan, on his last expedition, unhindered by serious blizzards. The plan was progressively to reduce his personnel to a party of six, which was said to go north of latitude 87° 47′ N. No explanation is offered for taking so large a unit for the final dash, when every argument pointed to a smaller one being much more advantageous. A party of six was incapable of the speed that a small unit could maintain. The normal unit on this expedition was one of four men. Yet Peary took Henson and four Eskimos, after dismissing Bartlett, as if for the deliberate purpose of making his 180 miles in two days as incredible as possible.

Of any two men, one will be the better walker and the faster sledger; from which it follows that every man added to a party reduces its speed. Four-men units are the largest that have done any authentic high sledging speeds, such as Cagni's on the pack and Rasmussen's in Greenland. Nansen's journey was made with one companion. A party of six on an important trip, with only one white man, is a mob.

Captain Scott adopted four-men units, and no doubt they were the most suitable for his purpose. They are, of course, safer than parties of three men, an example of which may well end this section. Captain (now Rear-Admiral) Evans was sent back with Scott's last supporting party of only three men. When Evans became too ill for travelling farther, Crean went on alone for help, leaving Lashly with the invalid. A blizzard broke half an hour after Crean arrived at Hut Point. Had this blizzard come on an hour sooner, it is highly probable that this whole party might have perished. Whether a companion with Crean would infallibly have saved the situation is problematical; it would depend upon the companion.

14

5. *Supporting Parties.*—Peary said: "It would be a physical impossibility for any man to reach the North Pole and return" without both pioneers and supporting parties.[1] It had not been a "physical impossibility," if we may believe his records, for him to travel a longer distance in Greenland without them than that from Cape Columbia to the Pole. The journey across the ice-cap in 1895 would not be an event to look back upon with satisfaction; yet the three-man party reached a point 600 miles away without support, and they returned, though by a narrow margin. This, however, was not on the polar pack, where Peary wished his supports to keep the trail open for his return. His statements on this, as on so many other points, are conflicting.

His main reason for using supports appeared to be the necessity of carrying "all the way to the Pole and back" the whole of the supplies.[2] In other words, depots cannot be left on the outward journey to be picked up on the return, because of the movement of the ice. Peary then proceeds to explain, at some length, how the supports "keep the trail open for the rapid return of the main party." This, he said, was done by knitting "together all the faults and breaks in the trail"; and he further explains that "the passage of the supporting party," on its return, "would itself renew the broken trail . . . packing down the ice and snow."[3] Thus it seems clear that, where the outward trail is faulted, as he wrote, "either to the east or west," *a new trail* is made by the supports for the return of the polar party.

Peary then adds a statement that appears to contradict all this, when he says that "the snow igloos built on the outward journey" are "reoccupied on the return journey."[4] If this were possible, depots could be left, and no supports were necessary; but how

[1] *The North Pole*, p. 204.   [2] *Ibid.*, p. 206.
[3] *Ibid.*, p. 207.   [4] *Ibid.*, p. 208.

could it be possible on drifting ice? If the last
supporting party is followed back to land soon enough,
its trail and igloos could, of course, be used; but
Peary seems careful not to make this clear, lest it
should appear that he did not go far beyond Bartlett's
turning-point.

The explanation may be found in the necessity of
accounting for the miraculous speed after Bartlett's
dismissal. Peary wrote that from 50 *to* 100 *per cent.*
greater speed than that of the outward journey was
possible in returning over the existing trails. Even this
would not have enabled him to reach the Pole, to which
he had to make his own trail for the last 150 miles.
The speed as far as Bartlett's turning-point averaged
about 10 (9·3 geo.) m.p.d. Fifty per cent. more is
15 m.p.d. and 100 per cent. more is 20 m.p.d. Peary's
speed was from 30 to 75 m.p.d., if he reached the Pole,
or from 200 per cent. to 500 per cent. faster! Had he
been recording what actually happened he could not
have made such mistakes.

In concluding this part of the subject we should
notice, perhaps, that Mr Stefansson made journeys of
about 1200 and 1000 miles, in 1915 and 1916, with
one or two companions, largely over the pack-ice and
entirely without supporting parties. He cannot fairly
be compared with other Arctic travellers because of
his dependence on the chase for support, and he used
no more than six or seven large dogs, which pulled the
greatest weight on record, or as much as 240 lb. each.
It is good to know that he brought all his dogs back
with him, alive and well.

CHAPTER XII

EXAGGERATIONS, MARVELS, AND MYSTERIES

" Travellers of every station
Draw long bows of every nation ;
Nothing but exaggeration
Of the climes where they have been.
Neighbours, since ye thus beseech me,
I'll my little story teach ye ;
May such dangers never reach ye
As have caused me fearful strife."

Old Song.

1. THE MYSTERY OF THE MARVELLOUS MARCHES. 2. THE MARVEL OF SLEDGING WITHOUT SLEEP. 3. EXAGGER-ATED PRESSURE RIDGES. 4. MINOR MYSTERIES.

1. ROBERT E. PEARY was a remarkable traveller. When he walked twelve miles a day over the pack-ice, he tells us that, ten years earlier, he would have said the distance was "fully fifteen miles." On the same journey, when only Eskimos and a negro were with him, he affirmed that he walked at 30 m.p.d., and added that his Eskimos (who would say anything to please him) "said forty." When his only chance to reach the North Pole was by walking 180 miles in two days (none but his Eskimos and faithful negro again being with him), he subsequently said that he did no more than sixty miles on one day, and he proved his physical fitness for such feats by walking fifty miles in *two* days!

No ordinary man could say and do these things; but Peary was unique. An attempt to delineate his original character will be made in the last chapter. We must now consider more fully a few of his remarkable sayings and doings.

The mystery that enshrouds the world's sledging record of 150 miles of latitude in less than 2¼ days still lures us on, for it is of surpassing interest. Let us first notice the peculiar manner in which this magnificent performance was presented to the world.

Peary began the account of how he left the Pole by devoting a page to the perils of the path back to land. He then outlined his plan of making *double* marches on the return journey, eating lunch at one of the igloo-camps built on the outward journey, and sleeping only at each alternate outward camp. The distance between these camps, from the Pole to Bartlett's farthest north, averaged about thirty-six miles, and the ice is ever in motion; yet nothing is said to indicate that there would be any difficulty in carrying out this part of the novel programme. Distances of 70 m.p.d. over the polar pack had no terrors for Peary. Open channels and drifting floes are there, indeed, described; but not as if the writer felt they had any power to endanger, or even delay, his progress.

After two and a half pages, the story of the actual journey is begun. Two pages [1] are devoted to the account of the whole distance from latitude 89° 57′ N. to latitude 87° 47′ N.; of which the first half-page is occupied with the record of taking a sounding. For, be it noted, Peary has ample time, not merely to perform this operation, but also, in the calm assurance of his latent power, to complete his tale of leagues.

Thus, only one page and a half remain for the description of the most marvellous sledge journey ever made by man. It is a curt manner in which to treat a miraculous performance. We are merely told that "the first camp at 89° 25′ was reached in good time." The distance to this point, apart from deviations and drift, was 36·8 statute miles; and these miles were walked by exhausted men and dogs, who had

[1] *The North Pole*, pp. 304–306.

tramped, immediately before starting, forty-one miles about the Pole, *without any sleep in between.*

We are asked to believe that after twenty-four hours' incessant activity, another thirty-seven miles, at least, could be done. No more is said about the second stage of the return than about the first. After sleeping "a few hours," Peary wrote, "hurried on again, Eskimos and dogs on the *qui vive,*" [1] as if another thirty-two miles could flash past like a weaver's shuttle; after which a further 28¾ miles had to be got in somehow before 9th April, which Peary appears to keep for his last 51¾ miles to Bartlett's last camp.

Peary claimed to have made the world's record for speed over the pack on his previous expedition in 1906. This was one degree of latitude in two days, if we can accept that somewhat dubious statement, performed at the rate of about three miles an hour. He slightly exceeded this daily average on the last day of his final spurt to the Pole, in 1909, according to his account, by covering thirty-two minutes at a slightly lower speed per hour. Suddenly he nearly trebles his own world's record, though that was hardly above suspicion. Any such distance is absolutely unprecedented in the whole history of polar travel, and is comparable only to the world's walking record, made in a few ounces of clothing. Now comes the deepest part of the mystery, if mystery it be: *Peary carefully abstains from mentioning a word as to the portentous distance he has done!*

Consider what this means. In all his earlier writings he had given great prominence to the speeds and distances he had attained, whenever they were good. He always took great pride in a long march and a quick journey. It was one of his forms of sport, and was most commendable, except for his tendency to exaggerate his exploits, and for his uniform rule of suppressing his poor performances. With pardonable pride he expatiated upon his thirty miles a day in 1906;

[1] *The North Pole,* p. 305.

pardonable, that is, if he did it. Why then did he not point out how, in 1909, he walked thrice that distance in the same time? He actually leaves us to find out his mileage from the latitudes; this is no difficult matter, but it is one that the general public could not do. Is not this a peculiar, not to say a suspicious, circumstance? Everyone knows that to hide his light under a bushel was not one of Peary's failings. His silence, therefore, is a positive portent. He must have had some very good reason for suppressing all reference to this new world's record, as such a thing is absolutely unique in all his writings. It was foreign to his nature. He always suppressed his short marches; but this is the only occasion when he suppressed his distance because it was too great. We cannot credit the exception.

In considering Peary's speed on his return, it must be remembered that when he and his equipage left the Pole, as stated in his story, they had already travelled at least 545 geographical miles since leaving the ship. During the five or six days previous to leaving the Pole they had averaged over 30 m.p.d. They had travelled forty miles about the Pole, and were setting out on their return with very little rest. So that, while they *may* have been fit enough to make fairly long marches, though this is somewhat doubtful, certainly they were not sufficiently fresh for any record-breaking speeds. Indeed, we have Peary's previous experience to confirm this, for he wrote, concerning the start of his return in 1906: "The interest and excitement of the advance were gone, the reaction had come and my feet dragged like lead. As a matter of fact the return journey, after the eagerness and excitement of pushing ahead is over, is always the hardest part of the work." [1]

All this was accentuated in 1909 by the increased strain of the greater distance, and by their pronounced exhaustion, as the result of the final spurt, to which

[1] *Nearest the Pole*, p. 139.

reference is made several times. We are now in a
position to examine, and to reconstruct, Peary's record
of his return to Bartlett's last camp.

TABLE No. 10

PEARY'S RETURN TO BARTLETT'S LAST CAMP

(Worked out at a speed of 2½ geographical miles an hour)

1909.		Lat. N.
April 7	4 p.m. Started from Camp Jesup	89° 57′
	6 p.m. Stopped for sounding	89° 52′
	8 p.m. Started 27-miles march.	
8	7 a.m. First sleep, 4–5 hours	89° 25′
	1 p.m. Started 28-miles march.	
	12 (midnight). Reached lunch-igloo	88° 57′
9	3 a.m. Started 25-miles march.	
	1 p.m. Second sleep	88° 32′
	10 p.m. *45 miles to march in less than 2 hours!* To 87° 47′	

Peary left Camp Jesup at 4 p.m. on 7th April, and
after going five geographical miles stopped to take a
sounding. The speed could hardly have been more
than 2½ geographical m.p.h., for this was the speed
given for the final spurt from Bartlett's last camp. The
party might have slightly exceeded this rate for short
spells, but the only safe assumption, in the absence of
definite information, will be to keep to this rate of
travel through the return to latitude 87° 47′ N. They
were not in good enough condition to have increased
it for any length of time, and their average, during this
remarkable part of their journey, was most probably
less than this. Hence, it would be about 6 p.m. when
they stopped to make ready the sounding apparatus.
It was recent ice, the thickness of which is not given.
They had to chop through it, and as they found 1500
fathoms with no bottom, it must have been at least
8 p.m. and possibly 9 p.m. before they resumed the

trail. They abandoned the sounding apparatus, which weighed 18 lb.

They had to travel twenty-seven geographical miles to the last outward camp, in latitude 89° 25′ N. They would arrive here, if they could do the distance without a halt, at about 7 a.m. or 8 a.m. on the 8th. It is extremely doubtful if they would be able to march the whole distance without stopping, for on the final spurt to the Pole they had made a halt, half-way, for tea, and they were in better form on the outward journey than on the return. We are told that they had their old tracks to follow, but this is dealt with elsewhere. At latitude 89° 25′ N. they slept "a few hours," of which four or five would be very few indeed, as will be seen when it is remembered how little sleep they had obtained during the last week.[1]

The very shortest halt that we can assume they made here is six hours, during which they would have two meals and four or five hours' sleep. It would then be from 1 p.m. to 2 p.m. on the 8th when they started off again, if they could do so after so little rest. Assuming that they were still able to maintain a speed of 2½ geographical m.p.h., it would be about midnight of the 8th to 9th when they reached the lunch-igloo, twenty-eight miles away, in latitude 88° 57′ N., again supposing that the whole run could be accomplished without a halt. This is very unlikely, to say the least of it, and perhaps impossible, with tired dogs. The weather was fine, we are told. Peary said that it was necessary to rest the dogs here, which is quite natural after over 600 miles of sledging on the polar pack, ending with a week at 30 m.p.d. before leaving the Pole; but it scarcely accords with the energy necessary to cover 150 miles in two days.

Three hours would not be much rest for the dogs. Assuming, however, that they had no more than this, they would leave the lunch-igloo at 3 a.m. It was

[1] See next section.

twenty-five geographical miles to the next outward camp, in latitude 88° 32′ N., and we cannot believe that they could maintain the high average of 2½ m.p.h. throughout this march, for this speed is very nearly the highest Peary ever claims to have done, and his dogs were getting played out. Let us give him a better chance than he could actually have had, and assume something nearly, if not quite, impossible, that it would be 1 p.m. on the 9th when they got their second sleep after leaving the Pole.

Human and canine endurance had at last been strained to its limit, and we are told that they could scarcely keep awake to eat their supper. This rest must have been a longer one, for outraged nature always takes her revenge. They must have slept at least eight or nine hours. Nine hours would bring the time to 10 p.m. on the 9th; but *Peary says that they had done a further forty-five geographical miles by then*, or the "night" of the 9th, which must be before midnight. This is the miracle that he ignores.

One other aspect of the subject requires more attention than it has received hitherto. The attempt we have made to compile a connected and credible account of Peary's return from the Pole to Bartlett's last camp, out of his own materials, credits men and dogs with powers which, from his own statements, they were most unlikely to have possessed at the time. Yet, although the speed assumed was about the highest he had ever maintained, it left forty-five geographical miles that could not have been done in the time recorded. He exerted his party to the utmost on the final spurt, when he wrote of their freshness and energy; but they could not exceed 2½ m.p.h. then, and he admitted that, in three marches, they were getting played out by that speed. He often mentioned their exhaustion when in the polar area, yet his claim to have attained the Pole rests upon a belief that they could travel *greater distances when they*

were exhausted than when they were fresh. Peary told
us that, on the return, they covered the same distance
in two days instead of five, or an average of 65 geographical m.p.d. when exhausted and 26 m.p.d. when
fresh. On p. 285 he complains of "the physical
exhaustion of the forced marches of the last five days,"
at *only* about 30 m.p.d. Then with an incredibly
small amount of sleep, they travel forty miles about
the Pole and embark on their miraculous journey.
Their speed actually increases with their advancing
weakness. After insisting on the exhausted state of
the whole outfit, as the result of five days at 30 m.p.d.,
Peary expects to be believed that he could treble this
speed. His exhaustion at the Pole is insisted upon in
his biography.[1]

Sixteen or seventeen years after this attempt to
hide an impossible performance, yet one that had to
be performed in order to claim the Pole, Commander
Green's excellent biography appeared.[2] Great were
our hopes that light would be thrown upon this dark
portion of Peary's record. What do we find?

We read, on p. 306, how the hero bids farewell to
the Pole, and then: *"The future—ah, how it beckoned:*
(his italics) for the long trek south was a cold and
bitter penance. . . . The biting wind penetrated. . . .
Thought of the bright future sustained the plodding
traveller . . ." and so on. *"Hurry-hurry"* (his italics).
"We rushed on to-day, 12th April. . . ."[3] *Too late.*

We yearn for light, and, behold, darkness! The
gloom has deepened with advancing years. Here is a
perfectly transparent evasion of the one thing that
matters. The crucial difficulty in accepting Peary's
claim to have reached the Pole is deliberately omitted.
Unless Commander Green could explain how Peary
did his 150 miles of latitude in two days, it was vain

[1] *Peary the Man who Refused to Fail*, Fitzhugh Green, pp. 303, 305.
[2] *Ibid.*
[3] *Ibid.*, pp. 306–307.

purpose had been achieved, so they had "a few hours of absolutely necessary sleep." He said that he could not sleep for long, however, and it must have been for less than six hours. He was far too busy, afterwards, travelling his forty-one miles about the Pole and taking observations to think of resting until the afternoon of the 7th. Then he was too excited to rest properly; and as he could not get to sleep when he tried, he started his dusky companions off on the return.

They must have been in the exhausted state that Peary emphasises; but how could men and dogs, in that condition, dash off nearly a hundred miles in a day?

On reaching latitude 89° 25′ N., on their return, "a few hours' sleep" was taken, after travelling 89 miles without any, and 131 miles on less than six hours of it. No sleep was permitted at the next camp, 37 miles farther, so we can well believe that "it took all our will-power to reach the next igloo," *another* 30 miles on, where Peary said: "We did it, and were asleep almost before we had finished our supper." [1] Thus they had done 67 miles since the previous short sleep, 156 miles with no more than four or five hours' sleep, and 198 miles on two naps, one of them being of less than six hours' duration.

3. *Exaggerated Pressure Ridges.*—Some of Peary's extraordinary statements may be accounted for partly, though not justified, by his genius for exaggeration. He was by no means alone in the possession of this ability. There are men, usually of a boastful kind, who magnify nearly everything they refer to; whose stories ascend, like those of an American skyscraper, to dizzy heights; and who are said to deceive themselves, eventually, into believing their own inventions. Peary's powers will be seen by a reference to the height of the pressure ridges he reported. It is not surprising that a man who could walk 180 miles in two days, near

[1] *The North Pole*, p. 305.

TYPES OF PACK ICE: IV.

facing p. 222

the Pole, and with scarcely any sleep during the process, should also be obliged to negotiate, at other times and in other places, the Brobdingnagian hummocks that Peary found strewn across his path.

The *lowest* ridges mentioned by Peary were "twenty-five to fifty feet" high.[1] Dr Nansen writes: "In the accounts of Arctic expeditions one often reads descriptions of pressure ridges or pressure hummocks as high as fifty feet. These are fairy tales. The authors of such fantastic descriptions cannot have taken the trouble to measure. During the whole period of our drifting and of our travels over the icefields in the far north, I only once saw a hummock of a greater height than 23 feet."[2] It would be unreasonable to expect that Peary could pause in his headlong flights for the purpose of measuring the heights of the ridges. It is most reasonable, however, to remember that, while Peary's course over the pack-ice was meteoric in its swiftness, Nansen dwelt for three years on it, and was, moreover, a scientist whose word can be trusted.

The *highest* pressure ridges mentioned by Peary lay about seventy miles north of Cape Neumeyer, on the north coast of Greenland. These, he wrote, were "from the size of paving-stones to literally and without exaggeration the dome of the Capitol."[3] One must not, perhaps, take such statements quite literally, even when Peary tells us to do so. Nor need we seek for the height of the dome, for he intends us to understand that these ridges were approximately the height of the Capitol, which is 275 feet.

Dr MacMillan was sent, subsequently, to take soundings to the north of Cape Morris Jesup. This cape is on the same coast as Cape Neumeyer, and here also Peary had reported stupendous ridges. The

[1] *Nearest the Pole*, p. 327 ; see also *The North Pole*, p. 275.
[2] *Farthest North*, vol. i, p. 241.
[3] *Nearest the Pole*, pp. 146–147.

depth in latitude 84° 15′ N., or about twenty miles nearer land than the "Capitol" ridges, was 91 fathoms. This indicates approximately the position of the edge of the continental shelf, near which Peary's 200-foot ridges must have been. The continental edge is the 100-fathom contour line. Pure ice has eight parts submerged to one above the water-line. Most ice, being less solid, floats with from four to six parts submerged. Hence, ice 200 feet high would have a depth of from 800 to 1600 feet, unless it was aground. It could float a few miles farther from the coast than the continental edge; but we have insufficient data for definite conclusions. We can only be sure that to report pressure ridges, seventy miles off the coast of Greenland, of twice the average height of Antarctic shelf ice, is a very "tall story."

On returning from his polar attempt in 1902, when a little south of latitude 84° 17′ N., Peary wrote: "Our tracks [1] now disappeared under a huge pressure ridge, which I estimated to be from 75 to 100 feet high." [2] Cape Hecla, his objective, lies in latitude 82° 50′ N., so this monster was about 100 miles from land. It was seen near the position (85 miles north of Cape Columbia) where, in 1909, 825 fathoms were found. It seems impossible that this ice could have been aground, and consequently its height is unaccountable.

Glaciologists are not satisfied about these ridges, as we shall see, more particularly, very shortly. Ice of 100 feet in height must be from 500–600 feet thick. Perhaps we are wasting time in taking this matter seriously; but Peary persuaded the world to take his polar claim seriously. Every effort has been made to believe his statements, with somewhat indifferent success.

In his last book he is content to affirm that the pressure on his route was "a few rods" in height.

---

[1] *I.e.* the outward tracks they were then retracing.
[2] *Nearest the Pole*, p. 345.

This has to be translated into less vague terms before it can be dealt with. We cannot say that "a few" is less than three; on which assumption the ice may have been from three to six rods, or approximately from 50–100 feet in height.

Let us turn, with relief, to the assured results of modern science. We have quoted Dr Nansen to the effect that, during three years' continual residence among pressure ridges, he never saw one as much as thirty feet in height. Mr J. M. Wordie, as a glaciologist,[1] endorses from the Antarctic Nansen's information. During fifteen months "in the Weddell Sea it was quite exceptional for any ridges to be as much as fifteen to twenty feet high."[2] This sea occupies a huge re-entrant angle in the coast of Antarctica, an alignment that would tend to increase, rather than diminish, the normal height of ridges, as compared with those found on an open ocean. Mr Wordie rightly says: "There has always been a tendency to exaggerate this feature." Messrs Wright and Priestley (our latest glaciological authorities) state, from their observations on the opposite side of Antarctica to the Weddell Sea, that 15–20 feet is the normal height of the *biggest* ridges.[3]

Admiral Kolchak estimates "the average height above water of floating hummocks to be 12 feet."[4] The above has reference only to ice that is floating freely. The pack will pile itself up against land to 80 or 100 feet, as Captain Sverdrup found on the coast of Axel Heiberg Land.[5] Ice that is aground, again, on shoals at a distance from land, is another problem. Mr Stefansson has measured ridges, under these circum-

[1] Mr Wordie was Chief of the Scientific Staff on Sir Ernest Shackleton's *Endurance* Expedition, and is now Fellow of St John's College, Cambridge.

[2] *Trans. Roy. Soc. Edin.*, vol. lii, part 4, No. 31.

[3] *Glaciology* (British *Terra Nova* Antarctic Expedition), p. 397.

[4] *Problems of Polar Research*, p. 102.

[5] *New Land*, vol. i, p. 375.

stances, as high as 78 feet.[1] With reference to ridges of more than about 25 feet high, Dr Nansen wrote: "I cannot believe in the possibility of them occurring in the open ocean." [2]

Peary, on several occasions, affirms that he saw them of 50 to 100 feet high. One fact, however, is transparently clear: that when his attempts to reach the Pole were unsuccessful, the ice was phenomenally rough. When, on the other hand, he was beating Cagni's record or attaining the North Pole, the pack resembled the frictionless plane of theoretical mechanics, on which distances of from 30 to 90 miles in a day could be performed.

Traveller's tales, from the earliest times, have been full of exaggerated statements; but modern science, sometimes by the simple process of measuring, reduces the absurdities to within the limits of the truth. It is only fair to add that Peary was by no means the only recent explorer who exaggerated. Others, with better reputations, have enlarged upon the immensity of their discoveries; though some have taken scientists with them, who have reduced their leaders' statements to more exact dimensions. Peary would not permit scientific men to behold his greatest wonders. He was an excitable man, who magnified his minnows into whales. Hence his statements are unreliable, and always in the same direction; he never reduced the scale of nature, except on his maps. It was perfectly natural for him, therefore, to over-estimate his speeds and distances.

4. *Minor Mysteries.*—The following sketch illustrates one of Peary's minor mysteries. In the photograph entitled "Approaching the peaks of Cape Columbia," [3] on the return from the Pole, the sledges

---

[1] *The Friendly Arctic*, p. 514. See *Journal of Manchester Geographical Society*, 1921-22.

[2] *Farthest North*, vol. i, p. 241, footnote.

[3] *The North Pole*, opposite p. 318.

appear to be running along a line that is very nearly parallel to the coast, instead of at right angles to it. Had they been returning on a course anywhere near the meridian of the cape the scene would have been different.

Peary's whole theory of his journey to the Pole and back assumed that he never deviated from this meridian. His distances were those on the meridian and no more; but the camera cannot lie, and it shows a line of sledges, represented as being Peary's, approaching the cape *from the west*.

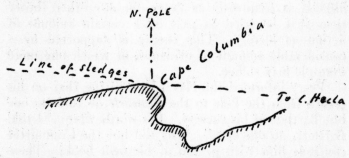

While this might not be anything more than the hitting of the coastal ice some miles in that direction, it may, on the contrary, mean much more. Peary says nothing to indicate any lateral drift, or otherwise, during the last day or two of the return. His assumption is a dead straight line between Columbia and the Pole, as shown on his chart.

To realise what may be indicated by this photograph we must remember that, on the only occasion when Peary's orientation could be tested, it was most inaccurate. All his cardinal points were swung round, from Land's End, *to the west*. As his return to Columbia appears to have been from this direction, it looks as if he had actually located the Pole somewhere in the north-west!

Many of the affairs of life are not what they seem. Some laws are kept only in theory and are broken in

practice. Institutions are capable of maintaining a
dignified appearance when they are rotten at the core.

Similarly, Peary tried to write an account of his
attainment of the Pole that would be accepted by the
world. It showed no high opinion of the acumen of
geographers; but, what he actually did appears to
have been a different matter. He did not record all
that happened, because it did not always suit his
purpose; and he recorded as history events that were
impossible.[1]

It would be a mystery how any man could contradict
himself as frequently as Peary, on any other theory
than that he tried to pass off a certain amount of
fiction as history. This theory is supported by a
considerable amount of evidence, of which one more
example may suffice.

Peary informed the Naval Committee that on his
return from the Pole to the *Roosevelt* he told no one
but Bartlett of his success. His words were: "I told
Bartlett, no one else." Why did not the Committee
confront him with p. 326 of his own book? There
we read: "I, therefore, at once started two Eskimos
off for Greenland with a sounding apparatus and a
letter informing MacMillan and Borup of our final
success."[2] Borup confirms this, in his interesting
little book, where he quotes from Peary's letter to
MacMillan, as follows: "April 28, 1909. Arrived
on board yesterday. Northern trip entirely satisfactory. No need of Greenland depots."[3] As Mr
Edwards wrote: "As soon as Commander Peary
reached the *Roosevelt*, he sent couriers in all directions
. . . telling of his success."[4]

Lest Peary should find a loophole through which
to slip, by reason of the indefinite terms employed
above (for the Pole is not actually mentioned), we must
proceed to notice that Borup also wrote: "We knew

[1] See Postscript, p. 275.   [2] *The North Pole*, p. 326.
[3] *A Tenderfoot with Peary*, p. 231.   [4] *Toll of the Arctic Seas*, p. 417.

he had the Pole"; [1] and again, "We hustled aboard
to congratulate the Commander on winning the four-
centuries' race to the Pole." [2] The complete contradiction of Peary's statement to the Congressional
Committee, with which they should have faced him,
was in the "Permanent monument" he had erected
at Cape Columbia (to commemorate in perpetuity his
"conquest of the Pole"), of which he had given full
particulars, accompanied by a photograph.[3] From
this account, and from Borup, who also mentions the
monument, it appears that everyone in the expedition
knew that Peary claimed to have reached his goal.
This great signpost, indeed, could not be erected
secretly; and its purpose was to blazon forth the
conquest.

Peary could not have forgotten all this. He may
have had excellent reasons for not wishing the committee to know what had been done and said; but
even so, few men would have had the nerve flatly to
contradict their own official records. This incident
is the final proof of the value of Peary's assertions.

A man of this kind, we must suppose, would not
think much of claiming to have done 180 or any
number of miles in two days; but someone must
have told him that it was virtually a contradiction in
terms. Thus he reduced the distance, in a belated
attempt to bring it within the limits of credibility.
What he failed to realise was that *both* his statements
could not be true; and that, if his distance to the Pole
could be altered at will, it would be evident he had not
been there.

A few fragments now need gathering up, before
we attempt to focus the various parts of the subject
on to a conclusion.

[1] *A Tenderfoot with Peary*, p. 233.
[2] *Ibid.*, p. 258 ; see also p. 259.
[3] *The North Pole*, pp. 325–326.

CHAPTER XIII

VARIOUS NOTES AND COMMENTS [1]

" It is not only ignorance but also romance that retreats before the advance of knowledge."

V. STEFANSSON.
The Friendly Arctic.

1. PEARY'S "BIG LEAD." 2. OCEANIC CURRENTS ACROSS PEARY'S PACK. 3. A BRIEF COMPARISON OF CONDITIONS IN 1906 AND 1909. 4. HOW PEARY'S CLAIM WAS ACCEPTED. 5. HIS PHYSICAL FITNESS IN 1909. 6. HIS PROBABLE COURSE IN 1909.

1. ON every journey over the polar pack Peary was confronted with one large channel, that he eventually called the "Big Lead." Our consideration of his work as an explorer would be incomplete if we omitted to mention a feature that seemed to him of great importance. It may well be introduced by a quotation from a letter, received by the present writer from one who has travelled a great deal in pack-ice. The letter reads as follows: "The last point which I wish to refer to is much more important, namely the use of the term 'Big Lead.' I have always objected to Peary's use of the term, as it was founded on very insufficient observations, and rather scanty knowledge of pack-ice. You probably know that Peary considered nine-tenths of the ice which he crossed on the way to the Pole as derived from the so-called 'glacial fringe.' In turn he regards the 'glacial fringe' as of land origin. This is sufficient to make one doubt any remarks which he makes about pack-ice. He thinks on the question of the origin of the Big Lead

[1] Sections 1, 2, and 3 of this chapter are somewhat technical.

that it tends always to occur in a certain latitude as a place of separation between the 'glacial fringe' (if this really is glacial) and the more actively moving pack-ice. I doubt very much whether there is any reason to suppose that a big lead should form where Peary says it does, any more than in any other part of the polar regions. Unfortunately Big Lead has been taken up by almost every writer, and it has now assumed an unnecessary prominence.

"I am quite convinced that the Big Lead was simply an ordinary lead, which was naturally very important to Peary, as it held him back for a certain period. I have seen similar pack-ice forms in various parts, and I can state definitely that their formation is fortuitous. . . . One thing seems quite clear, and that is that the majority of leads run at right angles to the direction of the wind which forms them. As pack-ice on the average moves with the wind, one therefore expects the majority of leads to run at right angles also to the average direction of the moving pack-ice. Most of the leads on Peary's journey would run north to south, so that in this way he saw very little of them."

Let us see what information we have on this channel.[1]

On 13th April 1902 Peary was held up for one day by a large channel that he named the "Grand Canal." Its latitude is not given, but it may have been about 83° 35′ to 83° 45′ N. There is no reason to assume that this was his "Big Lead" of later years. Its position was from about twenty to about seventy miles south of where big channels were found in 1906 and 1909. On his return, in less than a fortnight (in 1902), all we are told is that the place was "almost unrecognisable." [2] We are not told what the changes were, but pressure, rather than open water, appears then to have been the trouble.

[1] Chart No. 2 should be referred to.
[2] *Nearest the Pole*, p. 345.

In 1906, on 26th March, a great "river" was found in latitude 84° 38′ N., or from sixty to seventy miles north of where the Grand Canal had been met with. Peary named it the "Hudson River," in the text of his book, and the "Big Lead" in the heading of his chapter. It slowly widened day after day until, on the 31st, it was two miles wide, "the northern ice" being "slowly in motion to the *west*" (our italics) during this time.[1] Peary made no comment on this unusual direction of the drift, and it may have been only *apparent* motion. Both sides of the channel may have been drifting eastward, with the southern side, on which Peary stood, moving more rapidly than the northern side. The same movement appears to have continued, as the channel widened, during the 27th and 28th. It seems probable that this was actual westerly drift, but Peary seldom admitted movement in this direction.

On the 31st a stiff breeze is recorded from the S.S.W., and the ice ceased its apparent motion, though it may have been that the sides of the channel had equal motion. "An easterly movement of the northern ice" is mentioned on 1st April, which probably was due to the southern ice being more easily retarded. It is difficult, however, to understand what is meant by "The set of the current was still to the west," [2] unless Peary assumed that the ice on which he stood was then moving in that direction. He crossed on 7th April, after being held up for seven days, and wrote: "This lead . . . is undoubtedly the tidal crack between the land ice of Lincoln Sea and the central polar pack." It may be well to regard this as a matter still under consideration.

During the return to Greenland from his farthest north, Peary said: "We crossed the scar of the 'Big Lead.' By scar, I mean where the edges of the 'Big Lead' had been driven together and had frozen fast. There was no mistaking it." [3] No latitude is given,

---

[1] *Nearest the Pole*, pp. 115, 116.   [2] *Ibid.*, p. 118.   [3] *Ibid.*, p. 142.

but it would appear to have been about that of the "Hudson River." Peary immediately proceeds to show that, on his theory of a great and more or less permanent "tidal crack," he had been mistaken about the "scar"; for, two marches nearer land, "there was our friend the 'big lead,' a broad band of black water, perhaps half a mile wide." [1] It lay thirty to forty miles south of the latitude of the "Hudson River." Peary was held up, apparently for several days, while the channel broadened out to a width of over two miles, the northern side "drifting steadily eastward." The famous crossing then was made, on thin ice, to the "frozen Hades" on the southern side.

In 1909 Peary met his old enemy for the last time, on 4th March, forty-five miles to the north of Cape Columbia. This was farther south than the "Hudson River," or in about latitude 83° 53′ N., and he said there was no lateral movement of the ice. The channel was then about a quarter of a mile wide, and had opened through heavy floes, reported to have been 100 feet thick. It appeared to turn southward, a few miles to the east of the camp, and to extend for many miles in that direction. Peary said it "had every resemblance" to "the Hudson" of 1906, and referred to it as the "Big Lead." A sounding was made in 110 fathoms, or over the edge of the continental shelf.

During the night of 5th March the channel narrowed a little and then opened wider than before, under the influence, Peary thought, of the tidal wave. It did not close until the 11th, after imposing six days' delay. On that day the expedition crossed seven other channels, to the north of the large one, on young ice; each of these being from half a mile to a mile in width. During the return, on 21st April, the large channel, at about fifty miles from land, was frozen over and easily crossed.

On each of Peary's three principal journeys over

[1] *Ibid.*, p. 143.

the pack, he had to cross one, but not, apparently, more than one, very large channel. The latitude of the "Grand Canal," in 1902, is very uncertain; it was probably, however, within a few miles of the latitude of the "Big Lead" of 1909, or approximately 83° 50' N. The wide channel crossed during the return in 1906 also lay in *approximately* this latitude, but it was 150 miles to the east. On the outward journey of that year the "Hudson River" was met with forty miles farther north. Each of these channels extended so far to east and west that no attempt could be made to get round them.

They were met with as follows:—

Year.	*Lat. N. on Out-ward Journey.*	*Lat. N. on Return Journey.*
1902	about 83° 40'	(Unrecognisable)
1906	84° 38'	about 84°
1909	83° 53'	83° 48'

No notice must be taken of the way the "Big Lead" is marked on Peary's map, attached to his *Nearest the Pole*, where it is shown twelve to fifteen miles wide, and extending to east and west of all his routes for distances of 200 to 300 miles. There is not a particle of evidence for this, it is pure conjecture, and is, unfortunately, only one more example of the methods Peary employed. He did not, of course, invent all the particulars he has given with reference to wide channels. Until everything here has been verified, or otherwise, by scientists nothing definite can be decided about the channels.

Peary's theory as to the pack-ice, for what it may be worth, seemed to have been somewhat as follows: (1) Land-adhering ice, extending some miles from land, his " glacial fringe." (2) Adjoining the above, a zone of floating floes, for some distance farther from land.

(3) The drift of the pack, farthest from land, being assumed parallel to the coast, there must be a line of cleavage between the oceanic pack and the ice that adheres to the "glacial fringe"; and this line is the "Big Lead." He regarded this lead as a huge tidal crack.

2. *Oceanic Currents across Peary's Pack.*—We cannot enter fully into the interesting subject of the Arctic currents, as a whole; nor into a discussion as to how far the drift of the pack-ice is due to the winds. These matters have been dealt with by Dr Rudmose Brown [1] and other writers. [2] A movement of ice across the polar basin, from Siberia to Greenland, has been proved.

We are concerned only with a portion of the Western Arctic, that we may term, for convenience, Peary's pack. Admiral Kolchak writes: "North of the coast of Greenland the motion of the pack has a very complicated character." [3] That this should appear to be so may be due, to some extent, to the sporadic and conflicting information given by Peary, who has been the only traveller there, far from land. We should expect a possible splitting of the trans-oceanic current against the north of Greenland; but until we have definite data we cannot be sure as to how complicated the drift here is.

Considering the number of journeys made by Peary over his pack, we have a right to expect some reliable information with regard to its movement. We have none. We are sure of the great East Greenland Current; of weak and intermittent movements of the ice, to the south, through Robeson Channel; and of, apparently, a somewhat strong current entering Nansen Sound from the ocean. [4] Beyond this, Dr

[1] Chapter VIII of *The Polar Regions*.
[2] See especially *Problems of Polar Research* (in Bibliography).
[3] *Ibid.*, p. 130.
[4] *Four Years in the White North*, pp. 76–77.

Rudmose Brown says: "L. Koch reports a westward drift on the north coast of Greenland to the west of Cape Bridgman and an easterly drift to the east of it."[1] This would be expected; but the westerly drift conflicts with Peary's evidence, most of which, on this matter, has been given. There is a little further evidence, however, that we must now collect.

One of his objections to the Greenland route to the Pole, in 1900, was the danger of being swept into the East Greenland Current. The prevailing drift of 1902 was said to have been from west to east; and 1906 was notorious in this direction. In 1909 the pack was nearly motionless, in spite of transverse winds, for Peary to make his journey.

The one piece of scientific work accomplished by Peary during the race to land in 1906, was recorded by him as follows: "In the next march, after sighting the land, we came upon the trunk of a tree imbedded in a large floe. The part projecting from the ice was about nine or ten feet long, and the diameter at the ice level some ten or twelve inches. The wood was soft, apparently fir, and a small specimen was taken to permit of possible identification later on."[2] No account of this identification, if it was made, appears to be given.

This log was seen some few miles north of Cape Neumeyer, off the north coast of Greenland. In 1882 Lieutenant Lockwood, of Greely's expedition, had found a log, 100 miles along the coast, to the southwest of this cape. He wrote: "About half a mile from the coast I found an old piece of driftwood about six feet long, four inches wide, and four inches thick, pine or fir apparently, and evidently split from the body or branch of a tree. It was partially buried."[3] The place was near Repulse Harbour, towards the Black Horn Cliffs.

[1] *The Polar Regions*, p. 74.   [2] *Nearest the Pole*, p. 148.
[3] *Three Years of Arctic Service*, vol. i, pp. 308–309.

A much larger log was discovered by this expedition in St Patrick's Bay, Grant Land, on the shore of Robeson Channel. General Greely's record reads: "Privates Connell and Frederik found a large coniferous tree on the beach just above extreme high-water mark. It was about 30 inches in circumference, some 30 feet long, and had apparently been carried to that point by a current within a couple of years." [1]

These three logs were, almost certainly, Siberian conifers that had drifted completely across the Arctic Ocean. As evidence of this drift, Nansen and Sverdrup found logs about half-way across, not to mention all the evidence collected by the former before the drift of the *Fram*, nor that of the Melville casks. Nansen's log appeared to be of Siberian larch, and was found in latitude 85° 30′ N., on his route. Sverdrup's log was in about latitude 85° N., not far from where Nansen's log was found, and was the only complete specimen, of all the driftwood we have mentioned, that was secured. Sverdrup took it aboard the *Fram*.

The track of the transpolar current is largely conjectural, but it is supposed to cross Peary's part of the pack. Before he recorded his alleged west-to-east current, Lockwood had suspected the same, when he "attempted to obtain tidal readings in a crack one-quarter of a mile" off Cape Bryant, North Greenland. "The strong movement of the line to the eastward would seem," Lockwood wrote, "to indicate a current in that direction." [2] The following year, 1883, the evidence on this point seemed conclusive. While Lockwood was held up at the western end of the Black Horn Cliffs, he saw that "*the polar pack was moving rapidly towards the east.*" [3]

All this evidence is corroborated by Peary's experience until 1909; and even then, as we have seen, the easterly current is affirmed as a scientific result

[1] *Three Years of Arctic Service*, vol. i, p. 100.
[2] *Ibid.*, vol. i, p. 342.　　　　　[3] *Ibid.*, vol. ii, p. 22.

of the expedition. This is in direct opposition to
L. Koch's evidence. Also, had much current been
sweeping across Peary's trail to the Pole in 1909 he
could not have returned, as he asserts, over his outward track to his starting-point. We cannot pretend
to solve these mysteries, which require more exact
data; but it was thought that, by collecting whatever
evidence we possess at present on such disputed points,
the best service would be rendered.

Perhaps we should notice, before leaving this part
of the subject, that Peary's route of 1906 is incorrectly
marked on his chart. The longitude given on p. 117
of *Nearest the Pole*, at the big channel, is "74° W.
approx."; the chart shows it at about 72° W. If 74°
was correct, this would seem rather a large allowance
for the west-to-east drift. Was it evidence of a certain
amount of east-to-west drift? We cannot be sure of
Peary's data.

Proper scientific work is urgently needed on Peary's
pack. While a transpolar drift is established, the
course of the current, or even the existence of any
regular current, across Peary's pack, is not settled. It
may be that, as in the Beaufort Sea, the drift of the
ice here is entirely dependent on the winds, and that
they may not prevail for any long period in one
direction. Peary's evidence would seem to imply,
however, that westerly winds prevail; though this has
his own data of 1909 against it, when the reverse
happened and he was driven to the west.[1]

3. *A Brief Comparison of the Adverse Conditions in
1906 and* 1909.—Peary claimed that he would have
reached the North Pole in 1906 had not "a series of
unusually violent and continued winds disrupted the
polar pack. . . ."[2] This statement, from Peary's own
information, is untrue.

[1] See Postscript, p. 276. The subject of Arctic Currents and Ice
is well treated by Dr Rudmose Brown in chap. viii of his *Polar Regions*.
[2] *The North Pole*, p. 2; see also p. 31.

Table No. 12 gives a comparison of the most important relevant conditions on the two journeys. The latitude said to have been reached in 1906 was 87° 6′ N. At the end of the march on 27th March, 1909, latitude 87° 1′ N. was reached.[1] This is the nearest complete march, for the purpose of comparison, and is within five miles of the 1906 latitude. As this was only half a day's journey, on the 1909 average, it is near enough for our present purpose. The percentage of the total number of days on each journey, to these points, forms a basis for comparing the statistics.

TABLE No. 12

	1906.		1909.	
	Days.	Percentage of Total.	Days.	Percentage of Total.
On journey . . .	47	..	27	..
High winds . . .	13	27	5	19
Held up by bad weather	7	15	0	0
Held up by big channel .	7	15	6	23
Troubled with active ice	7	15	8	29

The whole week lost in Storm Camp, in 1906, was a serious delay that had no counterpart in 1909; but this did not rob Peary of the Pole, though it accentuated his main cause of failure. We saw, in Chapter IV, that his average speed to this camp was 3·6 minutes a day, and was little more than 5 m.p.d. for the whole outward journey. Had he not been held up for a single day he could not have gone more than about 30 miles beyond his turning-point. He was most anxious, however, to hide the real cause of his failure,

[1] *The North Pole*, p. 251.

which was the slowness of his progress, and the bad weather was a specious excuse.

The pack was disrupted actually less, and proportionately much less, in 1906 than in 1909; but he took three weeks longer than on his later journey to reach within five miles of the same point. One week of this, it is true, was due to the long blizzard, for the season was worse than that of 1909. Nevertheless, to blame the weather for failure, when it was known to have been the result of slow progress, looks very much like a deliberate attempt to deceive.

4. *How Peary's Claim was Accepted.*—The scientific aspects of polar exploration are a pure delight. In dealing with Peary, unfortunately, less attractive and even unattractive matters have to be faced. They cannot be avoided, if truth is to be served, however distasteful they may be.

Thus, the question has now become insistent: "How in the world could the great geographical societies and universities accept such a claim as that of Peary to have reached the North Pole?" One aspect of the reply to this can be mentioned more conveniently in the next chapter. Another aspect will be given now. All the main facts appear to be on record, and will be surveyed as briefly as possible.

The "National Geographic Society" of the United States did the trick. In Appendix III of *The North Pole* Peary gave the "Report of the Sub-Committee of the National Geographic Society on Peary's Records." This states that: "Commander Peary has submitted to his sub-committee his original journal and record of observations, together with all his instruments and apparatus, and certain of the most important of the scientific results of the expedition. These have been carefully examined by your sub-committee, and they are unanimously of the opinion that Commander Peary reached the North Pole on 6th April 1909."

What is the "National Geographic Society?" The

reply is given in official papers of the United States Government. The *Congressional Record* states that, at the second examination of Peary by Sub-Committee No. 8, on Saturday, 7th January 1911, Peary read two letters. The first was from the President of the Royal Geographical Society, acknowledging the copies of Peary's observations, and the second was from Mr Douglas Freshfield, referring to the same matter. Mr Freshfield added that the "scientific instructor" of the Royal Geographical Society "takes the same view of them as that taken by the Committee of the United States Geographical Society, on whose report the Council of the Royal Geographical Society acted."

We must note that the Royal Geographical Society supposed the "National Geographic Society" to be some kind of official institution, whose pronouncements could safely be accepted without question.

Mr Congressman Helgesen then stated: "The National Geographic Society is looked upon in England as really 'national.' This erroneous idea is shared by many persons in this country. In this connection the following letter from our Department of State is of interest.

Washington, 5.12.13.

Sir,—In response to your letter of December 2, I am directed by the Secretary of State to advise you that the National Geographic Society of this city is not a bureau of this Government.—I am, Sir, your obedient servant, J. A. TONNER,
Chief of Bureau.

"The above letter should prove to the most enthusiastic member—that is, subscriber to the *National Geographic Magazine*—that this society is 'national' in name only.

"In this connection I will also quote from a resolution (H. Res. 709) introduced in the House of Representatives on 21st January 1915, by Hon. F. O.

16

Smith of Maryland: 'Whereas the National Geographic Society is not national (in the sense that it
is not a bureau of nor connected with the National
Government in any capacity whatsoever), is not
geographic, is not scientific, and is not a society, but
is simply and solely a private publishing house, no
special privileges should be granted to it.'

"Yet this is the 'Society' that posed before the
world as a geographic, scientific, national arbiter of
Peary's claim to the discovery of the North Pole. . . ." [1]

The Report on which Peary's claim was acknowledged by the world is signed by Henry Gannett,
C. M. Chester, and O. H. Tittmann. [2] Mr Gannett
and Mr Tittmann gave evidence before the Naval
Sub-Committee. The latter, who was Superintendent
of the Coast and Geodetic Survey, was asked by a
member of the Committee if it would be possible for
anyone to 'fake' astronomical observations, 'without
actually going to the place.' Mr Tittmann replied:
'In a four days' journey, perhaps, he could; yes, I
think he might possibly do it in so short a journey. . . .
I don't think Mr Peary could.'

" MR ROBERTS. The point is, I have heard the statement made by men who I think have some knowledge,
and they claim that they could sit right here in
Washington and make up observations of latitude and
longitude for that immediate vicinity that could not
possibly be disproved.

MR TITTMANN. That might be so in so short a
journey; that is a matter of opinion.

THE CHAIRMAN. Professor, for myself I could not
comprehend how anybody would be so untruthful as
to say that he reached the North Pole if he did not;
but at the same time I wish you would state in some
way the observations that were made by Peary. You
see, I do not know how they were made; I know

---

[1] *Congressional Record*, 12th February 1916, p. 2847.
[2] Appendix III of *The North Pole*, p. 364.

nothing at all of astronomy, but I would like it to appear in the record the sort of an observation he made, the instruments with which he made it, how he made it, and what it showed, so that any scientific man may know, by looking at that observation, how you reached your conclusion and how it enabled you to reach your conclusion.

MR TITTMANN. I think Mr Gannett could give you all of that, as you have him here. I am really due before the Appropriations Committee." [1]

In Appendix III to *The North Pole* there is a footnote to Mr Gannett's name, as follows: "Henry Gannett, *Chairman of the Committee*" (Peary's italics) "which reported on Commander Peary's observations, has been chief geographer of the United States Geological Survey since 1882, etc." We now return to the *Congressional Record*.

"Mr Gannett was next examined. He said he was 'called geographer' of the Geological Survey, but the Director of the Survey has stated in writing that Gannett held no administrative position and had only been in the temporary employment of the Survey from time to time." Mr Helgesen exposes the deceptions of Peary's friends that his records were examined *officially*. "As a matter of fact, not one of the men who at that time 'examined' Peary's data did so in his official position." [1]

Mr Tittmann said that Peary's original records were on "loose slips of paper." Gannett said that Peary's original journal was "in a little book, a note-book, you know." Peary managed to get nearly a year's delay before showing them to the Congressional Committee, and then they were on different paper to either. [2]

It may have been noticed that the three friends of Peary who professed to "examine" his records were

[1] *Congressional Record*, 12th February 1916, p. 2819.
[2] *Ibid.*, p. 2795 ; see also Appendix.

inadvertently referred to as *his* sub-committee.[1] That they merely registered Peary's decrees is seen in the following quotation, with reference to their "examination" of the "instruments and apparatus" mentioned in their report, as given at the beginning of this section. This quotation was so astounding that the present writer submitted a copy of it to Washington, D.C., for official verification. It is here given as corrected by the Librarian of Congress.

"MR ROBERTS. First, how did the instruments come down?

CAPT. PEARY. They came in a trunk.

MR ROBERTS. Your trunk.

CAPT. PEARY. Yes.

MR ROBERTS. After you reached the station and found the trunk, what did you and the committee do with regard to the instruments?

CAPT. PEARY. I should say that we opened the trunk there in the station.

MR ROBERTS. That is, in the baggage room of the station.

CAPT. PEARY. Yes.

MR ROBERTS. Were the instruments all taken out?

CAPT. PEARY. That I could not say. Members of the committee will probably remember that better than I.

MR ROBERTS. Well, you do not have any recollection of whether they took them out and examined them?

CAPT. PEARY. Some were taken out, I should say; whether all were taken out I could not say.

MR ROBERTS. Was any test of those instruments made by any member of the committee to ascertain whether or not the instruments were inaccurate?

CAPT. PEARY. That I could not say. I should imagine that it would not be possible to make tests there.

[1] See p. 240.

Mr Roberts. Were those instruments ever in the possession of the committee other than the inspection at the station?

Capt. Peary. Not to my knowledge." [1]

This could not have happened without his knowledge. A copy of the complete Report may be seen at the British Museum. Gannett admitted that the only occasion on which the committee ever saw the "instruments and apparatus" was at the Pennsylvania Railway Station at Washington!

This would appear to deal the death-blow to Peary's polar pretensions. He always insisted that the only absolute proof of attainment was by expert examination of the original records and instruments; but he took very good care that his own never received this attention. They have never yet been examined. Why have they been withheld from proper scrutiny? If there was nothing the matter with them, why all this subterfuge and chicanery?

Perhaps one point should be made a little more clear. In Peary's evidence the instruments alone are mentioned; but in that of Mr Gannett, and he was chairman of Peary's committee, the discrepancies discovered were with respect to the original journal, so that all Peary's records are involved. On p. 15 of the above Report the Chairman says: "It will be seen that Mr Gannett, after his careful examination of Captain Peary's proofs and records, did not know how many days it took Captain Peary from the time he left Bartlett to reach the Pole and return to the *Roosevelt*, that information being supplied by a Mr Grosvenor." There was also a serious discrepancy in the equipment for the final dash, Gannett giving Peary four men, two sledges, and either thirty-two or thirty-six dogs, while Peary stoutly maintained that he had six men, five

[1] Congressional Report, Private Calendar No. 733, Sixty-first Congress, Third Session, House of Representatives Report No. 1961, pp. 21, 22.

sledges, and forty dogs.   As the chairman said, these were vital points.

Peary had successfully established the tradition that he was the only man who could ever reach the Pole.   Hence, when he said that he had been there, *his* committee obediently registered his decree.   The societies of other nations never questioned the reports of kindred bodies, and had themselves begun to imbibe the American Peary tradition.   This is one explanation of the mistake made in 1909; but the climax is not reached until a certain number of the *National Geographic Magazine* is seen.   In the issue for January 1923, among other issues, the following advertisement of the National Geographic Society appears: "The Society also had the honour of subscribing a substantial sum to the historic expedition of Admiral Peary, who discovered the North Pole."   The people who paid Peary were also the sole judges of his success.   Their verdict, therefore, was a foregone conclusion.

The following evidence from the Congressional Committee clears up another important point:

"Mr Macon. Did this (the Royal) Geographical Society have a full copy of the records that you have furnished to this committee?

Capt. Peary. They did not have all the material that is here to-day.

Mr Macon. What did they have?

Capt. Peary. They had copies of all of my observations, and they had copies of a considerable portion of my journal." [1]

None of Peary's *original* records were examined by any competent and impartial authority.

Some of the members of the Congressional Committee drew from Peary the admission that his practice had been to eat pemmican with his bare hands, and that this food was "distinctly greasy"; also that he wrote up his journal afterwards, "with the bare hand

[1] *The Congressional Record*, 12th February 1916.

usually." The Committee wished to examine the journal, but Peary refused, saying: "I do not care to leave it with the committee or anyone. I do not care to let it out of my possession; it never has been."

"Mr Roberts. If the members of the committee care to, I would like to have the book examined particularly with reference to its condition and state. It shows no finger-marks or rough usage; a very cleanly kept book." [1]

We shall not be expected seriously to consider the last expedition as a whole; its most important parts have been dealt with, and there seems nothing to be gained by attempting to separate, further than we have done, the wheat from the chaff.

5. *Peary's Physical Fitness in* 1909.—Sir Douglas Mawson, if judged by the wealth of the scientific information he has acquired and the amount of land he has discovered, is the greatest modern polar explorer. Hence, he will be accepted as one of the highest authorities on the physical fitness of men for sledging. He holds very strong opinions on the question of long journeys for men of over fifty years of age. In a recent letter to the present writer he said: "After the age of thirty-five no man can stand up to continuous high physical strain as he can from twenty to thirty-five years. But few men will admit this, unless it is brought home to them practically. . . . I have seen it several times in the field." Captain Scott wrote: "I have little doubt as to the value of youth for polar work." [2]

Peary's biographer, writing of the year 1895, says: "He had passed the crest of his physical hardihood." [3] A little later he writes: "Peary was thirty-nine, and had failed, and his physical strength had begun to ebb." [4] Once more he refers to Peary's "physical

---

[1] *Ibid.,* p. 2838.
[2] *The Voyage of the " Discovery,"* vol. i, p. 67.
[3] *Peary the Man,* p. 145.　　　　[4] *Ibid.,* pp. 150-151.

depreciation" at the age of forty-two. It was unwise of Commander Green to stress this, though the fact is perfectly natural, as Sir Douglas Mawson shows. It was unnatural, to the point of being grotesque, for any man of fifty-three to claim that he could walk at nearly double the speed, over a rougher surface, than the best he could do at the age of thirty-nine.

Peary seems to have been a normally healthy man, but he does not appear to have been strong enough for the heavy tasks he set himself. He overtaxed his strength. We have noticed his long periods of inactivity in the field, not during the winter, but in the sledging seasons, two of which were wasted on the *Windward* Expedition. We must now observe that each of these mysterious periods followed an excessive output of energy. Peary's temperament tended to exhaust his strength, and he suffered from pronounced reactions, during which he was incapable of doing anything.

Had he possessed any energy at these times he would have put it to good use, for he must have chafed at the inaction. He was not really a very strong man, and not sufficiently robust for the continual rough work that he wished to accomplish.

A man must be very tired by his day's work when he cannot add to it the labour of getting bubbles out of a thermometer. Yet Peary inadvertently admits, in this manner, that even the short marches (less than ten m.p.d.) he had made up to that time, about 18th March 1909, tired him. He wrote: "When I was not too tired I got the bubbles out." [1]

This is perfectly natural for the average man of fifty-three, but not for a superman who can walk more than 150 miles in two days. The truth slips out again on 25th March, when he said he was "tired with the long march" of twenty miles.[2] Of course he was tired, but no man of fifty-three, who was naturally

[1] *The North Pole*, p. 243.   [2] *Ibid.*, p. 253.

tired by a twenty-mile, and even a ten-mile, walk should have written afterwards of averaging 30 m.p.d. for about 800 miles.

Whether he was, or was not, past his prime, as his biographer says, at thirty-nine years of age, is not so pertinent as that, when he claimed to have reached the Pole, at the age of fifty-three, he was unquestionably far beyond "the crest of his physical hardihood." He incautiously admitted, "I was a little past the zenith of my strength." [1] He was considerably beyond it. His biographer affirms that his strength was declining fourteen years earlier, and this was quite normal. As the years advanced, after forty years of age, and especially after forty-five years, he, like other men, became progressively capable of less and less endurance.

He was unable, at the age of thirty-nine, to exceed 20·7 m.p.d. on the relatively easy surface of the inland ice; hence, it would have been a physical impossibility for him, when he was fifty-three, to have averaged 33 m.p.d. for a longer distance than in Greenland, including eight days at 50 m.p.d. and two days at 90 m.p.d.! Unless he accomplished all this he did not reach the Pole.

Commander Green, writing of Peary's health seven years later says: "He had lived a clean life, but one that had crushed much of his reserve energy away." [2] This was very true. Peary was not the type of man who possessed great reserves of vital force. His troubles and hardships in Greenland temporarily broke him down; and the bitterness he showed, after the failure of the *Windward* Expedition, was another example of the undoubted fact that he had not the strength to rise above his misfortunes, as the strongest men do, and retain their self-complacency.

During the European War, when Peary was about sixty years of age, we are told that "he said, 'I am very tired.' He was. And he never again got quite

[1] *Ibid.*, p. 9.　　　　　[2] *Peary the Man*, p. 383.

rested. . . . It was here, as much as through Arctic hardship, that he laid the foundation of his mortal illness." [1]   He had done too much for his strength and, as must befall anyone who does this, he paid the penalty.   Everything we know about him, with one exception, is consistent with natural law.   He gradually succumbed to pernicious anæmia at the somewhat early age of sixty-eight.   The strongest constitutions would not have suffered so.   On the other hand, any man of fifty-three who could walk 800 miles on the polar pack at over 30 m.p.d. must have had a most exceptional physique.

6. *Peary's Probable Course in* 1909.—The following sketch shows a course over the pack-ice that it was more probable Peary followed than his meridional line, which, indeed, we know he could not follow.   The course suggested no doubt could be improved upon, as it was not thought worthy of prolonged attention; but its main purpose is to mark the contrast between a real and a fictitious course, and at the same time to get nearer the truth on Peary's course as a whole.

He admits being blown southward by northerly winds.   Hence, he must have been blown laterally by easterly and westerly winds; but he had no means of finding out the amount of his leeway.   He was groping blindly over the pack.

When out of sight of land he could only have been on his meridian fortuitously; and the chances were heavily against him being near it again, unless he happened to have been drifted across it once or twice during the earlier part of the journey.   The easterly gales, however, would drive him far to the west.

They blew for the first three days after leaving land. He would endeavour to counteract them by setting an approximately north-easterly course; but he would soon see that the extra distance necessary to keep him on his meridian would be very great.   Possibly for

----

[1] *Peary the Man*, pp. 384, 385.

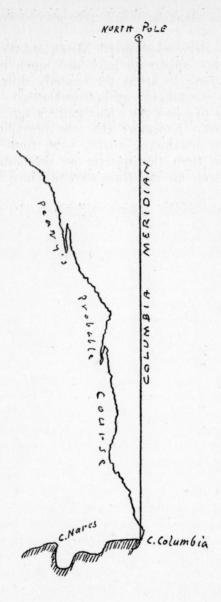

this reason alone he would take no observations for longitude.

The westerly winds of 4th March and the following days do not appear to have had much more than sufficient force to arrest the westerly drift; and on the 15th the wind came again from the east. It would be tedious to follow the whole journey again in detail, but we must remember that the prevailing winds, during the northward march, were from the east. They blew from this quarter on seven days, while from the west on only three days of which we can be sure.[1]

[1] The north-westerly course is practically proved by Bartlett; see p. 276.

CHAPTER XIV

CONCLUDING REMARKS

" There are many reasons which send men to the Poles. . . . But the desire for knowledge for its own sake is the one which really counts."
APSLEY CHERRY-GERRARD.
The Worst Journey in the World.

1. SUMMARY OF FOREGOING.   2. TRUE AND FALSE VALUES.
3. THE POSITION OF THE LEARNED SOCIETIES.   4. CONCLUSION.

1. IT is proposed to conclude, in this chapter, our consideration of the Peary Problem; and then to add an estimate of the man, that, if possible, his weatherbeaten form may emerge above the mists of controversy.

To study his life as an explorer is to become involved in the ramifications of his claim to have reached the North Pole. For this he lived; and after claiming success, he gave up exploring. The incredibility of his success bears a certain resemblance to the credibility of the evolution theory, for both depend upon the cumulative effect of a mass of evidence. The most important parts of the Peary evidence having been given, they can now be summarised.

It may be said of Admiral Peary, as Macaulay remarked of Southey: "It has never occurred to him that there is a difference between assertion and demonstration." This was a great pity, if only for the sake of his friends.

His claim to have attained the North Pole consisted exclusively in his own assertions, written and oral, that he had been there. He had no proofs, and not a single witness, to substantiate his claim. On the contrary, he disproved it himself, by:

(1) Contradicting his own statements on vital points;
(2) Not travelling the distance necessary to reach the Pole;
(3) Admitting that he neither measured his distances nor took observations for longitude or for compass variation.

In the official account of his last expedition he recorded a two-days' travel of over 150 miles; whereas he told a Congressional Committee that his best day's travel was about fifty miles. He tried to conceal the longer distance, in spite of the fact that, unless he did it, he could not have reached the Pole; and his biographer, recently, has deliberately evaded this difficulty.

The credibility of his unsupported word is disproved by the foregoing and other contradictions; by his claims of discoveries that had no existence; by the uncertainty of his most northerly latitude in 1906; by his "mistake" in a date when he wished to forestall a competitor; by the prodigious distances said to have been travelled without sleep; by his exaggerations, and the multitude of his inaccuracies.

He could not hide from the members of his expeditions that the distance travelled was greater than that made good on the northerly course; so 30 *per cent.*, as Borup said, was allowed, during the journey of 1909, for deviations. Yet, in the record of the journey, *the additional 30 per cent. is left out, because his unwitnessed speeds would then have been obviously impossible.*

The distances that he claimed to have sledged, and which he admitted were "extraordinary," were only his latitudes, or about 75 per cent. of the distance to the Pole. He was therefore over 100 miles short of it, even if only 25 per cent. is allowed for deviation, as seen on next page.

His maps were so inaccurate that they had to be withdrawn from the schools of the United States.

	Geo. Miles.	Stat. Miles.
The distance that had to be travelled from land .	516	593
Peary's distance.	413	475
Peary's distance was short of the Pole by . .	103	118

His navigation was so inaccurate that he could not fix his position on the inland ice of Greenland in 1886; he thought the North Pole was in the north-west in 1906; and he had no means of locating this point, in 1909, when he claimed to have reached it.

His *witnessed* evidence as to the character of the ice on his route is in general agreement with that of other travellers, and with what the flying men have found recently at and near the Pole; but his *unwitnessed* descriptions of smooth ice, which presented few sledging difficulties, are unsupported, and even contradicted by others.

His *witnessed* sledging speeds are slower than those of other polar travellers; whereas his claim to have reached the Pole depends upon exceeding the world's sledging records by *several hundred per cent.*

His physical condition in 1909 made these phenomenal speeds and distances impossible.

His records of his last two polar journeys are unsatisfactory, ambiguous, and even contradictory.

The only possible conclusion is, therefore, that Admiral Peary did not attain the North Pole, and that he should not have been honoured for a "discovery" he could not have made.

No party of six men, of whom one was fifty-three, and another forty-two years of age, ever sledged any distance remotely approaching 150 to 180 statute miles in two days over the polar pack, or averaged

30 m.p.d. for 800 miles on this rough and moving surface.

Suspicions that were aroused by Peary's departure from the recognised custom of other explorers, in making public their daily journals, are seen to have been well founded. His private diary of the last journey probably will remain the secret document it has been up to the present.

Commander Green says that, by the year 1903 or 1904, Peary "had grown more conservative in his claims, but more fulsome in his support of them . . . experience had taught him *finesse*."[1] This was most true.

On the other hand, Peary is to be credited with the discovery of a large amount of land; though his results, for six expeditions, were comparatively moderate. He was a fine pioneer, but of an obsolete type. He was not a great explorer.

2. *True and False Values.*—It is important to discriminate between two widely different forms of human activity; they may be termed the idealistic and the materialistic. The first of these, in relation to our subject, is variously described as the advancement of learning, the extension of knowledge, and the progress of science. The other class to which we refer is self-interest, the advancement of an individual for his personal gratification.

All explorers justly entitled to be called "Great" are of the former class. Some of these win public favour and applause, while others are little known, for this is not their main purpose. Their zeal for knowledge and their sense of duty urge them forward; and the world owes them a debt it will never repay. They steer homeward the "more truly treasure ships than the gold-bearing galleons of Spain," as Dr W. S. Bruce so well expressed the truth. We need to distinguish between real and fictitious values.

[1] *Peary the Man*, p. 236.

The second class of action to which we have referred includes men who may have various objects in view when they go exploring, but who do not travel in order to bring back their ships laden with golden knowledge. Sometimes they try to use science for the furtherance of their own ends; though they only pay lip-service to it, and their hearts are full of other ambitions. Their main purpose may be purely self-aggrandisement, and so they accomplish little that is of value. They appeal only to those who do not realise the difference between true and false values. Of this class was Robert Edwin Peary.

Commander Byrd, at the time of writing, is establishing his great expedition in Antarctica. It was Byrd who won for the United States the honour of first seeing the ice at the North Pole. He and his fine country are to be congratulated on this achievement. It was fitting that an American should be the first there, as it was fitting that a Norwegian should be the second. One has hoped, for many years, that the United States would do itself more justice than it has done in the past, by sending out one or more modern and scientific expeditions to the Arctic or Antarctic.

Excellent work has been done, by General Greely, Dr MacMillan, and especially by Mr Stefansson; but America could do still better. Byrd's expedition promises to fulfil the highest expectations, and we wish it every success.

3. *The Position of the Learned Societies.*—The public has yet to learn that universities and other learned institutions are not sent by heaven to protect innocent victims from charlatans. The granting of honours is no proof that the claims of those on whom they are bestowed are true. It was naturally supposed that Peary was honoured because he had reached the North Pole. This was not so.

As no institution undertakes to test the accuracy of explorers' claims, this work must fall upon individuals, or be left undone. Should this be? Should the whole burden, and possible animus, incurred by the purification of geographical truth be left to any chance investigator? Is it fair to leave the lone volunteer to fight the battle for the right singlehanded? It is true that the learned societies have national and social, as well as scientific, aims to pursue; but should their technical responsibilities be sidetracked by other activities?

Mr Lewin made the following suggestion, in 1911, as to the position of the Royal Geographical Society: "The Society may have been influenced by certain diplomatic considerations"; and he thought that it could not well refuse to recognise Peary because of "international complications." [1]

The Royal Geographical Society represents the dignity of His Britannic Majesty, in matters geographical, before the world. Hence, its recognition of an explorer may be formal and functional rather than scientific; though it took the very necessary precaution to bestow its medal on Peary, *not* for reaching the North Pole, as he said, but "for Arctic Exploration, 1886–1909." [2] He wrote that this medal, among others, was "awarded for the attainment of the Pole." How seldom the truth seemed to suit his ends!

The Society has been asked to investigate Peary's claims, and has, perhaps rightly, refused. It considers that the initiative should come from America. The result is that, as often in history, truth is not invariably associated with institutions. As long as the learned societies refuse to investigate this claim, so long will many people be led astray.

Several Fellows of the Royal Geographical Society have told the present writer that, while in general agreement with him, they cannot become involved in a controversy that, across the Atlantic, has been of

[1] *Did Peary Reach the Pole?*, pp. 84–85.
[2] *The North Pole*, pp. 364, 365.

such an undignified character. This attitude is quite reasonable; but it is a cynical comment on human affairs, that if wrongdoers become sufficiently degraded they escape the just reward of their deeds!

There is no present indication that the Peary Problem will receive further consideration, except that given it by individual students. The United States is not likely to take the initiative. Our polar authorities believe that the truth will be known eventually, and with that we must be content; but the truth never will be known if those who hold it keep silence.

4. *Conclusion.*—The only adequate reply to the foregoing critique would be the production of Peary's original journal, if he kept one. The evidence on this, as usual, is uncertain. There seems little hope of any such satisfactory solution of the problem. Had there been any documents to prove Peary's claim, they would have been produced when his pension hung in the balance. No document could prove that he walked 130 geographical miles in two days.

If there are no original documents for students to examine, the verdict of history may be severe, but no complaint could be made if it were so. The best use will be made, no doubt, of such data as we have. If they contain contradictions and impossibilities, judgment will be entered accordingly.

It will be noticed that the methods Peary employed, such as the removal of all witnesses, were the methods that would have been employed by anyone who intended to deceive. Dr Cook is the only other polar explorer who has attempted to reach either of the Poles without civilised witnesses. Sir Ernest Shackleton made the first attempt to reach the South Pole, in 1907, and he took Dr Marshall, Lieut. Adams, and Commander Wild. Three members of this party were professional navigators, and the fourth was an accomplished surveyor.

Men who refuse to do things properly, and stoop

to the use of subterfuges, are always in danger of being found out, in spite of abundant camouflage. Peary may have died in the belief that he had escaped detection, and probably he confided the truth to no one; but though "the mills of God move slowly they grind exceeding small." An Antarctic explorer once remarked to the present writer that Peary never imagined students sitting down to submit his writings to serious examination.

Political influence is carried to such excesses, as it seems to us, in America, that no public man can expect to be credited by more than about half the country. This encourages recklessness. It does not matter what is said or done, provided one's own party support one. Your opponents would tear you to a "frazzle" if you were an angel.

History will not fail to give Peary full credit for what he did, but it will not be able to credit him with reaching the Pole. There is no difficulty about this; neither is there much doubt as to the course of events by which he received honour for a "discovery" he did not make. The present position of the matter is, however, most unsatisfactory, one reason for which must be given.

Many noble institutions have been bequeathed a troublesome problem. They are gradually finding out the truth; but their dignity is at stake. Some of them may have hoped that public interest, traditionally ephemeral, would evaporate sufficiently to permit of Peary being decently buried in oblivion. What good, they may ask, can result from disinterring the hatchet?

Before replying to this question, the awakening of one learned institution to the facts must be mentioned. "Honorary membership in the Manchester Geographical Society" is given among the honours appended to Peary's book.[1] The present writer has been a member of this excellent Society for about ten

1 *The North Pole*, p. 365.

years, and has had the honour of bringing the Peary Problem prominently before it. Hundreds of its members have heard the evidence; ample opportunity has been given to contest the conclusions, yet there has never been a single voice raised in support of Peary's claim. How many of the other institutions which accepted Peary's word have since found out their mistake?

There are two good reasons, the one moral and the other historical, for not leaving Peary's claim unchallenged. That a lie should triumph was unthinkable; yet it does! The whole army of true scientists, whose lives are spent in pursuit of truth, will understand that this has been the driving power behind the task, now near completion. Could time be employed better than in tilting a lance at the ranks of error?

The second urge has been an attempt to prevent the falsification of history. Peary's claim is already generally accepted. Encyclopædias, school and other books, state that Peary reached the North Pole in 1909; that Amundsen reached the South Pole in December 1911 and Scott in January 1912. The first of these statements is not merely untrue; it is too closely related to the other facts not to be unfair to Amundsen and Norway, as well as to the ever-glorious memory of Captain Scott and his associates. It is unfair, also, to the memory of Sir Ernest Shackleton, who got as near to the South Pole as Peary did to the North Pole, but honestly admitted his splendid defeat.

Further, while making no pretence at correcting all the mistakes in Peary's biography,[1] the assertions in one chapter must be challenged. Chapter VII is entitled "First Crossing of Greenland," and refers to Peary's journey of 1891; the writer proceeding to say that Peary "set about crossing the inland ice to find out what lay within Greenland." [2] This was known several years before 1891, and not by skirting a coast,

---

[1] *Peary the Man who Refused to Fail.*   [2] *Ibid.,* p. 80.

as Peary did. The historical facts are well known. That great explorer, Baron Nordenskjöld, penetrated directly towards the interior for seventy-three miles, in 1883, and sent two Lapps on farther, who were said to have reached a point 218 miles from the coast. Another, perhaps even greater, explorer, Dr Nansen, made the first crossing of Greenland in 1888.

There appears to be a deliberate design to falsify history. We have suffered too much from this in the past; and we should have learnt, by now, that no trouble is worth consideration if it can prevent the defilement of the fountain of knowledge.

The alternatives seem plain. Either those who have been hoaxed may honestly admit it, or they may be liable to the charge of aiding and abetting an untruth. It is most improbable that Arctic history will be falsified. Historians may have two conflicting sets of documents to consult; but, as Peary's official record is so unsatisfactory, the result cannot well be doubtful. If all is to be known, institutions which sacrifice, if sacrifice be necessary, their own dignity in the cause of righteousness will receive the praise of posterity that will be their due.

"This question may be settled in our lifetime, it may only be settled a hundred years or two hundred years hence, but it is certain to be settled eventually by the supreme court of geographical discovery, the historical geographers, who will render a verdict biassed neither by partisanship nor by fear of ridicule, but a verdict based solely on the facts." [1]

[1] Edwin Swift Balch, *The North Pole and Bradley Land*, p. 82.

ROBERT EDWIN PEARY

facing p. 262

CHAPTER XV

AN ESTIMATE OF PEARY'S CHARACTER

" There are more people who innocently tell what is not the truth than there are people who deliberately concoct malicious lies."

LORD CARSON.
In the House of Lords.

1. A HUMAN being is a complex organism, and cannot be treated like a piece of protoplasm. Analyses and dissections, when applied to human character, have dangers unknown to the chemist and anatomist. Hence, Robert Edwin Peary must be seen as a unit, even though our purpose may be to examine his work, rather than the man himself.[1]

Within these limits, a sketch such as it is now desired to delineate, will show that Peary's life, as an explorer, consisted of two equally important parts: the obtaining of the means for his Arctic activities; and the end for which he strove, or his northern journeys. The former of these, or the province of preparation, concerns us only in so far as it throws light on his methods, character, and claims.

His purpose in life was simple, but it was pursued with intense earnestness. While so many men have no definite object, and while the efforts of others are comparatively feeble, Peary strove with the concentrated force, we might almost say the fury, of a powerful will, for fame. The result was that he attained his ambition, by means that we have seen, and reaped all the glory that he desired.

Civil engineering was his original profession, as it was that of the present writer; but, also like the writer,

[1] For the domestic aspect of Peary's life, and its fuller treatment generally, Commander Green's biography naturally will be consulted.

263

Peary did not find in engineering his true vocation. On the inland ice of Greenland, during his first reconnaissance, he felt an inspiration for polar travel; this was a path that promised to lead him to the notoriety for which he yearned.

Probably as much energy was required for the campaigns at home as for those in the Arctic. His connection with the Navy became farcical. He was continually clamouring for leave of absence, and had to adopt a strenuous system of wire-pulling to obtain it. Americans, who naturally understand their own methods better than is possible for others, will fully realise the amount of "machinery" that Peary had to set in motion before some of his expeditions could be launched. Commander Green's account of how, on one occasion, even the President of the United States had to use his autocratic powers for Peary's ends, is most entertaining and enlightening.[1]

Peary's biographer makes no attempt to disguise the fact that wire-pulling was the secret of Peary's success; no doubt this is a recognised custom in America. It was essential for the raising of funds, and for the obtaining of leave, which became almost continual. Peary gradually worked up a connection of influential supporters, by whom he achieved all his objects. They obtained him leave, they supplied him with money, and lastly, they supported his claim to have reached the Pole.

This solves the mystery of how so crude a claim could be acknowledged. It is seen in the remark of one of Peary's supporters during his examination by the Naval Committee. The moment it was discovered that three pencils had been used to write Bartlett's observations,[2] the following digression arose:

"Mr Butler. We have your word for it, and we have these observations to show that you were at the Pole. That is the plain way of putting it—your word

---

[1] *Peary the Man*, pp. 165–167.   [2] See p. 164.

and your proofs. To me, as a member of this committee, I accept your word; but your proofs, I know nothing at all about." [1]

Most British people have little conception how things are worked in America. Money and influence can do much in England, but they are paramount in the United States. The ramifications of political influence, and the power of the "almighty dollar," extend everywhere.

When an obscure civil engineering assistant in the Naval Dockyards was able to obtain sufficient influence, as Peary was able, to defy the head of his Department, in addition to obtaining the strong financial support necessary to equip expedition after expedition for over twenty years, it is not difficult to understand how he could get a mere geographical claim recognised, especially as it was made a matter of national honour and patriotism.

Yet time after time Peary failed, and his prestige became low. He had to clutch at "straws" to save his whole life's ambition from being wrecked. In 1895 he clung to the meteorites "as a drowning man clutches wildly at the trifling flotsam in the vortex of his dying struggles. For not only was Peary's mood now one of desperation, but the naked facts of his case were too damning for him to elude." [2] Again we read: "Drowning in disaster, as he felt himself to be, Peary clutched at the straw of scientific interest in the prize meteorites." [3]

Thus the first period of his Arctic activities held out no promise for the future; yet he never wavered. He merely set out for the North Pole more openly than before, on the four years' *Windward* Expedition. This was the darkest period of his life. We read: "For four terrible years he failed, not gloriously as he had upon the inland ice, but so dismally that to

---

[1] *Congressional Record*, 12th February 1916.
[2] *Peary the Man*, p. 145.   [3] *Ibid.*, p. 147.

the end of his life he never wrote more than a few curt pages about that awful period; and he wrote them only because he felt it his duty to make some sort of report to those who had backed him. The story of those years was all failure. He failed and failed and failed." [1]

We have seen how, in 1902, he returned to the dockyards as "a faded romance, a broken bubble, an exploded theory." [2] His life's ambition for fame seemed blighted. Then, for the third time, he renewed his efforts on behalf of his northern fetish. Again he got money, no less than a hundred thousand dollars from two wealthy men, and the *Roosevelt* was built.

The first expedition in his new ship placed him one stage nearer to his goal; it also proved to him, more clearly than before, the impossibility of making a high speed over the pack, and the uncertainty of being able to reach the Pole. He never admitted this, but it is obvious from his experience in 1906. He found, on his return, that one more chance would be his last, and he considerably strained the truth in his account of how he had set up a new record. One discovery that he made, however, put *a claim* for the Pole within his grasp. His biographer writes: "It was his combination of strength of purpose *with strategic cunning that carried him through*" (our italics). [3]

2. Human life is so remarkable that it seems possible, occasionally, to *crack* God's laws without a breakage! Many a good man has departed from the truth under the stress of desperation. Such men are not "common or garden liars," but their word is unreliable. Peary appears to have been no worse than many a respected business man. He was not without his parts. He had dauntless courage and an iron will; but these, perhaps strangely, were allied in his character with the mind of adolescence. His reason-

[1] *Peary the Man*, p. 156.   [2] *Ibid.*, p. 234.   [3] *Ibid.*, p. 14.

ing faculties never developed fully. Hence, his lapses from our accepted ethical code are perfectly transparent, for he was not experienced in evil ways.

To acclaim Peary as a great explorer would be to use the extravagant language to which he was prone. A great explorer has powers that Peary was denied. He must be a born leader of men, endowed with a sound and well-balanced judgment; he should have a love for knowledge, be devoted to the sacredness of truth and, perhaps above all, he must have a keen and unselfish sense of duty.

Peary was a poor leader. On nearly all his expeditions he had difficulty in getting white men to follow him, and on some of them they definitely refused to do so. His biographer admits: "He was not the born leader in the sense of being able automatically to inspire his men"; [1] also that, on the *Windward* Expedition, "he had to face a party of white assistants that were now wholly out of sympathy with his plans. Moreover, in addition to the regular party of co-explorers, he had a thoroughly sullen ship's company." [2] Again we read of "the mass of maledictions that were hurled in his direction from time to time by those who had been north with him"; [3] and that "many in Peary's command used to return hating him in a way that murder couldn't satisfy." [4] This may have been their fault as much as their leader's; for his assistants on the *Roosevelt* seemed happy with him. Still, he was not a great leader, and was forced to employ natives to do most of his sledging because he could not get white men to follow him. The Eskimos naturally regarded him as a kind of god, as they regard any man who rewards them handsomely.

His zeal frequently overran his knowledge and discretion. His explosive energy, with little to balance it, caused most of his troubles. He lacked

[1] *Peary the Man*, p. 397. [2] *Ibid.*, p. 207.
[3] *Ibid.*, p. 399. [4] *Ibid.*, p. 324.

counterpoise. Truth and accuracy he failed to understand in the scientific sense. His one, and that a
consuming, aim was self-aggrandisement.

We have noticed many examples of his want of
judgment, of reason, and of discretion; in making
desperate journeys, such as his second journey across
Greenland, obviously to no purpose; in taking
excessive risks without sufficient reason, as in the
winter journey when he lost his toes; in wasting whole
seasons at great expense, though this appears to have
been the result of sheer physical exhaustion; and in
the published records of his last two expeditions,
particularly of his final attempt on the Pole, from
which it is impossible to glean precisely what he
accomplished.

He had not a clear head. He was one of those
men who make contradictory statements because
they forget what they have said previously. Thus
he was inconsistent to a degree. With characteristic
instability he was continually expecting both to keep
his cake and eat it.

In spite of these failings, Peary always passed as
a "fine man," and he was a great pioneer. He culti-
vated, like William II of Germany, an "impressive"
personal appearance. He was built of the stuff from
which heroes are made, but of an ancient type. He
was a blundering enthusiast, nearly all emotion, and
devoid of trained intellect as well as love of truth.
He accomplished something in life, though his means
were disproportionate to his ends.

He discovered his "short cut" to world fame by
Arctic exploration at a bad time. The mind of the
American public was then filled with the horror of
the Greely disaster. Peary had an uphill fight to
alter the false conceptions, but he won it. He taught
his countrymen that, instead of man being beaten
by the grim forces of nature, an American could
conquer them, though not as completely as he claimed

to have done. In this sense he was, in Commander Green's happy phrase, "the man who refused to fail." It was a bitter struggle nearly to the end; but Peary could not give way because he became too old, before achieving much success, for embarking on any fresh career. When he could not force his will on the ice he could resort to some of his "strategic" expedients.

Peary's character was of the *daimonic* type, and his *daimon* drove him mercilessly. The American newspapers called him "a weather-beaten fanatic." [1] He was such an enthusiast that it was no idle boast to his mother that he would never be content until he was world famous. Yet the strain nearly broke him down, as it does so many "climbers." He was probably the only modern explorer whose troubles came near to turning his brain. On the loss of his big depot, in 1894, he wrote that "it seemed as if . . . I should lose my reason."

That his difficulties must have been great to drive him to this may be gathered from the fact that he was a very hard man. He could stand any amount of physical pain, and stumped about for weeks, after losing nearly all his toes, with eight open wounds on his feet! He had an iron will and would never give way. From this it followed that he was not of the sensitive type, though he was very kind to his friends, one example of which should be given.

Dr MacMillan was injured by a gun accident on the *Roosevelt* in 1909, and Borup tells us: "When the Commander heard the news he was very much upset, and came into Mac's room and told him, with tears in his eyes, he'd a good deal rather have had it happen to himself than to Mac., and we could see that, if ever a man meant what he said, Peary did." [2] There is no need to make allowances for the tenderfoot's worship of his hero, for Peary was never unkind.

While his emotions were normal, he was no ordinary

[1] *Peary the Man*, p. 236. [2] *A Tenderfoot with Peary*, pp. 296–297.

man of his age. He more resembled the heroes of olden times in his simplicity and strength; but he was mercurial. This he may have inherited. He was something of a prodigy at the beginning of the twentieth century, as seen in the following quotation from his letter to Mr Henry Bryant, President of the Philadelphia Academy of Sciences, dated 17th January, 1903: "It has always seemed a peculiar thing to me that neither Nansen nor Sverdrup has ever moved to repeat his attempt" (to reach the North Pole). "If the method [1] is such a certainty, why with their experience do they not try it again, and do the thing. You know as well as I that the talk of having secured all the scientific information that is desirable, and not considering the Pole alone of any especial value, is all rot. You and I are no longer chickens, and we both know that no man would give a few facts of so-called scientific information the slightest weight, if balanced against the Pole." [2]

No one but Peary could have written that. It reveals at once his peculiar mentality, his lifelong infatuation for an *ignis fatuus*, and his jealousy. From the only true, that is the intellectual, standpoint, what Peary wrote was nonsense. All true geographers have long been agreed that the Geographical Poles were not worth reaching, apart from the moral and physical benefits of all exploration, unless solid scientific data were obtained there. This point has been dealt with already.[3] The Poles, for a few years, were a lure to the popular imagination, and so to Peary; but this was quite childish. The presence of a great mind, such as that of Dr Nansen, at 200 miles' distance from the mathematical focus of the meridians, did more in one hour for the advancement of knowledge, the most worthy object in all exploration, than would have been possible for Peary had he reached his goal and been able to remain there for ever.

[1] *I.e.* of drifting, as the *Fram* drifted.
[2] *Peary the Man*, p. 239.   [3] See pp. 3, 191, 197–198, 256–257.

It is waste of time, of energy, and of money, for men with infantile minds to visit remote places; for nature has withheld the capacity for them to bring anything valuable back. Thus it is a misfortune for simple people to be endowed, as Peary was endowed, with excessive will-power; they merely increase the difficulties of life.

" Power, reft of wisdom, falls by its own weight."

One of the worst effects of the association of a powerful *daimon* with a small mind is seen in the grotesque attempts to escape from the embarrassments into which unwisdom has led. A species of cunning is forced to do duty for reason, with pitiful results.

Lower types of mind, on the other hand, are often successful in the petty affairs of life. Peary was not intellectual, but he was intensely practical. His ability in this direction is evident on every expedition: in his attention to detail, such as food and equipment, that suited his need, in the end, admirably, though not perfectly. Eskimo methods, for the most part, were adopted, some of which were unscientific. As one example of these, contrast Peary's unwieldy sledges with the light and strong "Nansen" type. Again, the fan system of dog traction, used by Peary, in which much of the animals' strength is wasted, may be contrasted with the efficient double tandem, used by Amundsen. For the model of modern sledging the world turns to Amundsen, not to Peary.[1] Peary did nothing to help progress in this or in other matters. He worked unblushingly for himself.

His practical nature is seen, more clearly, perhaps, in his polar ration of one pound of pemmican, one pound of biscuit, and two quarts of tea per man per day. This is a good example of his methods, because it is simple and free from over-refinements, not scientific, and yet of proved efficiency. He lavished fresh meat

[1] See *The South Pole*, vol. i, opposite p. 192.

on his men, and so never had one case of scurvy on any expedition. In polar clothing, too, Peary was seen at his best; this he thought, judging by his portraits, in a sense not intended. He could sleep in the open air of the Arctic, without tent or sleeping-bag, by pulling his hood over his face and withdrawing his hands inside his sleeves. The whole costume was of fur. He adopted snow igloos, as a general rule, instead of tents; these reduced the constant weights of the sledges, at the cost of half an hour's extra time in camping.

Peary's winter *régime* for his men has never been equalled, in the present writer's opinion, even by the greatest explorers. He believed in moderate work for all, during the dark season, instead of the immoderate play of earlier polar expeditions. Thus the men were kept occupied and healthy, while the work of the following season was well begun. As Commander Green remarks: "He permitted no vacation period during the dark months. . . . Of course there were blizzards, and the days grew inky black in December when the moon was absent. But this did not lead to any sort of indoor life which would have softened the men. . . . And since his men were in condition from a winter of hard work he was able to start early in the Arctic dawn." [1]

3. Dr V. Stefansson, in the course of an interesting correspondence with the writer, drew a sharp distinction between the ethics of science and of sport. He intimated, further, in one of his works,[2] that Peary should be judged by the latter. This does not seem the place in which to enter upon a discussion (that could not, by its nature, be very brief) of this suggestion; but it would not be quite fair, perhaps, to Peary's memory, to omit it altogether.

Scientific expeditions are modern. From the earliest times until the nineteenth century (with few exceptions), whatever the ethical basis, if any, of

[1] *Peary the Man*, pp. 290–291.   [2] *The Friendly Arctic*, p. 31.

exploration, it could not have been that of natural science. Most explorers, before the scientific era, probably could be termed, not altogether inaccurately, muscular Christians; they usually subscribed to some moral code, though it was punctured at times by customs that are offensive to us.

Peary was the last, or one of the last, of this older order of geographical pioneers. The whole order was doomed, by the advancement of science, to extinction. Whether he was a good exemplar of the moral principles of his, now defunct, order the reader must relieve the writer of all responsibility for deciding. The reader, furthermore, may form his own opinion as to whether the ethics of sport regulated the conduct of this obsolete order of explorers or that of Peary as an individual, as well as on the question: "Are the ethics of science and of sport widely different?"

The fundamental distinction between right and wrong, truth and error, will remain until all evil is annihilated. Lord Acton convicted Bishop Creighton of error in his attempt to "whitewash" the Popes. What is more to the point now is the essential difference between the mentality of scientists and of others. There may be a more fundamental diversity of minds than this, but it is enough for our present purpose to realise the intellectual segregation of the seeker after truth. It may be impossible for one species of mind perfectly, or even sufficiently, to understand another mental species. Peary had no semblance to a scientific mind, and with this undoubted truth we must end.

It is the heroic aspect of Peary's life that is his greatest merit, and it fills us with admiration. He was, for the most part, an old-fashioned hero, with the faults and virtues attributed to those of the past. He was almost an anachronism; but he must not be deprived of the glory that is his by right. All men have human shortcomings. On the other hand,

18

bravery and strength have ever been the qualities
most admired, and these Peary had to the full. His
life was a battle in which he never faltered nor feared.
He fought his nerve-racking fights in America, and
he measured his strength against the grim forces of
nature in her most awful forms. Never did Peary
flinch or show the want of courage. His spirit
triumphed over all adversity, and his body conquered
every obstacle—except the polar pack.

POSTSCRIPT

"THE LOG OF BOB BARTLETT"[1]

This interesting book came out after the foregoing had been written. Captain Bartlett is a fine man, whom one has always admired, and he is a splendid seaman. Something more than loyalty to his old chief, however, is necessary to prove that he reached the Pole. As no new data are given, this breezy book fails to help the cause that its author has at heart. He gives nothing bearing on the crux of the problem, except personal opinion ; he adds little to the information given in Commander Green's biography ; and he is like Commander Green in giving a wide berth to all the real difficulties. The only new argument seems to be the old one, said to have been of feminine origin : " It is *because* it is ! "

This fact is nothing less than portentous. Here is a second book published, like the biography, with the evident purpose of propaganda. Yet, for the second time, an opportunity of proving Peary's claim has been lost. His supporters, doubtless, have done all they could for his memory ; but the proofs that he did not reach the Pole are totally unaffected.

Why did not Captain Bartlett elucidate the mystery of the three pencils he appeared to have used in his record of the observations taken in latitude 87° 47′ N. ? This is one thing we want to know, and only he can tell us. He avoids all reference to the subject.

Why, if he expects Peary's polar claim to be accepted, does he not make some attempt to reconcile his Commander's contradictions ? Captain Bartlett, like Commander Green, is careful not to say one word about Peary's 90 m.p.d., or about his contradiction of this, that left him a great distance short of the Pole.

Bartlett artlessly assumes, with his cheery optimism, that his old Boss was capable of performing all the marvellous tricks, when out of sight, that he said he performed. But no explanation is suggested to account for the 800 miles at over 30 m.p.d.

These are the things that matter. Even " Captain Bob's " opinion cannot alter them. Facts can be refuted only by facts, and proofs with proofs. Bartlett frankly admits he is " prejudiced " ; and it is clear that he has no new light to throw upon the problem. This fact, be it noted, is valuable ; for it seems to show that nothing

[1] By Captain Robert Bartlett, Master Mariner (Putnam, 1928).

more can be said in defence of Peary's claim.   The biography, indeed,
as the penultimate word of his supporters, was enlightening, though
not, perhaps, altogether in the manner intended.   Should *The Log
of Bob Bartlett* be the last word on behalf of that claim, the result of
our examination, in the present volume, may prove to be the verdict
of history.

Bartlett tries to help Peary by saying that he did not hurry his
own return from latitude 87° 47′ N.   Perhaps not, though he had
admitted previously to a rapid journey ; he went faster than on the
outward journey ; and Peary spoke of it as a " forced march."   A comparison of his speed with Peary's, however, is not material to the
problem.   If Bartlett is entirely eliminated, the miraculous speed of
his Commander is unaffected.

One sidelight is unwittingly thrown on the central figure when
Bartlett says that Peary " knew more about red tape than any three
average men," and so " he didn't have much trouble fixing me up
with a job." [1]   We have seen that this was how Peary managed to
get his claim to the Pole " fixed up."

One further point is of great interest.   Bartlett writes anent his
return from the polar journey : " On 17th April I reached Cape
Nares."   This cape lies to the west of Cape Columbia ; *so that is
where the trail had got to !*   This may explain the photograph, commented upon on p. 227 ; for Peary said he followed Bartlett's track,
a day or two later, from the " Big Lead " to land.   Peary represented
a different state of affairs from this.   His whole story demands a
perfectly straight course, both from Cape Columbia to the Pole and
back again from the Pole to Cape Columbia.   If he made any deviations from his meridian his total mileage is wrong, and his speeds are
greater than he admitted them to be.   He distinctly said he followed
Bartlett's trail from the Big Lead to Cape Columbia ; but now
Bartlett says he landed at Cape Nares.

Bartlett's evidence is that the drift of the pack had been *from east
to west* during Peary's absence from land.[2]   One of Peary's " Scientific
Results," as we have seen, was the existence of a current flowing *from
west to east !*   As Cape Nares was over 20 miles to the west of Cape
Columbia, " Captain Bob " has done Peary a sorry service by telling
the truth !   Perhaps, however, we should say that the recognised
Peary tradition of contradicting previous statements has been worthily
upheld.

[1] *The Log of Bob Bartlett*, p. 290.
[2] See also Borup's evidence on this, p. 158.

APPENDIX

OTHER CRITIQUES OF PEARY

THERE have been at least eight other public criticisms, according to the information at my disposal, destructive of Peary's claim to have reached the North Pole. Six of the critics are Americans. Their names are :—

(1) His Serene Highness the Prince of Monaco.
(2) Major-General Adolphus W. Greely, United States Army.
(3) Mr Edwin Swift Balch, Philadelphia, author of *Arctic Expeditions, The North Pole and Bradley Land*, etc., etc.
(4) Mr W. H. Lewin, author of *Did Peary Reach the Pole ?*
(5) Captain T. F. Hall, Omaha, author of *Has the North Pole been Discovered ? "*
(6) The Hon. H. T. Helgesen, Member of Congress.
(7) The Hon. R. B. Macon, Member of Congress.
(8) Mr W. E. Shea, Washington, author of articles in the *Boston Independent*.

There are others known to me, geographers, scientists, and polar explorers, who have satisfied themselves that Peary's claim was untrue ; but I am not permitted to mention their names. I do not think that anyone, who was competent to examine this problem, has ever arrived at any other conclusion.

Mr Lewin, Captain Hall, and both the Members of Congress, criticised Peary a considerable time ago. I did not see their critiques, however, until several years' consideration had been given to the subject. Hence this book is not *greatly* indebted to them. It is indebted, to some extent, especially to Captain Hall, and acknowledgments are gladly made. General Greely's, Mr Balch's, and Mr Shea's critiques are more recent than my own lecture, mentioned in the Introduction.

It seemed best to complete one's work as independently as possible, and add a *résumé* of what others have said. I am reluctant to omit their support, and wish it could be given more fully ; it broadens the basis on which this volume rests.

1. His Serene Highness Prince Albert of Monaco is the Prince, also, of oceanographers, having done more for the advancement of this branch of science than any other individual. He has conducted oceanographical cruises, and made many important surveys, accompanied by a scientific staff. He has trained some of the leading

oceanographers, such as Dr W. S. Bruce ; and has supplied expeditions with oceanographical instruments and equipment. He has built a palatial museum and laboratory of oceanography at Monaco. When it was opened in 1910 the navies of five European nations were represented.

The *Philadelphia Public Ledger* of 30th June 1922 published an article entitled : " Prince of Monaco denied Peary's discovery of the Pole." In this article the " celebrated oceanographer " is reported to have said that " Peary never reached the Pole. . . . The scientific data reported by Peary as of the Pole itself was fiction, and based on real observations made 80 miles away and very plausibly reasoned out from these observations. . . . The entire scientific and geographic world knows the secret, but out of respect for the personality of Peary and in regard for America's feelings their beliefs were never made public."

2. General Greely requires no introduction. His name is deeply engraved upon the annals of Arctic exploration. His expedition was the finest sent out by America until Dr Stefansson's time ; and his monumental work, *Three Years of Arctic Service*, is a worthy record of great work nobly done.

The veteran explorer is reported in *The Washington Star* of 25th January 1926 as expressing himself thus : " I am not calling either Dr Cook or Admiral Peary a liar, but I am convinced that neither one actually reached the Pole. . . . The claims of both . . . are based on their own statements, which are not supported. . . ."

3. Mr Edwin Swift Balch was a lawyer and a member of a distinguished legal family. He was also a historical geographer with a worldwide reputation for sterling scholarship ; and he was the author of eleven books and papers on polar matters. Correspondence with him was always a great pleasure. He said in one letter, dated 19th June 1926 : " The whole Cook-Peary matter has been an evolution with me. I floundered around at first, but slowly light came. . . . Then I worked at other things, the arts of primitives and savages principally, and did nothing more about Cook-Peary beyond reading and evolving fresh views, which I wrote down some four years ago and which *The Independent* published last year. . . ."

Mr Balch was then over seventy years of age, and he died a few months later. The following is an excerpt from the articles just referred to, entitled : " North Polar Questions " (*The Independent*, 21st and 28th November 1925) :

" The two most vitally important points in connection with Peary's claim of reaching the North Pole are, in my opinion : First, Peary's marches, contrasted with Bartlett's marches after they parted company at lat. 87° 47' N. . . . Second, the drift of the ice in the neighbourhood of 85° N. lat. during Peary's journey of 1906, and the lack of drift during his entire journey of 1909."

" Bartlett is a very strong man just approaching middle age. . . .
On the already broken trail . . . he takes, therefore, exactly 24 days
to cover 370 miles, or an average of a little over 15·4 m.p.d. Peary
. . . is . . . nearly past middle age and has lost some of his toes. . . .
He marches on an unbroken trail 133 miles to the Pole. . . . He
therefore takes exactly 25 days to cover 672 miles . . . an average
of 26·88 m.p.d. In judging such a phenomenal performance there
must be taken into account Peary's positive statements that there is
no smooth and very little level ice. . . . How was it possible for
Peary thus to make 302 miles more in 25 days than Bartlett made
in 24 days, especially considering that 151 of these miles were over
an unbroken trail ? How was it possible for Peary, an older and
slightly crippled man, to average a trifle over 5 miles for every 3
miles made by Bartlett ? But these are the exact results obtained
if one foots up the figures given by Peary himself in his book."

" Turning to the question of the drift," Mr Balch refers to the
" almost constant movement " of the ice, which he believes to be
" a sort of zigzag motion." He shows how Peary's experience of it
in 1906 agreed with all other travellers on the pack, and then contrasts with this his claim to have returned over his outward trail.
" For a period of 54 days there was absolutely no drift of any account
of the ice either east or west."

" The situation in regard to the discovery of the North Pole
apparently narrows down to this. . . . The majority of the public,
including many scientific men, without examining the evidence,
accept on faith the assertions that Peary reached the Pole and that
Cook did not. But all scientific questions are decided finally not in
beliefs, but by facts. Therefore in this case, also, the facts and the
evidence will eventually win out."

" The evidence shows that undoubtedly Peary and Bartlett went
very far north, the former almost surely beyond 88° N. lat. But
the evidence is distinctly against Peary's having reached the Pole."

4. Mr W. H. Lewin's book, *Did Peary reach the Pole? By an
Englishman in the Street*, was published by Messrs Simpkin, Marshall
& Co. in 1911. Its style is dispassionate and its writer is an admirer
of Peary ; but Mr Lewin contends that the return from the Pole
could not have been made at the speed stated, 37½ statute m.p.d.
for eighteen marches. There was " an entire absence of continuous
observations for latitude and longitude. Peary's book contains no
real sequence of observations," and " an entire absence of observations
for longitude." Peary was " unable to determine what his actual
deviations to east and west had been." As to the denial of lateral
motion, Mr Lewin well remarks, " The statement must be accepted
with considerable reserve," for Peary recorded strong winds from
east and west.

Peary's actual mileage is worked out, with only 10 per cent. added to the straight-line distance for deviations caused by pressure and channels, which, as Mr Lewin says, is " a very conservative estimate." Thirty per cent. more is added for the drift of the pack. This may seem excessive, but it is based on Nansen's journey, during which the drift caused a 40 per cent. addition to the straight-line distance. Thus Peary is considered to have travelled about 1500 miles in forty-five marches, occupying fifty-five days, at an average of 33⅓ m.p.d. This speed is rightly shown to be impossible. The actual distance covered on the pack is demonstrated by a sketch of a zigzagged line.

After a comparison with the speeds of other travellers, Mr Lewin concludes by saying : " A speed of 33⅓ m.p.d. is, frankly, impossible over the polar ice " ; but he repudiates the suggestion that Peary wilfully deceived the world, and believes that " a series of blunders occurred with the few observations taken."

There has never been any reply to this little brochure, published eighteen years ago, probably for the sufficient reason that no reply which could rehabilitate Peary's claim is possible.

5. *Has the North Pole been Discovered ?*, published in 1917,[1] is more pretentious than the preceding book, and contains 370 pages. The claim of Dr Cook, as well as that of Admiral Peary, is examined. A very brief outline of the portion of the book devoted to Peary must suffice here.

Mr Hall was " Captain of the barque *Egypt* in the eighteen-sixties," his father and grandfather also having been mariners. He first draws attention to the absence of accurate information in Peary's account of his last journey. Worse than this was the fact that " the location of the expedition was never known on any day during the journey, because no longitude was taken, even the compass variations were not known ; the drift of the ice floes is overlooked in the calculations and contradicted in the descriptions. . . . His photos at the Pole show shadows on the wrong side. He claims a rate of speed which is impossible," and his account, as a whole, is suspicious.

Peary's speed is then examined, and illustrated by several diagrams. The assumption of a permanent current across Peary's route, while justified by Peary's own " Scientific Results," cannot be accepted, and this vitiates some of Captain Hall's conclusions. During the seven days and thirteen hours that Peary was north of Bartlett's last camp, his average is worked out at 66 m.p.d.

Peary is considered to have discredited his own story, by betraying indications that he never expected to reach the North Pole. His equipment, organisation, and especially the dismissal of all his white supporters, are said to point to this. His sledges were about 90 lb.

---

[1] By Richard G. Badger, Boston.

in weight and carried only 500 lb., while "Amundsen's sledges weighed 53 lb. and carried loads of 880 lb." Peary's clumsy vehicles were "never intended to go very far from land."

Other matters, such as Peary's predictions and their literal fulfilment, are dealt with ; as well as the absurdity of his assumption that the polar pack stood still all the time he was on it. Many mistakes in his story are pointed out, as to the number of dogs, of sledges, and of marches made.

One of the most conclusive facts brought to light in this book is that the shadows in the photos Peary claimed to have taken at the Pole are in the wrong place ; and that they were cast by the sun at a height of 30°, while it was only 7° above the horizon when he was supposed to have been at the Pole. As Mr Hall observes : " Shadows are nature's witnesses. They never lie." For this reason " most of the shadows appear to be eliminated . . . others, in the same picture, are evidently . . . ' doctored.' "

Peary's alleged observations at the Pole are critically scrutinised by the old navigator whose book we are considering. He points out that Peary located Camp Jesup, in one statement, on the 70th meridian, and in another statement on the 170th meridian. Both statements cannot be true. " Such a glaring error cannot be accounted for in any way except that Statement No. 1 was an imaginary record of events." Professor Galle of Berlin is quoted as saying : " None of Peary's methods are reliable. Even if he did reach the Pole he would not know it."

In his ﬁrst published narrative, Peary wrote of 6th April : " In twelve hou we made 40 miles " ; [1] but in the next sentence he gave a latitude that made his distance 32 miles. No man who had made the march could have done this. It would be possible to evade the mistake by saying that the 40 miles were route-miles ; and this would admit a 25 per cent. addition for deviation, but it is clearly an error, for in the next revision of the story the distance is corrected to " at least 30 miles." Contrast this with the records of Scott, Shackleton, and Mawson.

Captain Hall shows that Peary, in his first published accounts, made several mistakes ; these were patched up as well as possible in *The North Pole*. Another example of this was his statement in the first account, that he hoped to reach the Pole in time for a noon observation. Anyone who had been there would realise that there was no other time at that spot. The words " Columbia meridian time " were therefore added in all subsequent publications.

"Years have elapsed since Peary's alleged visit to the Pole, affording ample time for correction, and yet no one can tell within 100° of longitude where Peary wishes to have Camp Jesup located." His

[1] In the *Outlook*, 18th September 1909.

facsimile observations contradict his verbal statements. From all of which it is clear that " Peary did not make the march and did not make the observations as he alleges. . . . In order to make all the various conflicting computations and locations correspond chameleon-like to such a march, the direction of the sun is necessarily falsified, the points of the compass are disregarded, and the time of the day is adjusted to suit each case." [1]

Chapter VII explains " How Peary obtained his honours " ; but it is of more interest to Americans than to others. The examination of Peary by the Naval Committee is shown to have been unsatisfactory. Why were not Bartlett, Borup, and MacMillan called to give evidence ? If Peary is found to have falsified one statement, " his testimony *all* falls to the ground as absolutely worthless." [2] It is particularly significant that Peary's journal contained no record for 7th and 8th April, and that several blank pages were left under these dates. These were the days on which Peary walked about 180 miles, so there was no time for writing.

Captain Hall proves that Peary could not have known his position when out on the pack-ice, adding : " There can be no area on the earth's surface more difficult to navigate by compass than that near to the North Pole, where the traveller is on a geographical meridian distant from the magnetic meridian ; there is no place where it is more important to know, each day, the variation of the compass. Such a route is the one from Cape Columbia to the North Pole. . . . Nobody knows the variation of the compass very far north of Cape Columbia." The British Admiralty charts " give only conjectural compass variations in the north polar sea. . . . These conjectural variations at Cape Columbia have been given in different years as being 135° W., 120° W., and in 1912 as 75° W." [3] Peary assumed the variation at Cape Sheridan to be 95°, while the chart for 1912 gives 70°. Diagrams are given to illustrate this.

Captain Hall shows " that Peary's alleged ' proofs ' can be faked," by giving a better set of observations than Peary's. He also quotes the Professor of Astronomy and Physics in Nebraska University that proof of having been " at or near the Pole would consist in the cumu-lative evidence furnished by many and various observations besides those of the sextant, such as his dead reckoning data, the readings of his chronometers, of his barometers, and the like " [4]

Captain Hall believes " that the story of the trip to the Pole is pure invention." He well says : " If one can . . . deliberately absent himself from available witnesses, and while absent smooth down the pressure ridges of the polar sea, close all open-water spaces, ignore all drift, conceal his meridian whereabouts, have all winds fair,

---

[1] *Has the North Pole been Discovered ?*, p. 207.
[2] *Op. cit.*, p. 227.   [3] *Op. cit.*, p. 245.   [4] *Op. cit.*, p. 252.

and augment his speed to suit his ends, one can readily travel back and forth, over any pack-ice . . . as readily " as one can pace a quarter deck.[1]

The mistakes, too, are those of an inaccurate writer of fiction. " If he were recording facts . . . he would not be likely . . . to mistake the clock time by six hours, the direction of the sun by 69°," and not know whether he walked north or south. " He could not write in a diary that he took an observation at *noon*, and then enter in that diary that same observation in figures as being taken at 12.50 p.m. and repeat these mistakes in every description and have all this happen at one camp, when each item in the circumstances was a matter of vital consequence. Such errors indicate unmistakably that they are fiction." [2]

6. The Hon. H. T. Helgesen made two speeches in the House of Representatives to prove that neither Admiral Peary nor Dr Cook reached the North Pole. With the latter we are not concerned. The speech on Peary has been quoted already, but we must refer to it again because it was the result of considerable research and was marked by conspicuous ability. It is reported in *The Congressional Record* for 13th January 1916, p. 1092 and following pages.

Mr Helgesen called for a new chart of the Arctic " that the map-makers and scientists of the world may know that the fictitious ' discoveries ' of Robert E. Peary, heretofore shown on our maps, have been repudiated and cancelled by the sworn officers and scientists of our Navy Department and of our Coast and Geodetic Survey, with the end in view that scientific truth shall prevail and that history shall not be perverted." (Applause.)

Mr Helgesen wrote to the Secretary of the United States Navy asking for the data on which the sounding of 1500 fathoms five miles from the Pole was placed on Chart No. 2560, and received reply that Peary had furnished it, but no data were sent. The correspondence with the Coast and Geodetic Survey is given, in which repeated requests are made for the data of Peary's sounding in latitude 89° 57′ N. and in which it is admitted that Peary's profile of soundings is " not susceptible of proof." Mr Helgesen shows that it is susceptible of disproof.

The line of soundings was stated by Mr Tittmann to be the only official evidence of Peary having got within striking distance of the Pole. Mr Helgesen proves, from Peary's own statements, that they were not taken in the positions assigned to them.

Mr Helgesen made it known that " the printed testimony given at the Peary hearing before the Committee in Naval Affairs . . . was carefully guarded from general distribution," so he decided to make it public. He believed that " a careful study of that evidence " would

---

[1] *Op. cit.*, p. 307.   [2] *Op. cit.*, p. 355.

" convince any unbiassed, fair-minded person that Robert E. Peary neither discovered nor reached the North Pole."

Peary managed to get nearly a year's delay before showing his original records to the Congressional Committee. Several of its members wished to see them, but Mr Gannett [1] demurred. We then read :

" MR BATES. Do you care to state why that record should be kept from the public ?

MR GANNETT. I do not know that I should like to. I would rather Peary would state his reasons himself.

MR ROBERTS. Now, let me ask a question : do I understand the papers or records in issue now are copies of Mr Peary's original journal ?

MR GANNETT. Yes, sir.

MR ROBERTS. And what other ?

MR GANNETT. Copies of his observations.

MR ROBERTS. Just what is included in the term ' observations,' in a general way ?

MR GANNETT. The altitude of the sun and latitude.

MR ROBERTS. Do I understand that Mr Peary objects to his observations as to latitude, and the position of the sun—objects to that being made public, or is it simply the journal of his trip that he objects to, or both ?

MR GANNETT. Both.

MR ROBERTS. In view of the statement we have just listened to, I would like to ask Professor Gannett when Mr Peary placed the injunction of secrecy on those papers ?

MR GANNETT. When he gave them to me two or three days ago."

With reference to Peary's artificial horizon, Mr Gannett said : " There was a slight modification made in it ; it was not possible to get the sun at very low angles."

" THE CHAIRMAN. Could you rely upon his report of the observations taken without any other fact and not knowing the man ?

MR GANNETT. Just simply the observations, without any knowledge of the man and without any narrative ?

THE CHAIRMAN. Yes.

MR GANNETT. No ; I don't think I could.

MR GREGG. The personal equation and confidence in the man would cut a considerable figure in aiding you to come to a conclusion ?

MR GANNETT. Yes ; and the other attendant circumstances . . ."

On Saturday, 7th January 1911, almost a year after the discontinuance of the hearings because of Peary's reluctance to make his records public, Sub-Committee No. 8 of the House Committee on

[1] Chairman of the Committee which stated that Peary had reached the Pole.

Naval Affairs met to continue the hearings and listen to Peary's own testimony. Peary admitted that he only *estimated* his distances. Note the following :

" Mr Butler. The last march reached what point ?

Capt. Peary. The last point, I judged, brought me near enough of the Pole so I could reach it from that point.

Mr Butler. Estimated at how many miles ? I remember from your book very distinctly that it was about five miles.

Capt. Peary. My estimate put me within three or four miles of the Pole. . . . The observation which I made at that time (noon of 6th April) . . . indicated our position as 89° 57′, which is about three miles from the Pole."

He had only taken one latitude sight in the last 130 miles ! As Mr Helgesen remarks : " Marvellous accuracy. . . . Can you beat it ? "

" Mr Butler. You must have been at the place to have made certain observations, and if you were there you were there, but would you have made the figures without having been at the Pole, and if you had made the figures without having been there, is there any way to detect your effort ?

Capt. Peary. That is a thing I can only answer in this way. There is a difference of opinion in regard to that. You will find that some experts will say that observations can be arranged and others will say that they can not.

Mr Butler. Observations, in other words, can be written down as having been made by a person who reports to have been at a certain place ?

Capt. Peary. That has been stated.

Mr Roberts. Mr Gannett and Mr Tittmann told us that it is possible for a person who has sufficient knowledge to sit down in a department here in Washington and make figures and claim to have been at a point where the so-called observations were made. In other words, that the figures themselves would not carry any proof on their face.

Capt. Peary. That is the opinion of an expert."

The journal was considered carefully by the Committee, who found that Peary estimated, not only his distances but also his temperatures, as follows :

" Mr Roberts. How did you get the temperature of that day ; where did you find that ? " (Peary having just admitted that all three thermometers were out of action, yet read a diary entry with a −50°. Also, incidentally, that Bartlett's *estimate* of the latitude had been 85° 30′ and Peary's 85° 20′.)

" Capt. Peary. It was an estimate. . . . I know that brandy will freeze up there somewhere in the fifties."

7. The Hon. R. B. Macon delivered a speech in the House of Representatives as reported in *The Congressional Record* of 16th February 1911, from which the following is taken : " I realise that my efforts to defeat the passage of the bill to promote and retire Captain Peary are herculean in their proportions when I consider that I have the combined influence of the administration, a paid lobby of the Peary Arctic Club, and the National Geographic Society to contend with, but having right upon my side as I see it I am going to do everything in my power to defeat it.

" The Geographical Society has found a favourable verdict ; . . . but according to the statements of the committee who investigated the case they were not impartial ; . . . they were friends of Peary and believed that he had discovered the Pole before they saw any of his proofs. That alone is enough to condemn their finding."

As to the Naval Committee : " Some of the Committee were in earnest in their desire for the real facts in the case, and insisted upon asking questions that they deemed pertinent, but the best information, or so-called proofs, that they could get from the alleged discoverer, when summed up, were a lot of guesses, speculations, assumptions, estimates, and evasions, and from these, four of the Sub-Committee of seven solemnly reported that the proofs were sufficient to establish the self-serving declaration of the gentleman to the effect that he had discovered the Pole."

Thus, Peary only escaped defeat by one vote.

" It will be seen, Mr Speaker, that it will not do to put bogus heroes upon pinnacles of fame, for it will not be long before they must come down. A real hero would not accept honour at the hands of his people when there was a shadow of a cloud upon his title thereto. . . ."

" Experts had examined the chronometer before Peary left New York and predicted that it would run slow, but when returned to the same experts for examination, after Mr Peary's return, it disclosed that it had actually gained time. . . ."

" I have given more time and thought to this alleged discovery than I have to any other public question that I remember to have undertaken to investigate in my whole life, and the more I have investigated and studied the story the more thoroughly convinced have I become that it is a fake pure and simple."

8. Two excellent articles on this subject, written by Mr W. E. Shea of Washington, appeared in *The Independent* of Boston. In the first of these (22nd August 1925) he pleads for a settlement of the controversy while witnesses are alive, and suggests that a proper inquiry may " prove helpful to Peary " by explaining doubtful points. Some of these are then considered. The average speed as far north as latitude 85° 23′ N. is given as 8 m.p.d. ; " but north of this point a clammy blanket of doubt enshrouds everything the expedition is

alleged to have done." Peary gives a facsimile of an observation said to have been taken by Marvin at latitude 86° 38′ N. It is remarkable that all Marvin's other possessions were lost with him, including "his diary, the samples of the ocean bed taken during soundings—all were lost except this one paper."

Peary's arrival at the ship three days after Bartlett is dealt with. Mr Shea shows that while success would have been duly celebrated, either failure or the thought of making "a fraudulent claim to success" would have led to Peary being "non-committal, vague, uncommunicative," as he was.

Mr Shea examines the contradictory statements *re* the condition of the ice near the Pole. According to his figuring Peary did "57 m.p.d. for eight days," if he reached the Pole. This article attracted attention in Europe as well as in America.

The second article (12th June 1926) began by saying: "There never has been a thoroughgoing investigation of Admiral Peary's claims to have discovered the North Pole that did not end in an adverse verdict." There have been two favourable verdicts, that of the National Geographic Society, already referred to; and that of the Naval Committee. An example of the inquiry conducted by this Committee is then given, showing that about half its members were shielding Peary from awkward questions.

Mr Shea next considers three methods of finding out how many miles a day Peary could have travelled over the polar pack: (1) The best day's march before the white men were sent back, which was 20 miles. (2) "A distance to be determined by the reader," as to how far men could go over the broken surface. (3) The speeds of Nansen and Cagni, whose best days were respectively 25 and 28 miles. These two were "admittedly competent explorers." Peary's greatest distances in one day are then given: two days of 40 miles, one day of 45 miles and one day of 71 geo. miles, "exactly as Peary sets them down in his book, . . . not allowing for detours around open canals, weak ice, impassable ridges, or for errors in setting a course by the compass." Yet "there is no escape from the conclusion that the expedition was in no shape for smashing records of pedestrianism." Thus Mr Shea.

Mr Lewin added 10 per cent. for detours and 30 per cent. for drift to the latitude distance. Captain Hall's tables [1] give "average statute miles plus 30 per cent. drift and detours." I believe that, while 30 per cent. or even 40 per cent. may possibly be no more than would actually have to be travelled, in addition to the latitude distance, the impossibility of Peary reaching the Pole is most clearly proved by adding only 20 per cent. He certainly travelled this amount, and probably more, over the whole course, if he reached his goal. His unwitnessed distance, about 800 statute miles, was only 60 to 70 miles

[1] *Has the North Pole been Discovered?*, pp. 40–43.

288   ROBERT EDWIN PEARY

TABLE No. 13.

A COMPARISON OF PEARY'S SPEEDS ACCORDING TO VARIOUS
INDEPENDENT INVESTIGATORS

	Route Miles.	Days.	Av. p.d.	Marches.	Av. p.m.	
Lewin : 40 per cent. added to latitudes	1500	55	..	45	33⅓	Cape Columbia to Pole, back to Cape Sheridan
	675	..	..	18	37½	Pole to Cape Sheridan
	103	2	51½	..	..	Cape Columbia to Cape Sheridan[1]
Hall : 30 per cent. added	461·9	31	14·9			Cape Columbia to Camp Bartlett
	497	7½	66·3			North of Camp Bartlett (lat. 87° 47′ N.)
	449	13½	33·3			Camp Bartlett to Cape Columbia
	263	2¾	95·7			Pole to Camp Bartlett
	722	16¼	44			Pole to Cape Columbia, *plus* miles at Pole
Hayes : 20 per cent. added	799	22	36			Total unwitnessed distance
	401	8	50			North of lat. 87° 47′ N.
	180	2	90			Pole to lat. 87° 47′ N.
Shea :	152	19	8			Cape Columbia to lat. 85° 23′ N.
	456	8	57			North of Bartlett's last camp

less than Captains Scott and Amundsen travelled to the South Pole. The great Norwegian sledge traveller, with his splendid equipment, including sledges that were half the weight of Peary's unwieldy vehicles, averaged 22 m.p.d. for the return journey of 870 miles. This was a little faster than the outward journey. Peary's speed was at least 36 m.p.d., for 800 miles, if he reached the Pole. More than half Amundsen's sledging surface was over the level Barrier, and only his mountain section was difficult.

[1] Eighty statute miles in straight line.

A SHORT BIBLIOGRAPHY

ABRUZZI, H.R.H. THE DUKE OF THE : *On the " Polar Star " in the Arctic Sea*, 2 vols., 1903.
AMUNDSEN, CAPT. ROALD : *My Life as an Explorer*, 1927.
AMUNDSEN, CAPT. ROALD : *My Polar Flight* (undated).
AMUNDSEN, CAPT. ROALD : *The South Pole*, 2 vols., 1912.
BALCH, EDWIN SWIFT : *The North Pole and Bradley Land*, 1913.
BARTLETT, CAPT. ROBERT : *The Log of Bob Bartlett*, 1928.
BORUP, GEORGE : *A Tenderfoot with Peary.*
BROWN, DR R. N. RUDMOSE : *A Naturalist at the Poles*, 1923.
BROWN, DR R. N. RUDMOSE : *The Geography of the Polar Regions*, 1928.
Bulletin of the American Geographical Society, vol. 4, No. 9, September 1909.
CHERRY-GARRARD, APSLEY : *The Worst Journey in the World*, 2 vols., 1922.
Congressional Record, The (passim).
EDWARDS, DELTUS M. : *The Toll of the Arctic Seas*, 1910.
Geographical Journal, The (passim).
GREELY, MAJOR-GENERAL ADOLPHUS : *Three Years of Arctic Service*, 2 vols., 1886.
GREEN, COMMANDER FITZHUGH : *Peary the Man who Refused to Fail*, 1926.
HALL, CAPT. THOMAS F. : *Has the North Pole been Discovered ?*, 1917.
Hampton's Magazine, May, August, September, 1910.
HAYES, J. GORDON : *Antarctica, A Treatise on the Southern Continent*, 1928.
HENSON, M. A. : *A Negro Explorer at the North Pole*, 1912.
Journal of the Manchester Geographical Society, vols. xxxvii–xxxviii, 1921–1922.
KOCH, LAUGE : *Report on the Danish Bicentenary Jubilee Expedition*, 1920–1923.
LEWIN, W. HENRY : *Did Peary reach the Pole ?*, 1911.
MacMILLAN, DR DONALD B. : *Four Years in the White North*, 1918.
MARKHAM, SIR CLEMENTS : *The Lands of Silence*, 1921.
NANSEN, DR F. : *Farthest North*, 2 vols., 1897.
NANSEN, DR F. : *The First Crossing of Greenland*, 2 vols., 1890.
NARES, ADMIRAL SIR GEORGE : *Narrative*, 2 vols., 1878.
National Geographic Magazine (passim).
PEARY, ADMIRAL R. E. : *Nearest the Pole*, 1907.

PEARY, ADMIRAL R. E. : *Northward over the Great Ice*, 1898.
PEARY, ADMIRAL R. E. : *The North Pole*, September 1910.
PEARY, ADMIRAL R. E. : *The Secrets of Polar Travel*, 1917.
PRIESTLEY, R. E.   (See WRIGHT, C. S., and PRIESTLEY, R. E.)
" Problems of Polar Research," A series of papers, *American Geographical Society*, 1928.
RASMUSSEN, KNUD : *Greenland by the Polar Sea*, 1921.
Report on the Danish Expedition to North Greenland. (See KOCH, L.).
Report of the First Thule Expedition, 1912.
Report of the Geographic Board of Canada. (See WHITE, JAMES.)
SCOTT, CAPT. R. F. : *The Voyage of the " Discovery,"* 2 vols., 1905.
Scottish Geographical Magazine, The, 1912.
Scott's Last Expedition, 2 vols., 1913. (Edited by his staff.)
SHACKLETON, SIR ERNEST HENRY : *The Heart of the Antarctic*, 2 vols., 1909.
STEFANSSON, V. : *The Friendly Arctic*, 1921.
SVERDRUP, CAPT. OTTO : *New Land*, 2 vols., 1904.
Transactions of the Royal Society of Edinburgh. (See WORDIE, J. M.)
WHITE, JAMES : *Ninth Report of the Geographic Board of Canada*, 1910.
WORDIE, J. M.: " The Natural History of the Pack Ice " (*Trans. Royal Soc. Edin.*, vol. lii, part iv, No. 31.
WRIGHT, C. S., and PRIESTLEY, R. E. : *Glaciology, British (Terra Nova) Antarctic Expedition*, 1910–1913.

INDEX

By the Same Author   42s. net

ANTARCTICA
A Treatise on the Southern Continent

Part I. Character, Scenery, Geology, Glaciology, Meteorology,
Nature Notes.

Part II. Recent exploration critically considered: Scott, Shackleton,
Mawson, Amundsen, and others. Cause of fatalities.

Part III. The Future. Uncharted spaces and their exploration.
Territorial rights. Three Addenda.

Glaciological Glossary; 22 Tables; 16 Photographs; 14 Charts; Index.

" This substantial volume is the work of an enthusiastic student of
polar exploration who has devoted years of labour to its preparation, and
has earned the gratitude of his readers by appending a full and accurate
index. . . . The programme is ambitious, and anyone who dares to
attempt it without personal experience of the polar regions or first-hand
knowledge of equipping and organising an expedition must possess courage
comparable with that of the explorers whose life's work he weighs in the
balance of his judgment. Our author has the courage ; his trumpet gives
no uncertain sound. . . . The value of the book rests mainly on the critical
remarks regarding each of the main British expeditions and the Norwegian
attainment of the Pole. The aloofness of the author from the leaders of
these expeditions and from the controversial atmosphere in which most of
them were kindled into being enables him to assume a position of detach-
ment unattainable by one who shared the hopes and fears, the successes
and failures, of those exciting years. Probably it is this fact which makes
it appear that Mr Hayes sees Scott, Shackleton, Mawson, and Amundsen
ranged alongside Cook, Bellinghausen, Biscoe, and Ross on the horizon of
history. His views thus acquire an interest as forecasting the possible
verdict of posterity. . . ."—Dr H. R. Mill in *The Geographical Journal*.

" The size and weight of the books published on South Polar exploration
may be taken as symbolical of the vastness of Antarctica, most of which,
though ' discovered,' is as yet unexplored. At all events, the physical
magnitude of Mr Gordon Hayes' treatise on the Southern Continent is
equal to that of the books which were the immediate product of the famous
explorations of Scott, Shackleton, and Sir Douglas Mawson. Our first
thought was that it was pretentious for an author, not an explorer himself,
to imitate the heroic form, but we were entirely wrong. A book such as
Mr Hayes has written was needed, and here it is. He has marshalled all
the principal results of the various expeditions, and by descriptions, maps,
and photographs has made us feel that we are almost as familiar with
Antarctica as with Australia or Arabia. He has done his work superlatively
well. The book is written with extreme care and in a scholarly, scientific
spirit, though as far as possible scientific phrases are avoided. It is a book
for both learned and simple."—*The Spectator*.

" Men of letters, geographers, naturalists, and physicists will read this
work with great interest and indisputable personal benefit ; they will know
henceforth whence to draw an authoritative documentation for their labours
and researches on the Antarctic. Past explorers will greatly add to their
knowledge and will be able to keep themselves in touch with recent discoveries. . . . Finally, and this is one of its greatest merits, this book,
although scientific, is written within the understanding of all. . . . *Antarctica*
is at the same time a remarkable treatise and a complete manual. It will
be read equally as an intensely moving true story. . . . One feels that this
book, born of really serious work, has been written with great feeling ;
it will be read with the same."—Dr J. B. Charcot in *La Géographie*.